HARD LABOR

ISSUES IN WORK AND HUMAN RESOURCES

Daniel J.B. Mitchell, Series Editor

WORKING IN THE TWENTY-FIRST CENTURY
Policies for Economic Growth Through Training,
Opportunity, and Education
David I. Levine

INCOME INEQUALITY IN AMERICA
An Analysis of Trends
Paul Ryscavage

HARD LABOR
Women and Work in the Post-Welfare Era
Joel F. Handler and Lucie White

HARD LABOR

Women and Work in the Post-Welfare Era

EDITED BY
Joel F. Handler and
Lucie White

M.E. Sharpe
Armonk, New York
London, England

Library of Congress Cataloging-in-Publication Data

Hard labor : women and work in the post-welfare era /
Joel F. Handler and Lucie White, editors.
p.   cm.—(Issues in work and human resources)
Includes bibliographical references and index.
ISBN 0-7656-0332-2 (alk. paper)   ISBN 0-7656-0333-0 (pbk. : alk. paper)
1. Welfare recipients—Employment—United States.
2. Poor women—Employment—United States.   3. Public welfare—United States.
4. United States—Social policy—1993– . I. Handler, Joel F. II. White, Lucie, 1949– .
HV95.H266   1999
362.5′8—dc21   98-8338
CIP

Printed in the United States of America

The paper used in this publication meets the minimum requirements of
American National Standard for Information Sciences—
Permanence of Paper for Printed Library Materials,
ANSI Z 39.48-1984.

BM (p)   10   9   8   7   6   5   4   3   2
BM (c)   10   9   8   7   6   5   4   3   2

CONTENTS

FOREWORD

Although it may have seemed to many that when Congress and the President made the decision to "end welfare as we know it," they had concluded a major chapter in public policy. In fact, they had just begun a new chapter. "Welfare as we know it" was created in the 1930s out of social currents of that era. It drew on earlier experience with state "mothers' pensions," essentially support programs for dependent mothers who had been widowed.

Implicit in such programs was the notion that mothers should not work, but should be left to care for their children. Absent from that era was the baggage welfare subsequently acquired relating to never-married mothers, teenage mothers, and the politics of race. And absent was the changing norm about women in the workforce that developed in the 1960s, 1970s, and beyond. After the 1970s, the strong presence of working women with children actually in the workforce tended to undermine public support for the tax support to those not working.

But other economic realities must also be considered. First, real wage trends at the lower end of the wage spectrum have been negative since the early 1970s. Although this tendency has been more pronounced for men than for women, it is present for both sexes. Moving from welfare to work is not necessarily synonymous with a rise in economic well-being. Second, a simple count of the number of minimum wage jobs compared with the number of women on welfare indicates that the move from welfare to work on a large scale will not be an easy undertaking.

In this volume, Joel Handler and Lucie White have assembled an impressive array of experts to deal with the job prospects for poor women. In Chapter 1, Handler provides an introduction to the empirical realities and the public policy options. Chapter 2, by Mark Greenberg, reviews the changes in welfare policy that have been adopted. As he notes, much attention has been focused on the degree to which welfare caseloads decline. But there are larger issues to be confronted about the well-being of the working poor and their longer term opportunities.

As it is, Julia Henly reports in Chapter 3, the low wage labor market is not an easy place to navigate. Informal networks often are the route to job-finding and not everyone has access to such networks. But as Susan Jones point out in

Chapter 4, if there are barriers to finding regular wage jobs, self-employment may be an option. And one concrete example of employment creation that lies somewhere between regular wage jobs and individual self-employment is cooperatives, as described by Peter Pitegoff in Chapter 5.

If there is to be a move of mothers from welfare to work, then various support services must be considered. Among the more obvious, Lucie White notes in Chapter 6, is child care. High-quality child care comes at a steep price, however, especially for a low-wage worker. And health care—which has been provided to welfare recipients through Medicaid—as Louise Trubeck points out in Chapter 7, also poses a challenge. For the non-elderly population, job-based health insurance is the largest form of coverage for workers and dependents. But low-wage jobs often do not come with health insurance. In the absence of a universal health insurance system, some extension of Medicaid dollars to the working poor and/or their children becomes a prime concern. Finally, because low-wage work is often intermittent, the operation of the federal/state unemployment insurance system must be reexamined, notes Lucy Williams in Chapter 8. Although ideal sources of support for the working poor are not available, Joel Handler and Yeheskel Hasenfeld, in Chapter 9, propose a model of community-based employment support services that could be useful.

With changes in the welfare system come changes not only for recipients but also for advocates of the poor. As Kathleen Sullivan reports in Chapter 10, the welfare debate has tended to reinforce stereotypical public images of poor women. And, as Fran Ansley points out in Chapter 11, the external economic environment will have an important role in determining the outcomes in the national effort to promote welfare-to-work. Most dramatic has been the direct impact of immigration. Although the exact impact of globalization is difficult to quantify, it has led to demands for labor standards linked to trade treaties.

In summary, this volume suggests that ending welfare as we know it is more than a budgetary exercise. It invites an examination of all of the social and employment-related policies that have grown up since the Great Depression. And its eventual ramifications are likely to be more far-reaching than advocates of welfare reform suspected.

DANIEL J.B. MITCHELL

PREFACE

This book features case studies by twelve scholar-activists who work in the areas of social welfare and low-wage labor policy, with a particular focus on low-income women with children. Our concern is with low-income women who are single mothers, as well as those who are married or in stable relationships with another adult. Overall, the book will address the following three questions in chapters that describe and analyze innovative policy and advocacy in which each of the contributors is engaged:

1. What barriers keep low-income women from entering into, staying in, and thriving in waged work?
2. What policy innovations—at the federal, state, and local levels—in social welfare law, in labor and employment law, and in other areas such as health, child care, domestic violence, and disability, can reduce or remove the barriers?
3. How can new lawyering and other advocacy strategies link community and work-site organizing, public dialogue, and policy advocacy to realize these policy innovations?

The contributors came together in 1994 out of concern over the increasing consensus in public discourse that women receiving Aid to Families with Dependent Children (AFDC) should become economically self-sufficient through waged work. On the one hand, our understanding of low-wage labor markets counseled us that this was an impossible policy goal. On the other hand, our advocacy work, as well as our study of the history of U.S. social welfare policy, counseled us that low-income women, particularly women of color, whether single or married, have always worked outside of the home. Most low-income women worked to support their families. Those who received government benefits worked to supplement them. Furthermore, low-income women have long sought to improve the conditions of low-wage work, both individually and through organized political action. They have long sought the support of national and state governments and concessions from low-wage employers that would make low-wage work a real option for them.

Our belief was that the occasion of welfare reform was a fit time for renewed focus by policymakers, lawyers, and grassroots activists on this historic agenda of low-income women. Thus, the idea for this book emerged. Drawing on the contributors' extensive experience as scholars, teachers, legal advocates, and grassroots activists on low-income women's policy issues, the book brings a unique focus to the policy debate over low-wage work and social welfare policy.

Each chapter centers on a description and analysis of the ground-level experiences of low-income women and their advocates as they grapple with the realities of low-wage work—gaining entry; negotiating child care, health care, and other social benefits; dealing with the uncertainties of the low-wage job market; sometimes seeking to set up enterprises on their own. The contributors also describe collaborative efforts, by low-income women, government officials, employers, and other actors, to shape innovative, local solutions to the multiple challenges that low-wage work poses for women. The chapters track the advocacy process and then examine the policy innovations that emerged. Special attention is paid to the lessons that can be drawn from each example, with respect to both change strategies and new policy ideas. Most of the chapters focus on local and state level policy innovation, which is appropriate in the current climate of increasing devolution of welfare policy to the states and local governments. The book demonstrates how a pragmatic, grounded approach to social welfare policy can generate ideas that are both politically feasible and genuinely responsive to low-income women's needs. Furthermore, it demonstrates how low-income women can be brought into the policy innovation process as partners, and indeed as leading actors, rather than the objects of expert scrutiny.

Thus, this volume seeks to move the debate over social policy regarding low-income women beyond the dichotomy between individually focused behavior and character-changing punitive policies, on the one hand, and broad calls for comprehensive national level welfare entitlement, or vague institutional change, on the other. Instead, the volume seeks to turn the attention of lawyers and policymakers back to real, street-level institutional sites, like workplaces, government agencies, and not-for-profit welfare-to-work services. It focuses on the real life circumstances of low-income women, as well as those of the low-wage employers, local and state level bureaucrats, service agency staff, and others with whom these women's lives are enmeshed. It acknowledges both the limited organizational capacities of the institutions serving low-income women, and the conflicting interests of the players. Yet it also describes niches where partnership and innovation present real possibilities.

Through all of the chapters, the book asks how low-wage work sites and social programs can change their practices, rules, and cultures so as to give low-income women access to real economic security. What policy innovations can make economic *enfranchisement* a realistic vision for low-income women? When is coalition between government, employers, the nonprofit sector, and low-income women realistic, and when is it bound to shortchange low-income women's needs? How can the state be brought back into low-income social policy, rather than be pushed even farther out? What will it take to enable low-income women to thrive, rather than scramble for their families' day-to-day survival, in waged work?

Chapter Outlines

Chapter 1. Low-Wage Work "As We Know It": What's Wrong/What Can Be Done

Joel F. Handler

Chapter 1 gives an overview of why it is unrealistic to expect low-income women to become self-sufficient through waged work. The focus is on the difficulties that low-income women, especially mothers, have in the low-wage labor market—the kinds of jobs that are available, the employment characteristics of these women, and what employers are looking for in new employees. It then summarizes where the latest welfare reform legislation left us with respect to low-wage work policy. It emphasizes how inadequate income support, child care, health care, and related programs, such as unemployment insurance, create barriers for low-income women who are seeking employment.

The chapter concludes with a summary description of the kinds of changes needed to increase the income and support in the low-wage labor market. The focus of social policy must change from individual women to the workplace and the labor market. This focus requires us to rethink, rather than write off, public benefits such as welfare, Social Security disability, unemployment, and the Earned Income Tax Credit. It requires us to redesign those programs—paring down, supplementing, expanding—so that they enhance women's best efforts to "make work work."

Chapter 2. Welfare Restructuring and Working-Poor Family Policy: The New Context

Mark Greenberg

Chapter 2 describes the key elements of the Personal Responsibility and Work Opportunity Reconciliation Act of 1996 (PRWORA) and the new federal block grant structure—Temporary Assistance for Needy Families (TANF). TANF fundamentally changes the structure of decision making from the federal government to the states and local governments. While the focus, thus far, has been on the dangers threatening welfare families, the chapter discusses opportunities under the new structure for working-poor families. By understanding what is permitted, prohibited, and possible, the new structure can play a role in promoting many of the policy proposals discussed in this book.

The thrust of the new law, as well as the preceding state waivers, is to increase the work requirements on welfare recipients. States have wide discretion—they can operate pretty much as before or they can sharply reduce benefits to poor families. While the emphasis thus far is on the "risks" of the new regime, this chapter discusses the opportunities to rethink social policy toward working and nonworking poor families that will not only encourage labor market entry and stability, but, at the same time, protect the well-being of children, provide for those who cannot work, and reduce poverty. With the new flexibility and the surplus funding, states can create separate programs, not tied to welfare, to fund public employment, wage subsidies, training programs, job retention programs, and child-care subsidies. Child support assurance can be provided for cooperating parents. Other areas include reforming the Earned Income Tax Credit and Unemployment Insurance (see Chapter 8), paid parental leave, and education and training. These initiatives might be more popular if they extend more broadly to the working population.

The first two chapters provide the background environment or the setting. The remaining chapters discuss specific, ground-level issues and opportunities facing low-wage women workers.

Chapter 3. Barriers to Finding and Maintaining Jobs: The Perspectives of Workers and Employers in the Low-Wage Labor Market

Julia R. Henly

Chapter 3 explores the problems and barriers that low-wage women face in finding out about jobs, applying for jobs, getting jobs, and keeping jobs. The principal method of getting a job turns out to be informal networks. Low-wage employers rely primarily on current employees to fill vacancies. This works to the advantage of the employers, since employees can both screen and vouch for applicants. It also may work to the advantage of the employees, since there are incentives on employers to work around work-related or family-related difficulties.

On the other hand, many low-wage workers, who are not already connected to networks of friends in the labor market and who may also have employment-related deficits, will have difficulty in obtaining jobs. They will have problems of information—what jobs are available, what employers are looking for, how to get these jobs, and then how to keep the jobs. There are many real or potential mismatches between the employment characteristics of the job applicants and those for which employers are looking. Then, when problems on the job arise, there are difficulties in learning about options and mustering the resources necessary to pursue these options. Examples include discrimination in the hiring process (e.g., in addition to race, having young children) and while on the job; sexual harassment; violations of protective labor standards; child-care and health care options; domestic violence; transportation; and so forth. This chapter draws on empirical work dealing with barriers to low-wage women's work in Los

Angeles. Community-based service models as sources of information, monitoring, and advocacy will be explored in Chapter 9.

Chapter 4. Self-Employment: Possibilities and Problems

Susan R. Jones

Chapter 4 explores the emerging field of microenterprise development as a strategy for the "economic enfranchisement" of low-income women. While self-employment may not work for all, it does represent an important opportunity for developing human capital and increasing employment. It is an important component of a larger Community Economic Development strategy.

The chapter examines self-employment demonstration projects, what has worked, why and for whom, obstacles to self-employment, and the legal and policy changes required for self-employment to become a more viable option and opportunity for low-income women. Drawing on the example of the George Washington University Law School's microenterprise development clinic in the District of Columbia and similar projects around the country, the chapter also explores how lawyering strategies can support and facilitate this movement. The chapter concludes with a series of policy recommendations designed to facilitate microenterprise development. The recommendations address the constraints on microenterprise development under the new welfare reform regime but also the opportunities under the new law—for example, linking microenterprise into state welfare-to-work strategies. Other state initiatives are proposed that will help microenterprise.

Chapter 5. Shaping Regional Economies to Sustain Quality Work: The Cooperative Health Care Network

Peter Pitegoff

Chapter 5 presents a case study of the Cooperative Health Care Network as an exemplary welfare-to-work model and as a sophisticated strategy to reshape regional economies for the benefit of the working poor. A consortium of worker-centered home health care companies in Boston, Philadelphia, and New York has crafted a sectoral approach to community economic development, targeting specific low-wage labor markets in order to upgrade the status of home health aides. With select alliances and managed care, the network is navigating the wake of welfare reform in the rough seas of a rapidly changing health care environment.

These social entrepreneurs represent an employer-based effort for job training and development, creating hundreds of quality jobs and informing strategies for business corporations, policymakers, advocates, and the working poor at a fluid moment in welfare policy. One clear lesson of this inspiring case study is that the successful transition from welfare to work, rather than a single event, is a complex process that occurs over a period of time and that requires systems for ongoing support. Another lesson is that an enterprise strategy infused with democratic values can bring about fundamental change for those individuals building new work lives and, moreover, for the political economy beyond the workplace. As a collaborative yardstick enterprise, the network's performance standards and values influence others in the health care industry and in the public policy arena.

The experience of the Cooperative Health Care Network foreshadows a changing policy context in which low-wage labor markets will be defined increasingly without reference to the current welfare regime. Although widely recognized as an effective welfare-to-work program, the network maintains a strategic integrity apart from the welfare system. Its effort is essentially an economic development strategy driven by social values—an approach that creates quality jobs, upgrades the status of the home health care work force, and demonstrates the capacity of poor working women for sophisticated enterprise.

Chapter 6. Quality Child Care for Low-Income Families: Despair, Impasse, Improvisation

Lucie White

Chapter 6 explores the challenge of providing child care for low-income families. It begins with several case studies that illustrate how the high cost of good-quality child care creates hardship for low- and moderate-income households. It then surveys the social science literature on child care to search for ways to understand the well- documented "trilemma" of cost, quality, and access in the child-care domain. The chapter then moves to a quick historical survey of the state's involvement in child care to show how caretaking services have long been subsidized by women's unpaid labor in our economy and to highlight how our current public policies regarding child care have left a legacy of scattered services, inadequate funding, and perverse incentives with regard to the care and education of children while their parents work. The system's particular failures in ensuring continuous care for low-income children as single parents cycle between contingent, low-wage jobs; unemployment; and welfare are emphasized, as is the challenge of devising policies that promote both parental involvement and class/race diversity in child-care services. The chapter will end by critiquing the child-care funding proposals of several advocacy groups, and arguing that to improve child-care policy, we must begin to rework the entire institutional landscape of work and care in innovative, politically realistic, and power-sensitive ways.

Chapter 7. The Health Care Puzzle: Creating Coverage for Low-Wage Workers and Their Families

Louise G. Trubek

Along with child care, the lack of access to health care constitutes a significant employment barrier for poor single mothers. Welfare carries with it Medicaid, and while not a good program, clearly it is better than what is increasingly the situation in the low-wage labor market. Many employers do not offer health insurance at all; others are increasingly restricting coverage to employees only. How, then, can a state reform welfare by moving recipients into the paid labor force and not provide for health insurance? But how can a state provide health insurance for low-wage workers who are ex-recipients and not for other low-wage workers?

Chapter 7 presents a case study of welfare reform in Wisconsin that is attempting to meet this challenge. "Wisconsin Works" (W-2), which replaces AFDC cash assistance, includes the creation of the W-2 Health Plan using Medicaid funding. The chapter describes the roles of the various actors in the development of the W-2 Health Plan—the legislature, the governor, the providers, the clients, and other government agencies. Each set of actors had internal conflicts and viewpoints and unique combinations of self-interest and concern for the poor. The study shows how the actors eventually came to collaborate on the final proposals.

Through a variety of strategies—lobbying, media contacts, agency debate, public education, and alliance building—the actors were able to modify the W-2 Health Plan legislation. They developed two approaches. The first was safeguarding the positive aspects of Medicaid: funding and managed care. The second was endorsing the W-2 aspiration to expand health care to uninsured working people. The two approaches were both divergent and congruent. The actors' endorsement of the conversion of Medicaid to a program to benefit all low-income working people impressed the welfare reform community. On the other hand, expansion will require additional funding and complex oversight. As the welfare program continues to unfold, the actors will continue to modify their strategies.

Chapter 8. Unemployment Insurance and Low-Wage Work

Lucy A. Williams

No matter how many barriers to entering and maintaining waged work are overcome, there will always be periods of unemployment for low-wage workers, in general, and low-wage mothers, in particular. Yet the unemployment insurance system, theoretically designed to provide for workers in times of unemployment, is structured in such a way that often benefits are unavailable for single parents who are low-wage and/or part-time workers. As we come to realize, the majority of welfare mothers are, in effect, low-wage workers struggling to establish a steady connection with the low-wage labor market, and they are forced to use welfare because of the unavailability of unemployment insurance. In other words, as this chapter documents, AFDC often has been the "poor mother's unemployment insurance."

Chapter 8 provides a critique of that system and proposes a number of interim recommendations that build on the author's experience serving on the 1994–97 congressionally established Advisory Council on Unemployment Compensation, and then envisions a restructuring of unemployment insurance that would incorporate into the costs of production a portion of the unpaid labor costs provided by parents.

Chapter 9. Community-Based, Employment-Related Services for Low-Wage Workers

Joel F. Handler and Yeheskel Hasenfeld

Chapter 9 proposes a community-based, employment-related social service agency for low-wage workers. The preceding chapters described the multiple barriers that low-income women face in trying to secure employment that will support their families. Common barriers include lack of information about the availability of jobs, how to go about obtaining the jobs, finding out about and monitoring day care, coping with postemployment problems, learning about and gaining access to health care, and coping with related government benefit programs, such as the Earned Income Tax Credit, Unemployment Insurance, disability, and so forth. Mothers often have inadequate information about child care, have difficulty qualifying for Unemployment Insurance or gaining access to health care.

Not only is there a lack of information, but there is also a need for monitoring and advocacy. There are many examples where locally based hotlines and advocacy services have proven extremely useful for particular issues—for example, Medicare. Several of the chapters described organizing and advocacy efforts tailored to specific problems or projects. What is proposed here is more general information, monitoring, and advocacy services that would be available to all low-wage workers in a given community. A community-based service would take advantage of ethnically based neighborhoods and networks. These services should prove useful, not only to workers but also to the local employers. The agencies could become reliable sources of referrals, especially since employers would know that the agencies would provide postemployment services.

Thus far, the authors, in varying degrees, call for proposals to help low-income women workers—improving their earned income, improving employment-based benefits, improving working conditions, encouraging self-employment, providing health care and child care, reforming unemployment insurance, and offering services for those who need more individual help. In the next chapter, Kathleen Sullivan reminds us that when the more powerful define the issues and do things for the less powerful, they still may not resolve the tensions and contradictions that these women face. Consequently, good intentions may not work for the best interests of these women.

Chapter 10. The Perils of Advocacy: Listening, Labeling, Appropriating

Kathleen A. Sullivan

Low-income single mothers, forced to provide for their families yet deprived of the means for doing so, have always been accused of neglecting their children, thereby justifying state intervention and societal stigma. In the recent welfare debates, negative images of mothers have been projected by the media and by politicians. All low-income mothers, whether or not they are receiving welfare, are affected by these negative stereotypes. Because public policy refuses to acknowledge the realities that these mothers confront in their efforts to support their families on inadequate welfare benefits and episodic low-wage jobs, they are typically forced to go "underground" to make ends meet. Yet these efforts— of supplementing their incomes through work that has been stigmatized or even criminalized—put them at risk of further stigma and criminal sanctions by welfare bureaucracies, and make them the target of child protection agencies. Chapter 10 explores this tension—the ways in which low-wage work, welfare, and child protection systems simultaneously require women to violate the system's rules and then sanction them for doing so. This chapter explores the dilemmas of lawyering for women who face this double bind. It suggests an approach to advocacy for low-income women that pays heightened attention to both their voices and their silence, attending carefully to what they say, guarding their privacy and autonomy, and respecting their need to keep some things "secret," while at the same time mapping the systemic contradictions in our work/welfare system that constrain the choices that they can make.

Chapter 11. Afterword: What's the Globe Got to Do With It?

Fran Ansley

There is the paradox of pessimism and optimism throughout the book. Clearly, the world of low-wage labor is harsh and bleak for those women who must both work and care for dependents. Yet, the chapters are optimistic in that they offer interventions and innovative strategies for low-wage workers and their allies. When we move to a larger frame—the current global economic and political change—we find the same paradox. Foreign and domestic labor markets interact and affect each other in complex and varied ways. The actual or threatened job loss, plus the exploitation of immigrants, serves to undermine the few remaining protective labor laws on the books. At the same time, governments, responding to the supposed strictures of conservative global economic theory, feel powerless to intervene. This is the disheartening side.

There are, however, counter trends. There is a growing chorus of protests to the global economic orthodoxy—from nongovernmental organizations, church groups, labor unions, human rights groups, and so forth. Ansley finds people all over the world working toward a more humane, equitable, democratic order. She concludes by discussing examples of grassroots, innovative exchanges between U.S. workers and workers from Mexico and other Third World countries. At these meetings, important similarities in experiences are exchanged. Workers gain strength from these interchanges, networks are formed, and there is the promising start of local political organizing. The lessons learned from the global economy can help those who are fighting against the current regime of exploitation, poverty, and injustice.

HARD LABOR

1

Joel F. Handler

LOW-WAGE WORK "AS WE KNOW IT"

WHAT'S WRONG/WHAT CAN BE DONE

Poor women have always had to work.[1] In the current labor market, they are finding it increasingly difficult to escape poverty, let alone achieve economic independence. Among married working couples, economic viability now requires not only two earners, but there is an increasing trend for three jobs per couple.[2] Married mothers, who still have the greatest bulk of child care responsibilities, are working longer hours in a poorly paid, gender discriminatory labor market. Single mothers have special, acute problems—indeed, much of this book is devoted to single mothers, not only in poverty, but often on welfare. In part, this is a reflection of the state of research—we know more detail about the day-to-day lives of welfare mothers than about working-poor mothers, in general. But, as we shall see, most welfare mothers are also working mothers. Their experiences shed important light on the issues that we are addressing.

Although this book is about working women, men also have to be brought into the discussion.[3] The economic position of working men has eroded, and this, in turn, has affected the lives of women.[4] The lack of employment among young adults—both male and female, and especially among African Americans, is truly ominous.[5] While women, especially poor women, have special, unique problems, we argue that long-lasting, effective solutions must apply to all the working poor.

Many people in poverty are working but still remain poor. Why is this so? While there is no single answer to this question, in this chapter we focus on the low-wage labor market. In subsequent chapters, we discuss other major barriers facing low-wage women workers.

The Low-Wage Labor Market

According to Rebecca Blank, "Among all poor families, almost two-thirds (63 percent) contain at least one worker."[6] Of the 36.4 million people living below the official poverty line in 1995, 7.2 million were employed more than half the year and about 60 percent of these worked full-time. There were over 4 million families in poverty, even though one or more members worked for at least half the year. While three-fourths of the working poor were white, poverty rates for blacks and Hispanics were two and three times higher, respectively, than the rate for whites. Working women have a higher poverty rate than men do.[7] Among the 30 million near-poor (150 percent of the poverty line), there were 6 million full-time and 5.5 million part-time workers.[8]

If so many people are working, why are they having such a hard time? The principal reason for the growing inequality and poverty is the decline in the real earnings of the less skilled, less educated workers over the past twenty-five years.[9] In 1973, for men, with 1 to 3 years of high school, the median income was $24,079 (1989 dollars); in 1989, it was $14,439. For men with a high school diploma, income dropped from $30,252 to $21,650. For women, with 1–3 years of high school, the median earnings were $7,920 in 1973; by 1989, they dropped to $6,752. For women with a high school degree, the figures were $11,087 (1973) and $10,439 (1989).[10] Furthermore, the decline in income was not due to the shift in jobs from manufacturing to service; real wages declined in both sectors.

While, in general, less-skilled women's wages have not experienced the same declines as men's wages, women still earn substantially less.[11] Women's relative progress vis-à-vis men will probably slow in the future, primarily because of increasing labor-market segmentation along race and gender lines. Women are concentrated in the lower end of the service jobs; and the growing use of involuntary part-time labor will increasingly block entry-level workers from traditional career-ladder jobs.[12] Since 1979, the hourly wages declined steeply for all women, but most severely for African American women without a high school diploma. Moreover, those who experienced the greatest loss in hourly wages also experienced the highest levels of unemployment. In other words, despite the long period of economic growth, the labor market has deteriorated for women, mostly with children, mostly black, and mostly without a high school diploma.[13]

With the decline in real wages, the poverty rate of full-time workers is increasing, especially for workers without a high school degree. In 1991, 31.2 percent of full-time workers earned less than the poverty line, which has increased by 30 percent since 1973. Women are more likely to earn poverty-level wages than men.[14] The earnings of young male high school graduates in 1991 were about 26 percent less than similar workers in 1979; for women, the decline was smaller (16 percent) but still significant. Not only did earnings decline, but so did employment for both high school graduates and dropouts. In 1995, the unemployment rate for high school dropouts was 17.2 percent and for high school graduates it was 6.1 percent.[15] It is this combination—declining real earnings and rising unemployment—that has resulted in increasing poverty among these young families, whether white, black, or Hispanic.[16] The real wages of the less-skilled worker have deteriorated so far that low-wage earners in America have lower earnings than similar workers in all other industrialized countries.[17]

Not only is there the increase of low-wage jobs, but the nature of employment is also shifting from full-time work for a single employer to various forms of "contingent" work.[18] Many workers are employed in part-time, temporary, contract, or other types of flexible work arrangements that lack job security. The contingent work force grew rapidly in the 1980s, and this percentage should increase again, since new jobs are expected to be almost entirely in the service sector, where contingent employment is most likely to occur. According to the Bureau of Labor Statistics (BLS), almost two-thirds of the new entrants into the labor force by the year 2000 will be women, and they are more likely than men to hold part-time and temporary jobs.[19] "While women are more likely to *choose* part-time work, they are also more likely to be *stuck* in part-time jobs against their will. The female rate of involuntary part-time work is 44 percent greater than that for men."[20]

Part-time jobs are more likely to be dead-end, for shorter periods of employment, often without health or pension benefits, and with a lower hourly wage.[21] Thus, families headed by part-time workers are four times more likely to be below the poverty line. By 1995, more than a fifth of all workers were part-time; but of poor workers, almost 70 percent were part-time.[22] Again, single-parent families were worse off—40 percent of these families were poor, and 26 percent were on welfare.[23] The significant portion of employees in part-time work, and the expected proportional growth of this form of employment, indicate that underemployment is going to be a continuing concern.

Despite the impressive growth in jobs in the United States, there are still the questions of whether there are enough jobs in the low-skilled labor market for those who want them and who will get those jobs.[24] While there are no systematic national data on job vacancies, local studies consistently show a job shortage. Estimates suggest that there are six times more people looking for jobs than there are vacancies.[25] A study by the California Employment Development Department projected that in Los Angeles through 1999 the total annual job openings for low-skill occupations will be 72,948. Of these openings, 48,374 would come from turnover and 24,614 would come from growth. However, the number of unemployed and discouraged workers is estimated to have been 595,300, in 1996; in addition there are may job-seeking welfare recipients, a figure that may be as high as 250,000.[26] A recent report on the New Hope Project reached a similar conclusion.[27] New Hope, a pilot demonstration project, operated in two areas of concentrated poverty in Milwaukee. The two areas were largely, but not exclusively, made up of people of African American and Hispanic origin. Although half of the adults were working, unemployment was very high (25 percent for all adults; 47 percent for African Americans). The project offered participants help in their job search. If they worked full-time (30 hours per week), if necessary, they would be given subsidies for health insurance and child care and additional income to move out of poverty. If a job could not be found, the project would provide a community service job.[28] The project served 1,357 people. However, despite the low unemployment rate, both in Wisconsin and in Milwaukee, the report concluded that approximately 9,700 of the eligible targeted population were unemployed and that to absorb this group, employment in these neighborhoods would have to be increased by a third. In other words, "as important as New Hope may be, it seems clear that its chemistry will work best when jobs reappear."[29]

When jobs are available, employers favor ethnic networks, primarily immigrants; African Americans are increasingly displaced. Moreover, these niches are remaining stable and not providing routes for upper mobility.[30] In a recent survey of over 3,000 employers in several large metropolitan areas, Harry Holzer reported that the vast majority of jobs require daily interactions with customers and literacy and numeracy skills; most employers require their employees to have a high school degree, previous work experience, and references and/or formal job training; only a small proportion of job seekers in the inner city would meet these qualifications. In the lower-skilled jobs, Holzer found a preference for hiring whites (clerical/sales) or Hispanics (blue-collar) over African Americans.[31] Waldinger, in a survey of employers of low-income labor in Los Angeles, also found a preference for hiring Hispanics and immigrants (with people skills) rather than African Americans.[32] In contrast, in the New Hope project target population, the researchers found not only very high unemployment (78 percent) but very low skills—over 60 percent had no high school degree and 20 percent had no full-time work experience. Most (71 percent) were women with children (59 percent), and almost half were on welfare. African Americans were disproportionately underrepresented in the project. In other words, despite the impressive growth in jobs, disadvantaged job seekers—women who lack a high school diploma, African American women, and mothers—will have a hard time getting and keeping a job.[33]

And how much will these jobs pay? A recent study reported that if a mother—say a former welfare recipient—worked full-time at a wage rate of between $7 to $8 per hour (1996 dollars), she would earn between $14,000 and $16,000 per year, which is higher than the 1996 official poverty line ($12,600 for a mother and two children).[34] In fact, because of the low number of hours worked, actual earnings were between $9,000 and $12,000. Supplements, such as the Earned Income Tax Credit and food stamps, as well as less payroll taxes, would increase the family income to $15,000.[35] On the other hand, child care expenses average $3,000 per year, thus putting the family below the poverty line.

Will a working-poor mother be able to move up the job ladder? A recent study, based on the National Longitudinal Survey of Youth, examined the employment patterns of young women beginning at age 18 and continuing through age 27. The study was concerned with transitions from bad jobs to good jobs—a job paying at least $8 an hour for at least 35 hours of work a week. As we shall see, low-wage women workers say that they need to earn at least $8 per hour, full-time, in order to cover child care, transportation, and other work-related expenses. The study found that whether or not a woman ever holds a good job or holds one steady job depends on her background, history, and personal characteristics. Women without a high school diploma, or who are African American, or who have children do not have much of a chance for meaningful employment even by their late twenties. "Only 47.4 percent of women who have completed high school ever work in a good job, and only 17 percent work primarily in good jobs by their late twenties." While those who have completed high school have a better chance, "It is only among women who have completed some post-secondary education . . . that one finds a majority (61.4 percent) working steadily in good jobs by the time they reach their late teens." The majority of mothers work steadily by their late twenties but not at good jobs. "Only one-quarter of women with one or more children work primarily in a good job by their late twenties" as compared to more than twice as many women without children (60.4 percent).[36] Over three-quarters of white women and two-thirds of Hispanic (and other non–African American minorities) women have good jobs in their late twenties as compared to less than a third of African American women. Finally, the women who are most likely to get only bad jobs are much more likely to become jobless.[37]

These employment prospects look especially serious for welfare recipients. The Personal Responsibility and Work Opportunity Reconciliation Act of 1996 (PRWORA) replaces the Aid to Families with Dependent Children Program (AFDC) with block grants to the states to establish a Temporary Assistance for Needy Families (TANF) program. The states are required to have increasing percentages of welfare families in work activities.[38] At the same time, skills and training are de-emphasized. Under the "work first" philosophy, the states are encouraged to place recipients in jobs as quickly as possible. The assumption is that any job is better than no job and that eventually the women will work their way up the ladder. We have seen that this assumption is questionable, at best. Given the lack of education, skills, and work experience, most of the recipients will be working in bad jobs. The Urban Institute study estimates that only 61 percent will have steady work by the time they are in their late twenties, with 36.9 percent working primarily in bad jobs and about a quarter in good jobs; of the remaining 39 percent, most will be jobless. And the more the women share the characteristics of long-term recipients, the poorer the employment prospects. The study predicts that only half of recipients who have not completed high school will work steadily by their late twenties, and only 15.2 percent will have good jobs. Again, the prospects are considerably worse for African American women. Only 16.5 percent of African American women, who have ever been on welfare, will have good jobs, as compared to 28 percent of white women and 31.5 percent of Hispanic and other minority women. The conclusions of the Urban Institute study are sobering, especially for low-skilled mothers. "Among women who had not completed high school and who worked steadily from age 18 to 25, only 40.4 percent worked steadily in a good job by ages 26 and 27. In addition, steady work is not the norm among women who share the characteristics of many welfare recipients. Only about half of high school dropouts and 60 percent of women with children worked steadily by their late twenties."[39]

The future does not look good for the less-skilled worker. Continued levels of unemployment exacerbate the problems of the less-educated worker. High school dropouts, older workers, women, and members of minority groups were less likely to be reemployed.[40] Other factors include the sectoral shifts in employment; wages in the service sector are lower but skill levels are higher. While the impact of immigration varies, there has been a large increase in less-educated immigrants and this has contributed to the decline in the labor market for high school dropouts.[41] There is the continuing uncertain effects of imports of manufacturing goods from Third World countries.[42] Nonwhite men and women still suffer from discrimination, especially African Americans who are associated with inner-city culture.[43]

This, then, is the labor market for the population that we are concerned with—overall declining real wages, increasing education and skills requirements (even more than high school) for the better jobs, and increasing low-wage, part-time jobs without benefits.

The second major reason for the growth of family poverty has been the dramatic changes in family structure. The future is particularly serious for the single-parent family.[44] Although most children still live in two-parent families, there has been a significant growth in single-parent households, mostly female-headed, accounting for about 25 percent of all children. Earnings opportunities are seriously affected by household composition. In 1960, about a quarter of female-headed families were poor; today, it is more than half (53 percent). These families are poor because there is typically only one earner, they usually have child care expenses, and women earn less than men, even when they work the same number of hours. Thus, while female-headed households represent about 10 percent of the population, they account for more than a third of the poverty population and more than half of the increase in poverty since 1990.[45]

Two-parent households will not necessarily escape poverty. In most of the poor households, there is only partial employment or unemployment, but even in families with two wage earners, a fifth remain poor. In these poor households, less than half of the unemployed workers receive unemployment compensation and jobs found after unemployment usually pay, on average, about a third less than the previous job.

Working-Poor Mothers

How do working-poor mothers survive? Here, we rely on ethnographic research done with welfare recipients. Contrary to the stereotype, most welfare recipients are part of the working poor. A large majority of recipients are either in the work force (packaging welfare with earnings) or have recently left a job and had to return to welfare. Then they try again to get off welfare and often succeed. Several studies have now documented that the most common route out of AFDC is through work.[46] Many attempt to exit via work, but for a variety of reasons— lack of health care, a breakdown in child care, low wages, and jobs that do not last—return to welfare. Of those who leave welfare through earned income, about 40 percent remain poor. The picture that emerges is that for most recipients, welfare is a safety net, rather than a "way of life." A large portion of those on welfare are relatively short-termers; another significant portion cycle back and forth between welfare and work, but eventually leave the welfare rolls after about four years; and a smaller fraction are long-term dependents. The long-term dependent is usually the young, poorly educated mother of color: in addition to suffering discrimination, she has more child care needs and less employment skills. But even here, long-term dependency is the exception.

The problem for most welfare recipients—which is also true for the nonwelfare working poor—is not a lack of work ethic, rather it is a lack of jobs that will enable them to become independent.[47] It is a story of low-skilled women in and out of jobs that disappear or who have to leave work because of child care or health or other family problems. There is no support for these wage earners. Because of the labor market and the lack of social support, recipients cannot make it on welfare or work alone. Even if they work full-time, their families remain in poverty. When we look at the characteristics of many of these women, we readily see how disadvantaged they are in competing even for the low-wage, entry-level jobs—they have very little education, have major child-care responsibilities, and uneven or sparse work experience, and many are of color. And even if they do manage to find and keep jobs, as previously noted, "the upper-bound estimate of their earnings should they work *full time-year round* . . . is no more than $12,000–$14,000; given their family sizes, this level of earnings will not remove them from poverty."[48] And this assumes full-time work. In fact, most of these women only find temporary jobs paying less than average wages. "Indeed, the typical former recipient earns about one-half of this 'outer limit' earnings level."[49]

According to the U.S. Census Bureau, at least 40 percent of welfare recipients averaged 1,800 hours over the years 1990 to 1992—which is about the average number of hours of all working mothers—either by combining work with welfare or cycling between work and welfare. They held an average of 1.7 jobs over that period, and 44 percent held two or more jobs, for about 54 weeks. The average number of hours worked per week was 34, which suggests that these women hold "sporadic full-time jobs rather than steady part-time jobs."[50] They averaged about 4 months either laid off or looking for work.

The jobs held by these women were cashiers, nursing aides, food service workers, janitors, maids, and machine operators; the average pay was $4.40 per hour (1990 dollars). Most held food service jobs, which were the shortest duration (30 weeks) and the lowest wages ($3.73 per hour); sales jobs and cleaning service jobs paid $3.94 and $4.08, respectively. The jobs in these categories were more likely to be part-time. The blue-collar jobs paid between $4.38 and $4.65; the white collar jobs paid between $5.24 and $6.40. There was no evidence that changing jobs improved the wages, length of employment, or duration of the jobs. The picture is one of intermittent, low-wage jobs.[51]

Kathryn Edin and Christopher Jencks examined the economic position of AFDC recipients in Chicago.[52] They found an extensive number of women who work for the simple reason that single mothers on welfare cannot pay their bills on welfare alone; they have to obtain additional income, often without telling the welfare department. At that time (1990), a single mother with one child, counting both the welfare grant and food stamps, received $399 per month, or $4,800 per year. Benefits rose per additional child to a maximum of $9,300 if she had four, but these families' total incomes were still only 60 to 75 percent of the poverty line.

Virtually all of the recipients obtained additional income, both legal and illegal, to cover their expenses, either by work or through friends and relatives. Recipients had to obtain additional income because unless they lived in subsidized housing, the AFDC check would not even cover rent and utilities. For those in unsubsidized housing, rent and utilities came to $37 more per month than the welfare check; those in subsidized housing would have $197 extra—still not enough to get through the month. Food stamps help, but again, very few were able to feed their family for the entire month on the stamps alone. Taking the sample as a whole, $314 was spent for food, rent, and utilities. This left only $10 for everything else—clothing, laundry, cleaning supplies, school supplies, transportation, and so forth. Edin calculated that her sample spent about a third of what the average mother in the Midwest spends on these items. Still, it amounted to $351 in excess of the welfare grant, and almost all of this money came from unreported income.

Almost half of the extra money needed to live was earned but not reported. Jobs varied. Some held regular jobs under another name and earned $5 per hour. Others worked off-the-books (bartending, catering, babysitting, sewing) earning an average of $3 per hour. A small number sold drugs, but earned very little ($3–5 per hour). The only high earners ($40 per hour) were occasional prostitutes (five in the sample).

The families' expenses were about $1,000 per month. The federal poverty line in 1990 was a little less than $10,000 per year. This meant that the recipients consumed $2,000 above the poverty line. The poverty line is considered low; most Americans think it should be considerably higher. Edin estimates that the public would put the figure for her sample at about $16,000, or $4,000 higher than the recipients were currently consuming. As a consequence, almost 90 percent of the respondents, in varying degrees, lacked basic necessities and material comforts. Edin reports that they lived in bad neighborhoods in run-down apartments, often without heat and hot water. Roofs and windows leaked. Members of the sample had no telephones or money for entertainment. They could not afford fresh fruits or vegetables. There were some small "extravagances" such as a home video, trips to McDonald's, cigarettes, and alcohol, but the amount spent on these items was only 6 percent of the sample's expenditures. Half of the sample could have cut their expenses if they had been willing to move into

Chicago's worst neighborhoods or the large public housing projects, but these options were considered too dangerous.

The Chicago results have been replicated in Cambridge, Charleston, and San Antonio.[53] Urban welfare mothers need about $1,000 per month to live on, which they get from work, family, male friends, and absent fathers. Working mothers need even more money to pay for transportation, clothing, and child care. These mothers typically spent between $12,000 and $15,000 per year.

If these mothers are so willing to work, why, then, are they also on welfare? The argument of the authors is that "single mothers do not turn to welfare because they are pathologically dependent on handouts or unusually reluctant to work—they do so because they cannot get jobs that pay better than welfare."[54] In fact, "Working mothers faced larger budget deficits than welfare mothers because they often did not get Medicaid and had considerable work-related expenses. Moreover, working mothers had far less time to work at a side job or solicit aid from community groups and charities. Thus, mothers generally found it more difficult to make ends meet when they worked than when they collected welfare."[55] Edin and Lein found that low-wage working mothers were able to survive primarily because they had more noncash resources than welfare recipients—for example, child-care subsidies (or free child care), shared living arrangements, lower commuting costs—in other words, more secure private safety nets, at least for the short term. On the other hand, work was far less stable than welfare.[56]

As stated, most recipients leave welfare for work. Moreover, a great many (more than half) leave during the first year. The problem is that many also return, and then repeat the process again and again. There is significant movement between welfare and work. At least one-half work for at least some of the time that they are on welfare. Although there is some variation depending on the survey, significant numbers—as high as two-thirds—of welfare exits occur when the mother finds a job or continuously works until she leaves welfare.[57] The failure to make a successful exit from welfare is not because of a failure of the work ethic—these women simply cannot make it in the labor market. Not surprisingly, those who are the most disadvantaged in terms of employability, are the least successful in staying off the welfare rolls.[58]

What happens when women leave welfare? Why do some return and not others? While most welfare recipients exit via work, others leave through a change in family circumstances, such as marriage or cohabitation, but remain off welfare only as long as their partner is working. Women who were most successful in remaining off welfare via work were those who had the most investments in human capital, were older (a proxy for work experience), and had an education, especially if it extended beyond high school. Education, in particular, had strong effects in increasing the likelihood of economic independence. The women who have these investments in human capital are often able to maintain their wage rates, continue to work, gain additional education and experience, reduce their poverty (although a third still remained poor after three years), and increase their chances of marriage or cohabitation.[59]

Summing up both the qualitative and quantitative research, most welfare mothers either work or try to work while on welfare, and most leave welfare via work. The "problem" of welfare dependency is the job market and the conditions of work. And for those who do manage to work, according to Edin and Lein, they find that (1) while work pays more than welfare, expenses are greater, often leaving the worker worse off than the recipient; (2) working makes pursuing other income-producing strategies more difficult; (3) work is less stable than welfare; (4) there is little hope for climbing up the employment ladder; and (5) work often conflicts with parenting.[60]

Conclusions: New Directions

The experience of both working and welfare mothers shows the difficulties that mothers have in surviving in the low-wage labor market. The effects of both poverty and low-wage labor reinforce each other. Children growing up in poverty approach adulthood already overburdened. They face a labor market that offers little rewards. Most of these young adults will work, but a great many will still remain in poverty.[61] Many, especially women and their children, will have to rely on welfare. They, too, will struggle in the low-wage labor market, but will most likely remain in poverty. Neither welfare nor work will greatly improve their lives or the lives of the next generation. Policymakers define self-sufficiency as not being on welfare. It has to be redefined to mean a decent life.

We start with the proposition that, at least in the near future, most low-skilled women will be trying to support themselves in the low-wage labor market. The first order of reform, then, is to make sure that jobs are available and to improve the earnings from these jobs. While the long-term goal for our society should be a full-employment economy with well-paying jobs, the reality of the near future, at best, seems to be a relatively full-employment economy with large numbers of low-wage jobs. Such an economy will not reduce poverty. What has to be done is to make work pay.

Current policies assume that jobs are available for all who want them. As discussed, although the precise extent of job availability is difficult to determine since no systematic data are being collected on job vacancies, available evidence does indicate that there are many more low-wage job seekers than there are available slots.[62] We know, for example, that in a labor shortage economy the employment opportunities of those most disadvantaged improve markedly. Richard Freeman found that in a tight labor market (unemployment rate under 4 percent) the employment opportunities and the hourly wages for disadvantaged young men improved considerably.[63]

What is required is an aggressive public policy to stimulate new jobs in economically depressed areas. Such a policy may include programs such as economic incentives to industries to relocate to or remain in these areas, public investments in the infrastructure of the local community, and ultimately public service employment.[64] Job creation programs, such as the Civil Works Administration (CWA) in 1933–34, and the Comprehensive Employment and Training Act (CETA) and the Youth Incentive Entitlement Pilot Projects in the 1970s suggest that, despite the political opposition to them by powerful business interest groups and exaggerated charges of "corruption," they have shown to be quite effective in combating unemployment.[65] CETA, enacted in 1973, provided for direct job creation in response to both cyclical and structural unemployment.[66] The record shows that a public service employment program, if well administered, can be quite effective in creating jobs during periods of high unemployment.[67] One of the legacies of CETA was the Youth Incentive Entitlement Pilot Projects (YIEPP), which represents one of the largest national demonstrations to test the feasibility and effectiveness of a job creation program in reducing youth unemployment. The demonstration was successfully implemented and created jobs for more than 76,000 youth in 11,000 work sites. Most jobs were of adequate quality and provided meaningful work experiences and not make-work. The project showed that a major reason for high minority youth unemployment is lack of jobs.[68] Reviewing the experience with these and other public employment programs, Levitan and Gallo argue that if adequately funded, such programs could be quite effective. They calculate that if we set as a target an unemployment rate of 4 percent, then the federal employment programs at their peek (1979) reduced the job deficit by 43 percent.[69] The bottom line is that any successful strategy to reduce poverty will require the assurance of employment to those who can work.

While the long-term policy should be an economy of well-paying jobs, in the near term, probably the best that we can hope for is higher levels of low-paying jobs. This is a starting point. However, in order to reduce the poverty of low-wage workers, these jobs have to be supplemented both in terms of earnings and benefits.

The Earned Income Tax Credit (EITC)

First enacted in 1975, the EITC has become a significant redistribution program, which, at least until recently, enjoyed strong bipartisan support. The EITC supplements earnings either through a tax reduction, or, if the family owes no taxes, a refundable tax credit.[70] Today, nearly 14 million families receive the credit. The benefits are substantial. For example, for a family with two or more children, earning $8,500 per year, the benefit will be $3,370 (39.7 percent), which brings them to just about the poverty line.[71] When fully phased in, more than six million working families with incomes below the poverty line will be eligible for benefits, the poverty gap will be decreased by $6.4 billion, and the incomes of 1 million taxpayers will be raised above the poverty line.[72] It will be the largest cash program directed at low-income families.[73]

To illustrate the effects of the EITC on a welfare family, in Eden and Jencks's study of working welfare mothers in Chicago, the jobs they had paid about $5 per hour. If a mother worked 25 hours per week, 48 weeks at $5 per hour, she would earn $6,000, less $460 in payroll taxes, and receive about $2,400 EITC The total—$7,940—is $3,140 more than that family would get from the state oı Illinois (AFDC and food stamps comes to $4,800 per year). We have noted that a majority of welfare recipients are already working, and more than two-thirds will exit welfare via work. Over time, the changes in the EITC should greatly accelerate that process.

The EITC has thus far remained popular because it encourages work and provides income for the working poor. However, the EITC is not trouble-free.[74] In addition to the issue of work incentives[75] and participation rates,[76] probably the most important problem right now with the EITC involves program integrity.[77] There is a high error rate; and it is hard to know how much is due to fraud or to ignorance. After all, a great deal of the population that is affected by the EITC lacks the experience and the skill in dealing with the Internal Revenue Service (IRS). Many of the error-producing aspects of the EITC can be cured by changing the rules and the forms, although there will be tradeoffs.[78] Granted there are problems of program integrity that have to be addressed; however, it is difficult to fathom why the EITC is now under attack. For more than two decades, it has enjoyed bipartisan support because it is an effective measure that both reduces poverty and rewards work.

Wage Subsidies

Haveman and Scholz argue that the EITC does not go far enough in correcting the employment barriers facing low-wage, low-skilled workers.[79] Despite high levels of employment, certain groups cannot get jobs primarily because they lack skills and education. Not only are such workers not profitable for business, but minimum wage laws, union wage contracts, and fringe benefits and payroll taxes further compound the market disadvantages of the low-skilled. They propose, in combination with the EITC, a permanent wage subsidy to increase hiring incentives. There would be the combination of a employer-based (demand side) and employee-based (supply side) incentives that would equalize the employment opportunities of the low-wage, low-skilled worker at a reasonable cost—certainly lower than providing jobs—and will raise the incomes of the low-skilled workers.[80] There are other subsidy proposals.[81]

Family Allowances; Refundable Tax Credit

All industrialized countries—except the United States—have a child allowance.[82] The United States may be moving toward this direction by means of the refundable tax credit. While similar to the child allowance, as far as family economics is concerned, administration is different. With a child allowance, every family receives a weekly or monthly check. With the tax credit, the worker would receive an offset to withholding. With no wage earners, the family would have to apply for the credit.

The cost of a $1,000 refundable tax credit would be $40 billion. But its antipoverty effects would be substantial. It is estimated that a $1,000 refundable tax credit (per child under 18), an assured child support benefit ($2,000 for the first eligible child), and national health insurance would reduce the poverty rate by 43 percent and the welfare caseload by 22 percent; it would also raise the annual incomes of poor families by $2,500, and result in more work hours for welfare recipients.[83]

Raising the Minimum Wage

In the decades prior to the 1980s, a full-time worker with a family of three, working at the minimum wage, would be above the poverty line. During the 1980s, the Reagan administration refused to raise the minimum wage ($3.35 per hour), and its value fell sharply. In 1991, it was finally raised to $4.25 per hour, but since then, its purchasing power has slipped; by 1996, the minimum wage sank to its lowest level in over forty years.[84] Finally, new legislation was passed raising the minimum wages in two stages—to $4.75 in October 1996 and to $5.15 on September 1, 1997. The Department of Labor estimates that when the full effect is in place, 9.7 million workers will have received a raise, and minimum wage workers will receive an additional $1,800 per year in potential income.[85]

Not everyone is covered by the minimum wage. The Department of Labor estimates that only 30 percent of all employers and approximately 70 percent of the work force is covered by the Fair Labor Standards Act (FLSA).[86] The most significant exemption is for small businesses; more than 11 million firms are below the FLSA minimum ($500,000). While most exempted employees are probably teenagers, it could be that exempt small retail businesses are likely employers of poor young mothers. And these wages are often substantially below the federal minimum wage.

The major argument against raising the minimum wage is that it will reduce employment.[87] However, in several recent empirical studies, based on the 1990–91 increase in the federal minimum wage, and the establishment of a teenage subminimum, the opposite was found—both employment, and hourly and weekly earnings *increased*.[88] And, unemployment continues to decline despite the recent rise in the minimum wage. Thus, it would seem that raising the minimum wage, at least modestly, should be continued. Raising the minimum wage *in combination* with the EITC, plus food stamps, will have a substantial effect in improving the returns from low-wage work and reducing poverty.[89]

The chapters that follow discuss specific barriers for low-wage women workers, for example, access to child care and health care, the failure of the unemployment insurance system, the need for basic information as to employment opportunities and support services, as well as the more general problems that women living on the edge have in dealing with professionals and government agencies. The poverty conditions of these women workers make most of these barriers more difficult to negotiate. This is not to say that increased earnings solve everything—for example, there will always be a need for health insurance for the working poor—but a vital, necessary condition is to reduce income poverty. A higher income allows more choice in child care, expands the opportunity to secure better housing and health care, and increases the ability to weather the vagaries of the labor market. Similarly, higher incomes are important for the case studies that discuss alternative employment opportunities—microenterprise and improving the quality of traditionally low-wage work. People starting businesses on their own, with family and friends, will also be depending on part- or full-time work to supplement their income. Businesses that strive to improve the quality of low-wage work will be at less of a competitive advantage. While the rest of this book is a series of case examples of particular barriers and strategies, an underlying goal is to reduce the income poverty of these low-wage workers.

Notes

This chapter is based on Joel Handler and Yeheskel Hasenfeld, *We the Poor People: Work, Poverty, and Welfare* (New Haven, CT: Yale University Press, 1997), chapters 3 and 5. Reprinted with permission from The Century Foundation, formerly the Twentieth Centuryy Fund, New York.

1. Alice Kessler-Harris, *Out to Work: A History of Wage-Earning Women in the United States* (New York: Oxford University Press, 1982).
2. Aimee Dechter and Pamela Smock, "The Fading Breadwinner Role and the Economic Implications for Young Couples," Discussion Papers DP# 1051–94, Institute for Research on Poverty, University of Wisconsin, Madison, 1994.
3. Rebecca Blank, *It Takes a Nation* (New York: Russell Sage Foundation, 1997), pp. 42–47.
4. Lawrence Mishel and Gary Burtless, *Recent Wage Trends: The Implications for Low Wage Workers* (Washington, DC: Economic Policy Institute, 1995).
5. In 1993, the male unemployment rate for African American high school dropouts was 42.1 percent and for graduates, 21.3 percent. For whites, the comparable figures were 18.3 percent and 10.8 percent. Jared Bernstein and Lawrence Mishel, *Trends in the Low-Wage Labor Market and Welfare Reform: The Constraints on Making Work Pay* (Washington, DC: Economic Policy Institute, 1995), Table 4.
6. Blank, *It Takes a Nation*, p. 31.
7. U.S. Department of Labor, Bureau of Labor Statistics, *A Profile of the Working Poor, 1995,* Washington, DC, August 1997, Report 914.
8. Hugh Heclo, "Poverty Politics," in *Confronting Poverty: Prescriptions for Change*, ed. Sheldon Danziger, Gary Sandefur, and Daniel Weinberger (Cambridge, MA: Harvard University Press, 1994), chapter 16.
9. See, e.g., Mishel and Burtless, *Recent Wage Trends;* Blank, *It Takes a Nation*, pp. 79–82.

11. Annette Bernhardt, Martina Morris, and Mark Handcock, "Women's Gains or Men's Losses? A Closer Look at the Shrinking Gender Gap in Earnings," *American Journal of Sociology* 101, no. 2 (1995): 302–28.

12. Ibid, p. 325.

13. Bernstein and Mishel, *Trends in the Low-Wage Labor Market,* p. 1; LaDonna Pavetti, *Moving Up, Moving Out or Going Nowhere? A Study of the Employment Patterns of Young Women* (Washington, DC: Urban Institute Press, 1997).

14. Mishel and Burtless, *Recent Wage Trends,* p. 2.

15. U.S. Department of Labor, *A Profile of the Working Poor,* p. 2.

16. Mishel and Burtless, *Recent Wage Trends,* p. 3.

17. Richard Freeman, "How Labor Fares in Advanced Economies," in *Working under Different Rules,* ed. Richard Freeman (New York: Russell Sage Foundation, 1994), p. 13.

18. U.S. Government Accounting Office, "Workers at Risk: Increased Numbers in Contingent Employment Lack Insurance, Other Benefits," report to the chairman, Subcommittee on Employment and Housing, Committee on Government Operations, 1991; U.S. Bureau of National Affairs, *Daily Labor Report* (Washington, DC: Bureau of National Affairs, 1994) pp. 28–29.

19. Rebecca Blank, "Are Part-Time Jobs Bad Jobs?" in *A Future of Lousy Jobs? The Changing Structure of U.S. Wages,* ed. Gary Burtless (Washington, DC: Brookings Institution, 1990).

20. Karen Holden, "Comment," in *A Future of Lousy Jobs? The Changing Structure of U.S. Wages,* ed. Gary Burtless (Washington, DC: Brookings Institution, 1990); Chris Tilly, *Short Hours, Short Shrift: Causes and Consequences of Part-Time Work* (Washington, DC: Economic Policy Institute, 1990).

21. Controlling for education, gender, and age, part-time workers receive about 40 percent less per hour than full-time workers in the same jobs.

22. *Profile of the Working Poor,* Table 1, p. 6.

23. U.S. Government Accounting Office, *Workers at Risk,* pp. 5–6.

24. See Phillip Harvey, "Combating Joblessness: An Economic Analysis of the Principal Strategies that Have Influenced the Development of Social Welfare and Employment Law in the United States." (Manuscript).

25. Ibid.; Gordon Lafer, "The Politics of Job Training: Urban Poverty and the False Promise of JTPA," *Politics and Society* 22 (1994): 349–88, 351. In a recent study of fast-food restaurants in Harlem, there were 14 job seekers for each vacancy. Kathleen Harris, "Work and Welfare Among Single Mothers in Poverty," *American Journal of Sociology* 99 (1993): 317–52.

26. *Homeless Workers: A Labor Market Analysis* (Los Angeles: Economic Roundtable, August 1997), pp. 39–40.

27. Michael Wiseman, *Who Got New Hope?* (Washington, DC: Manpower Demonstration Research Corporation, 1997).

28. One of the important findings is that despite aggressive outreach, only about 20 percent of the targeted adults ever heard of the program and less than 12 percent of those most likely to be eligible knew any of the details.

29. Wiseman, *Who Got New Hope?,* p. 46.

30. Roger Waldinger, "Black/Immigrant Competition Re-assessed: New Evidence from Los Angeles." UCLA Department of Sociology, preliminary draft, manuscript, 1995.

31. Harry Holzer, *Job Availability for Long-Term AFDC Recipients.* Institute for Research on Poverty, IRP Special Report #65, 1995, p. 17.

32. Waldinger, "Black/Immigrant Competition Re-Assessed."

33. Daniel McMurrer, Isabel Sawhill, and Robert Lerman, *Welfare Reform and Opportunity in the Low-Wage Labor Market* (Washington, DC: Urban Institute Press, 1997);

Pavetti, *Moving Up;* LaDonna Pavetti, *Against The Odds: Steady Employment Among Low-Skilled Women,* a report to the Annie E. Casey Foundation, July 1997 (Washington, DC: Urban Institute Press).

34. McMurrer, Sawhill, and Lerman, *Welfare Reform and Opportunity.*

35. For example, if a mother with two children earned $10,000 (which is slightly less than full-time at the new minimum wage of $5.15 per hour), the EITC would be $3,556 and the value of food stamps $2,400. Payroll taxes would be $765. McMurrer, Sawhill, and Lerman, *Welfare Reform and Opportunity,* p. 5. Payroll taxes would be deducted. The participation rate in food stamps is high. Collecting the EITC is more problematic.

36. Pavetti, *Moving Up.*

37. Ibid., p. 8–9.

38. In FY 1997, states are required to have 25 percent of the single-parent-family caseload in work activities; the participation requirement increases through FY 2002 when 50 percent is required to participate. Ibid., p. 2.

39. Ibid., p. 11.

40. U.S. House of Representatives, Committee on Ways and Means, *1992 Green Book: Background Material and Data on Programs within the Jurisdiction of the committee on Ways and Means* (Washington, DC: U.S. Government Printing Office, 1992), pp. 555–6.

41. Mishel and Burtless, *Recent Wage Trends,* p. 4; Panel on High-Risk Youth, Commission on Behavioral and Social Sciences and Education, National Research Council, *Losing Generations: Adolescents in High-Risk Settings* (Washington, DC: National Academy Press, 1993), chapter 2.

42. Richard Freeman, "Are Your Wages Set in Beijing?" *Journal of Economic Perspectives* 9, no. 3 (1995): 15–32; Mishel and Burtless, *Recent Wage Trends,* p. 6.

43. Panel on High-Risk Youth, *Losing Generations,* chapter 2.

44. Sheldon Danziger and Daniel Weinberger, "The Historical Record: Trends in Family Income, Inequality, and Poverty," in *Confronting Poverty: Prescriptions for Change,* ed. Sheldon Danziger, Gary Sandefur, and Daniel Weinberger (Cambridge, MA: Harvard University Press, 1994), p. 50; Mishel and Burtless, *Recent Wage Trends,* p. 1.

45. U.S. House of Representatives, Committee on Ways and Means, *1993 Green Book: Background Material and Data on Programs within the Jurisdiction of the committee on Ways and Means* (Washington, DC: U.S. Government Printing Office, 1993), p. 1308.

46. Kathleen Harris, "Work and Welfare among Single Mothers in Poverty," *American Journal of Sociology* 99 (1993): 317–52; Kathryn Edin and Laura Lein, "Work, Welfare, and Single Mothers' Economic Survival Strategies," *American Sociological Review* 61 (1996): 253–66.

47. Blank, *It Takes a Nation,* pp. 30–32, chapter 2.

48. Gary Burtless, "Employment Prospects of Welfare Recipients," in *The Work Alternative,* ed. Demetra Nightingale and Robert Haveman (Washington, DC: Urban Institute Press, 1995), pp. 71, 72.

49. Ibid., p. 34.

50. Roberta Spalter-Roth, *Making Work Pay: The Real Employment Opportunities of Single Mothers Participating in the AFDC Program* (Washington, DC: Institute for Women's Policy Research, 1994).

51. Ibid., p. 4.

52. Christopher Jencks, *Rethinking Social Policy: Race, Poverty, and the Underclass* (Cambridge, MA: Harvard University Press, 1992), p. 204.

53. Ibid.

54. Ibid.

55. Edin and Lein, "Work, Welfare, and Single Mothers' Economic Survival Strategies," p. 254.

56. Ibid., pp. 262–3.

57. Harris, "Work and Welfare Among Single Mothers in Poverty," p. 333. See also Mary Jo Bane and David Ellwood, *Welfare Realities: From Rhetoric to Reform* (Cambridge, MA: Harvard University Press, 1994), pp. 55–59.

58. As Gary Burtless puts it, "Even if welfare recipients had no young children to care for—and almost half have children under six—most face severe problems finding and holding good jobs. Limited schooling and poor academic achievement doom most AFDC mothers to low-wage, dead-end jobs." Gary Burtless,"Paychecks or Welfare Checks: Can AFDC Recipients Support Themselves?" *Brookings Review* (Fall 1994): 35.

59. Harris, "Work and Welfare Among Single Mothers in Poverty."

60. Edin and Lein, "Work, Welfare, and Single Mothers' Economic Survival Strategies," p. 263.

61. Panel on High-Risk Youth, *Losing Generations,* chapter 2.

62. Lester Thurow, for example, estimates that the unemployment rate in the U.S. is actually closer to 30 percent, when one counts all those who had dropped out of the labor force and were otherwise unaccounted for. Lester Thurow, "The Crusade That's Killing Prosperity," *The American Prospect* 25 (March–April 1996): 54–59 (http://epn.org/prospect/25/25thur.html).

63. In metropolitan statistical areas with a tight labor market in 1987, for African American youth with twelve years of education or less, the unemployment rate declined from 40.5 percent in 1983 to 7.2 percent in 1987. Richard Freeman, "Employment and Earning of Disadvantaged Young Men in a Labor Shortage Economy," in *The Urban Underclass,* ed. Christopher Jencks and Paul E. Peterson (Washington, DC: Brookings Institution, 1991).

64. Full discussion of these options is beyond the scope of this book, but see Collins, Ginsburg, and Goldberg, *Jobs for All: A Plan for the Revitalization of America* (New York: New Initiatives for Full Employment, 1994). Roberta Spalter-Roth, Heidi Hartmann, and Linda Andrews, *Combining Work and Welfare: An Alternative Anti-Poverty Strategy* (Washington, DC: Institute for Women's Policy Research, 1992), using a conservative estimate, suggested that the creation of 500,000 public service jobs targeted to welfare recipients will cost $6.6 billion (1990 dollars), affect 800,000 women, and save $1.7 billion. Harvey proposed a federal employment assurance program whereby the government would not only stimulate private employment but also supplement, as needed, the regular demand for labor with public employment. Phillip Harvey, *Securing the Right to Employment* (Princeton, NJ: Princeton University Press, 1989).

65. At the height of the Depression, the Civil Works Administration was formally launched on November 9, 1933, and ended on February 15, 1934. In that short period of time, the program provided jobs to 4 million unemployed persons. CWA was strikingly different from typical work-for-relief programs. First, there were no means tests. Two million relief workers were transferred, and 2 million workers were selected on the basis of their skill, training, and experience. Second, the projects selected provided the workers with real jobs paying living wages. Moreover, the workers were entitled to the same medical and compensation benefits as federal employees. The impact on the unemployed hired into CWA was dramatic. "In one stroke, 'clients' became wage earners who would receive cash for their labor to spend as they saw fit." Bonnie Fox Schwartz, *The Civil Works Administration, 1933–1934: The Business of Emergency Employment in the New Deal* (Princeton, NJ: Princeton University Press, 1984).

66. Clifford Johnson, "A Direct Federal Job Creation: Key Issues," National Committee for Full Employment, Job Creation Education Project, 1985.

67. As a strategy to combat structural unemployment, CETA has been shown to produce significant earnings gains, especially when it is targeted for highly disadvantaged populations. Johnson concludes that "Evidence suggest that public service employment programs under CETA enhanced the ability of participants to secure permanent jobs in the public sector, serving as try-out period and providing on-the-job training for adults with limited prior experience." Moreover, the jobs themselves were shown to be useful and meaningful.

One of the arguments against Public Service Employment (PSE) is job substitution, that is that state and local public employers shift their regular employees to the federal payroll rather than create new jobs. However, research by the Brookings Institution, following the 1976 CETA amendments found low rates of substitution. Indeed, when Congress tightened eligibility requirements and imposed wage and job duration limits, the rate of substitution declined further to about 10 percent. Moreover, direct public job creation has been shown to be more cost effective than indirect measures such as tax cuts.

68. Judith Gueron, *Lessons from a Job Guarantee: The Youth Incentive Entitlement Pilot Projects* (New York: Manpower Demonstration Research Corporation, 1984). Indeed, YEIPP created new jobs; for every one and two-third jobs funded by YEIPP, one new job was created. What was particularly impressive about the project is its impact on postdemonstration employment. One year after the demonstration, the earnings of the African American youth were 40 percent higher in comparison to those in the non-demonstration sites.

69. Sar Levitan and Frank Gallo, *Spending to Save: Expanding Employment Opportunities* (Washington, DC: Center for Social Policy Studies, Georgetown University Press, 1991), pp. 15–6.

70. Rebecca Blank, "The Employment Strategy: Public Policies to Increase Work and Earnings," in *Confronting Poverty: Prescriptions for Change,* ed. Sheldon Danziger, Gary Sandefur, and Daniel Weinberger (Cambridge, MA: Harvard University Press, 1994), p. 192. Three very important changes have been made in the Earned Income Tax Credit: (1) It now applies to welfare recipients; previously, at least 50 percent of income had to be from "earnings," (2) benefits have been raised significantly, and (3) EITC receipts are not counted against welfare income. For a short political history of the EITC, see Christopher Howard, "Happy Returns: How the Working Poor Got Tax Relief," *The American Prospect* no. 17 (Spring 1994): 46.

71. Robert Greenstein, *The Earned Income Tax Credit: A Target for Budget Cuts?* (Washington, DC: Center on Budget and Policy Priorities, 1995), p. 10. In 1996, the EITC rate is 40 percent of earnings for families with two or more children (a maximum credit of $3,370) and 34 percent for families with one child (a maximum of $2,040) and will also cover low-income childless taxpayers ($306). For families with two or more children, the EITC increases a minimum-wage job to $5.95 per hour ($5.70 for a one-child taxpayer).

72. Robert Haveman and John Scholz, "Transfers, Taxes, and Welfare Reform," *National Tax Journal* 7, no. 2 (1994): 17; John Scholz, "The Earned Income Tax Credit: Participation, Compliance, and Antipoverty Effectiveness," *National Tax Journal* 7, no. 1 (1994): 3.

73. John Scholz, "Tax Policy and the Working Poor: The Earned Income Tax Credit," *Focus* 15, no. 3 (1993–94): 2. By FY 1998, the EITC is expected to cost $24.5 billion a year (the federal share of AFDC will be $16 billion).

74. Anne Alstott, "The Earned Income Tax Credit and the Limitations of Tax-Based Welfare Reform," *Harvard Law Review* 108 (1995): 533; Barbara Kirchheimer, "The EITC: Where Policy and Practicality Collide," *Tax Notes* (October 3, 1994): 15–18.

75. The credit increases with earnings until a maximum; then there is a "phase-out"

during which the amount of the credit decreases until the break-even point. Critics argue that many workers are in the phase-out range; these workers are potentially the more productive, and it is bad policy to subject them to disincentives in order to provide a work incentive for a small number of welfare recipients. Many economists, as well as the General Accounting Office (GAO), argue that the expansion of the EITC will induce single mothers to enter the labor force with only a slight disincentive to other recipients. The two most important studies of the effects of EITC on labor supply are based on the Seattle-Denver income maintenance experiment. However, that study was done twenty years ago and may be no longer relevant today. In addition, practically all of the EITC is a year-end lump-sum payment; therefore, the disincentive effects on the phase-out may be less evident. Finally, the most positive effects of EITC are for households either not working or not earning much. The most serious negative effects are on households already working a significant amount. Blank, "The Employment Strategy," p. 193. See also Alstott, "The Earned Income Tax Credit," p. 546; Scholz, "Tax Policy and the Working Poor," pp. 8–9.

76. In order to receive the EITC, a family has to file a tax return. It is estimated that between 1.3 and 2 million eligible taxpayers do *not* get refunds. Scholz, "Tax Policy and the Working Poor," pp. 3–4.

77. Kirchheimer, "The EITC: Where Policy and Practicality Collide."

78. Scholz recommends that various nontaxable benefits should be excluded (e.g., military benefits, housing allowances), changing the support-based definition of a dependent (the GAO estimates that 9 million dependent exemptions were erroneously claimed) to rely on residency, and the age requirements for qualifying children, conduct outreach for the advance payment option, provide integration with AFDC and food stamps as proposed by the Michigan experiment, and possibly restrict the EITC to wage and salary income. Scholz, "Tax Policy and the Working Poor," p. 10. See George Yin, John Scholz, Jonathan Forman, and Mark Mazur, "Improving Delivery of Benefits to the Working Poor: Proposals to Reform the Earned Income Credit Tax Program," *Tax Notes Today* (October 29, 1993). Some reforms have been enacted, and others are proposed. In 1990, changes were made in many of the EITC eligibility rules, a new form was introduced, and IRS verification procedures (e.g., matching Social Security numbers, verifying numbers of children in EITC families, requiring additional documentation in selected cases) had been introduced. The GAO is of the opinion that these changes would remove principal sources of errors. Preliminary studies by the IRS indicate a significant reduction in the number of filers and in the error rates. Greenstein, *The Earned Income Tax Credit,* pp. 13–16. More recent legislation is designed to further tighten the EITC. Nonresident aliens are excluded; Social Security numbers are to be provided for children under age one; households with more than $2,350 in income from investments are ineligible. Additional tightening measures are proposed by the Treasury Department, the Senate, and the GAO. Greenstein, *The Earned Income Tax Credit,* pp. 29–31.

79. Haveman and Scholz, "Transfers, Taxes, and Welfare Reform."

80. For example, if the target wage were set at $10 per hour, then a worker taking a job at $6 would receive an additional $2 (or 50 percent). They estimate that the cost of providing public service jobs would be $17,000 per worker per year. The authors also propose capital accounts for young people and poor families. For a less sanguine view of the effectiveness of wage subsidies, see Laurie Bassi, "Stimulating Employment and Increasing Opportunity for the Current Work Force," in *The Work Alternative: Welfare Reform and the Realities of the Job Market,* ed. Demetra Smith Nightingale and Robert H. Haveman (Washington, DC: Urban Institute Press, 1995).

81. Edmund Phelps, "Raising the Employment and Pay of the Working Poor: Low-Wage Employment Subsidies versus the Welfare State," *AEA Papers and Proceedings* 84,

no. 2 (1994): 54–58. Some countries allow the long-term unemployed to use part of their unemployment benefits as vouchers to firms that hire them. An innovative approach to encourage welfare recipients to "make work pay" through wage supplementation has been tried in Canada's Income Assistance program (the equivalent to AFDC). Under the Self-Sufficiency Program (SSP), recipients who work 30 hours or more per week receive substantial financial incentives to work, while being subject to a relatively low marginal tax rate on earnings. The SSP supplement is equal to half the difference between the participant's gross earnings and a "target" earnings level. In British Columbia, the target was set at $37,000 (Canadian dollars). A recipient who worked for 30 hours per week at $7 per hour would earn $10,500 per year and receive a $13,250 SSP supplement. By comparison, the Income Assistance grant for a single parent with one child in British Columbia is $12,478. Eligibility for SSP is limited to recipients who have been on aid for at least a year, and the SSP supplement payments are limited to three years. The impact analysis of the first 18 months shows that there was a 13.1 percent increase in the employment rate (or a 50 percent increase relative to the average employment rate in the control group). The increase in average monthly earnings was $137 (or a 60 percent increase relative to the control group), even though the program group members were taking fairly low-wage jobs. There was also a 14 percent reduction in the proportion of the program participants receiving Income Assistance, yet the total income (earnings plus Income Assistance) increased by a monthly average of $235 (or 23 percent more relative to the control group). These findings are quite encouraging, showing how a combination of earnings and wage supplementation (in a form of income assistance) can lift recipients out of poverty. Yet, they also point to the fact that the participants were working in low-wage jobs, and unless their wages continue to improve after the three-year limit, they may have to return to welfare. David Card and Philip Robins, *Do Financial Incentives Encourage Welfare Recipients to Work?* (Vancouver, BC: Social Research and Demonstration Corporation, February 1996).

82. Irwin Garfinkel and Sara McLanahan, "Single-Mother Families, Economic Insecurity, and Government Policy," in *Confronting Poverty: Prescriptions for Change,* ed. Sheldon Danziger, Gary Sandefur, and Daniel Weinberger (Cambridge, MA: Harvard University Press, 1994), pp. 205–25.

83. Rebecca Kim, Irwin Garfinkel, and Daniel Meyer, *Interaction Effects of A Child Tax Credit, National Health Insurance, and Assured Child Support,* DP # 1047–94 (Madison, WI: Institute for Research on Poverty, 1994).

84. Robert Greenstein, *The Earned Income Tax Credit: A Target for Budget Cuts?* (Washington, DC: Center on Budget and Policy Priorities, 1955), p. 9.

85. Handler and Hasenfeld, *We the Poor People,* n. 90, p. 249.

86. Bradley Schiller, "Below-Minimum Wage Workers: Implications for Minimum-Wage Models," *Quarterly Review of Economics and Finance* 34 (1994): 131–43.

87. Richard Burkhauser, Kenneth Crouch, and Andrew Glenn, "Public Policies for the Working Poor: The Earned Income Tax Credit Versus Minimum Wage Legislation," Discussion Paper 1074, Institute for Research on Poverty, University of Wisconsin, 1995; David Card and Alan Krueger, *Myth and Measurement: The New Economics of the Minimum Wage* (Princeton, NJ: Princeton University Press, 1995), p. 4. Since most minimum wage workers are teenagers, the research applies mostly to that group. According to Ronald Ehrenberg, prior research has shown—*ceteris paribus*—that a 10 percent increase in the minimum wage would be result in a 1 to 3 percent decrease in teen employment. Ronald Ehrenberg, "New Minimum Wage Research: Symposium Introduction," Industrial and Labor Relations Review 46 (1992): 3–5.

88. Lawrence Katz and Alan Krueger, "The Effect of the Minimum Wage on the Fast-Food Industry," *Industrial and Labor Relations Review* 46 (1992): 6–21; David Card

and Alan Krueger, *Myth and Measurement: The New Economics of the Minimum Wage* (Princeton, NJ: Princeton University Press, 1995).

89. According to the Department of Labor, quoting a recent analysis by the Economic Policy Institute and preliminary work by the U.S. DHHS, 300,000 people, including 100,000 children, will be lifted out of poverty when the new law is in full effect. A family of four, with one worker working full-time year round at $5.15 per hour earns $10,300, plus a maximum EITC credit of $3,560, food stamps worth $2,876, less $788 payroll tax, for a total income of $15,600, which is above the poverty line. Furthermore, more female workers receive the minimum wage than men; most of these women (52 percent) are aged 25 years or older; therefore, raising the minimum wage will provide a modest pay raise to the poorest working women, many of whom are raising a family. Handler and Hasenfeld, *We the Poor People;* http://www.dol.gov/dol/esa/public/minwage/bottom.htm.

2

Mark Greenberg

WELFARE RESTRUCTURING AND WORKING-POOR FAMILY POLICY

The New Context

The 1996 federal welfare law represents the beginning of a new stage in U.S. policies affecting unemployed and working-poor families. Much of the initial coverage of the debates, legislation, and early state experience focused on the most apparent features of the new welfare law: time limits, work requirements for families receiving assistance, and restrictions on assistance to legal immigrants. However, over time, other aspects of the law that received less immediate attention are likely to generate significant changes in national and state policies affecting working-poor families.

For many people, the centerpiece of the 1996 federal welfare legislation was the repeal of the Aid to Families with Dependent Children (AFDC) program and its replacement with a new system of Temporary Assistance for Needy Families (TANF) block grants to states. Opinion about the effects of the new structure has been polarized, with proponents asserting that it has already resulted in dramatic effects—most evident by reduced welfare caseloads—and opponents emphasizing the contraction in support provided to poor families and the elimination of the basic federal guarantee of assistance. The 1996 legislation fundamentally changes the structure in which decisions about low-income family policy are made, and the ultimate effects of the legislation cannot be judged by the experience of the first year or several years. However, it is important that persons concerned about working-poor families and family policy understand how the context has now changed, because an understanding of that new context is crucial to understanding the risks and opportunities presented by the new environment.

This chapter describes the key elements of the new federal block grant structure that emerges from the Personal Responsibility and Work Opportunity Reconciliation Act (PRWORA) of 1996, and discusses some of the implications of the federal law change for state and local policy initiatives. The chapter provides a brief description of the prior structure of income support for low-income families, outlines the key features of the block grant structure, and then offers an analysis of some of the risks and opportunities presented by the new structure. Understanding what is permitted, prohibited, possible, and encouraged by the new structure can play a significant role in analyzing the viability of promoting many of the policy proposals outlined in this book.

Before 1996: The Prior Structure of Income Support for Low-Income Families

Until enactment of PRWORA in 1996, there were two principal government sources of cash assistance for low-income families: the Aid to Families with Dependent Children (AFDC) program and the federal Earned Income Tax Credit (EITC). Both were potential sources of income support for working-poor families, though only AFDC assisted families without employment income. In some important respects, AFDC was beginning to take on a greater role in supporting working-poor families at the time of its repeal. It is helpful to understand the pre-1996 structure in order to appreciate the full significance of the new policy context.[1]

The Role of AFDC

Until 1996, Aid to Families with Dependent Children (AFDC) was the nation's principal income support program for families with little or no other income; in 1995, nearly 4.9 million families received cash assistance averaging $377 each month. AFDC was a federal-state cooperative program; no state was required to participate though all states elected to do so. Federal law established a set of program requirements. If a state complied with those requirements, the federal government would pay half or more of the cost for assistance payments made to eligible families. States, in turn, had a responsibility to provide assistance to families who satisfied federal and state eligibility guidelines.

AFDC eligibility rules involved a complex mix of federal requirements and state options. Federal law set the basic framework: states were required to assist needy families that were "deprived of parental support or care"; in practical terms, this meant families where at least one parent was dead, absent from the home, or incapacitated. Under limited circumstances, two-parent families in which one parent was unemployed also qualified for assistance. In some instances, federal law was highly prescriptive; for example, there were detailed federal definitions of what counted as income or who must be counted in an "assistance unit" when a family applied for assistance. At the same time, states had very broad discretion in setting AFDC benefit levels, and, in practice, this effectively determined much as to whether families were eligible for assistance. Since there were no federal standards for determining benefit levels, the actual amounts paid varied widely between states: at one extreme, Alaska paid cash assistance of $923 a month for a family of three with no other income; at the other extreme, Mississippi paid $120. The typical AFDC family also received food stamps and Medicaid, but the combination of AFDC and food stamps only brought a family of three up to 65 percent of the U.S. federal poverty line.[2]

AFDC was not typically thought of as a program of assistance to working-poor families. A key moment in program history had occurred in 1981, when the Reagan administration sought and obtained amendments to federal law to restrict the eligibility of working-poor families in the interest of reducing program costs and targeting assistance to the most needy.[3] Under the 1981 changes, families with earnings became less likely to qualify for assistance. Moreover, an AFDC family entering employment became more likely to lose eligibility for assistance either immediately or within a few months. As a result, the share of employed families receiving assistance declined. In 1994, only 9 percent of AFDC families reported earnings in an average month; in 1973, the comparable figure had been 16 percent.

In and before its final years, AFDC was a program in transition, enormously controversial and deeply unpopular. The program was criticized both for failing to provide adequate support to needy families and for providing sufficient support to function as a work disincentive and as an incentive to the formation and maintenance of single-parent families. Perhaps the most common articulation of "the problem" with AFDC is that it had been created in the 1930s as a program intended to provide income support at a point where mothers were not generally participating or expected to participate in the paid labor force. Since that time, there had been a dramatic increase in women's labor force participation.[4] With that increased participation, it became increasingly problematic to have a program that seemed designed to discourage labor market participation. Thus, an increasing focus of reform efforts became how to redesign AFDC into a program that encouraged, supported, and required employment by parents who were able to enter the work force.

Before 1996, there had been several rounds of initiatives intended to strengthen the linkage between AFDC and employment. The last major federal legislative enactment before the 1996 legislation was the Family Support Act of 1988. The Family Support Act had a number of significant features: it expanded child support enforcement; provided additional funding to states for education, training, and employment-related services for AFDC families; increased the circumstances under which adults and teen parents could be required to participate in employment-related activities; required states to guarantee child care assistance for families receiving AFDC assistance; and required states to provide up to one year of transitional child care and Medicaid assistance for families leaving AFDC due to hours or earnings from employment.

Beginning in 1992, state initiatives under the Family Support Act began to be supplemented by a new set of restructuring efforts under what was known as the waiver process. A provision of federal law allowed the federal government to waive a number of program rules for states engaged in experimental demonstration research projects. Beginning in 1992, first the Bush and then the Clinton administrations began to freely grant waivers of federal AFDC rules for state demonstration projects. While much public attention focused on the more restrictive aspects of state rule changes, the actual state directions involved a mixture of expansion and contractions of program eligibility.

One significant aspect of state waiver initiatives involved expansion of assistance to working-poor families. In part, states were concerned that a structure that sharply reduced assistance when families entered employment did not provide sufficient incentives to look for and accept low-wage employment. In part, states were concerned that the lack of sufficient income in the initial months of employment could make it more difficult for families to retain employment. And, some states were simply concerned that many of the jobs available to the families with limited educations and work histories did not provide sufficient income to meet family needs and believed that supplemental assistance was appropriate as a means of reducing poverty of working-poor families.

As a result, new policies to expand AFDC support to working-poor families were one of the principal initiatives in the AFDC "waiver process." From 1992 to 1996, most states modified their rules to expand the circumstances under which working-poor families qualified for assistance. The most common approach was to change program rules concerning treatment of earnings, so that families receiving assistance did not face a dollar-for-dollar loss of that assistance after entering employment. States also modified their rules concerning treatment of two-parent families so that such families would not lose eligibility for assistance when working a limited number of hours per month.

Beside expanding the availability of AFDC assistance to working-poor families, states also used the waiver process to expand the availability of health care and child care for families leaving AFDC due to employment or for families who could be diverted from receiving AFDC by providing access to health care and child care.

Approaches to expand assistance to the working poor were not the only direction taken in the waiver process. Other common directions included:

- increasing requirements to participate in employment-related activities as a condition of receiving support;
- increasing penalties for families that failed to comply with work, child support cooperation, or other program behavioral requirements;
- expanding the circumstances in which two-parent families could qualify for assistance;
- removal of the most restrictive program asset requirements (i.e., the amount of savings or other assets that a family could have and still qualify for assistance);
- imposition of time limits on assistance; in some instances, requiring participation in a work program as a condition of further assistance after reaching a time limit, and in other instances, seeking to reduce or terminate assistance for families reaching a time limit;

- imposition of new behavioral requirements (e.g., penalties for failure to satisfy school attendance or preventive health care requirements, denial of assistance for children born while a family received assistance).[5]

The waiver process was sometimes viewed as allowing states to move in 50 different directions. In fact, it was more accurately viewed as resulting in 50 (or nearly 50) variants on a single direction. At the point at which the AFDC program terminated, many states appeared to be moving toward a new vision of a means-tested income support program, which combined strong requirements to participate in employment-related activities, time limits on the availability of program assistance, and increased support for working-poor families both inside the outside of the program.

The new vision created an obvious tension between the goal of using AFDC to expand income support to working-poor families and the goal of making AFDC assistance time-limited and temporary. This tension, apparent on paper, had not fully been experienced in practice at the point when Congress eliminated the program in 1996, because many of the time-limit provisions had only recently been implemented and there was little experience with what would happen as more families reached time limits.

The new vision also created a tension between the goal of using AFDC to promote and enforce employment expectations and the goal of ensuring that a basic safety net would exist to prevent destitution of poor families with children. If the only goal for states was the promotion of employment, then it might seem straightforward that termination of assistance after time limits and severe penalties for noncompliance with employment requirements might maximize the number of employment entries. Yet such policies could pose significant risks to the well-being of low-income families when parents cannot or do not find stable employment. Thus, a central question in welfare policy was becoming that of how (or whether) to strike a balance between the imposition of requirements and penalties and the policies needed to avoid more extreme deprivations for poor families.

The Role of the EITC

While the AFDC program was in transition, the Earned Income Tax Credit (EITC) was undergoing dramatic growth and coming to replace AFDC as the principal source of income assistance for low-income families (although AFDC still provided more support to families below the poverty line). The EITC is a federal tax credit primarily available to low-income families with children and employment earnings. The EITC began as a small program in 1975 but was repeatedly expanded (in legislation in 1986, 1990, and 1993). Although structured as a tax credit, the EITC is "refundable," meaning that if the amount of credit that a family qualifies for exceeds the family's tax liability, the federal government will make a payment to the family of that excess amount. By 1996, the total cost of the EITC to the federal government was $25 billion, an amount exceeding the combined federal and state costs for AFDC benefits; 86 percent of EITC costs involved direct payments to families, and 70 percent of EITC costs were for single-parent families.[6]

Mechanically, the EITC provides a tax credit that represents a percentage of earnings, up to a maximum amount, which is then gradually phased out. For a taxpayer with two or more children, the EITC in 1996 provided a tax credit of 40 percent of the family's first $8,890 of earned income, up to a maximum credit of $3,556. The amount of the tax credit would then remain constant until the family's earnings reached the phase-out level ($11,610 in 1996), at which point the EITC would begin being phased out at a rate of $.21 for each additional dollar of income.[7] Thus, the EITC provided its maximum assistance to a family in the $8,890 to $11,610 range, that is, weekly wages of $177.80 to $232.20 for a parent working fifty weeks a year.

Conceptually, then, the EITC works quite differently than state AFDC programs worked in providing assistance to working families. In AFDC, a family with no earnings would begin with an AFDC benefit level, and the benefit level would be reduced, either slowly or rapidly, as the family's earnings increased. In contrast, the EITC provides no assistance at all to a family with no earnings, and the amount of the EITC increases, rather than decreases, until the family reaches the point where the EITC hits its plateau. Thus, the strength of the EITC as a policy device is that it provides no assistance to those who do not work and has a continuing work incentive, at least until the family reaches the point where phasing out of benefits begins to occur. At the same time, the strength of the EITC is also its weakness: it provides no assistance to families when unemployed or unable to attain employment, and provides the least assistance to those who are able to earn the least.

The other most significant difference between the two approaches is, of course, the delivery mechanism: the use of the tax system versus the use of the welfare system. On the one hand, providing assistance through the tax system offers advantages in avoiding stigma, reducing administrative costs, and integrating income and tax policy. However, the tax system faces significant limits as a means of providing income support because it is primarily based on determining liabilities (or credits) retrospectively on an annual basis (i.e., determining the liability or credit for 1996 after 1996 has been completed). While there is a mechanism for projecting and providing a portion of the EITC that a family appears to qualify for, through a system of advance payments incorporated into the recipient's paycheck, this system is rarely used—in 1995, it was used in less than 1 percent of all cases.

Thus, until the point at which AFDC was repealed, the EITC and AFDC could have been viewed as playing complementary roles in assisting low-income families. AFDC provided its principal assistance on a monthly basis to families with little or no income, with the amount of assistance either gradually or rapidly reduced when families entered employment. The EITC typically provided once-a-year assistance, with a design ensuring that it provided the least assistance to the poorest families but with a structure intended to encourage increased work effort. Taken together, the programs provided both monthly and annual assistance to working-poor families, though with some significant gaps in coverage and with the increasing restrictions on AFDC limiting the potential role of that program as a source of ongoing assistance.

The New Block Grant Structure and the New Set of Choices

The landscape for decisions about the provision of support to unemployed and working-poor families changed in a fundamental way as a result of enactment of the Personal Responsibility and Work Opportunity Reconciliation Act of 1996 (PRWORA). The 1996 legislation affected a broad array of programs for low-income families and individuals.[8] This chapter focuses on a key component of the legislation that is likely to have a particularly notable impact on the shaping of working-poor family policy: the repeal of the AFDC program and the enactment of the Temporary Assistance for Needy Families (TANF) block grant. In addition, it describes some of the key provisions of the Child Care and Development block grant, as it will interact with TANF in important ways. The following sections outline the principal aspects of the changes, and then highlight some of the most notable implications for working-poor family policy.

Key Requirements of TANF

The TANF provisions of the 1996 law are sometimes described as turning over the AFDC program to the states, while imposing time limits and work requirements on those receiving assistance. The actual nature of the change is more substantial and more radical than that.

It is most helpful to understand the TANF framework as having seven key components, discussed in the following paragraphs.[9]

A Block Grant of Essentially Fixed Funding

First, AFDC and a set of related programs were repealed, and in their stead, each state is provided with a block grant of essentially fixed funding. The amount of the block grant is approximately what the state received from the federal government for AFDC and a set of related programs in 1994, 1995, or the 1992–1994 average. A minority of states qualify for 2.5 percent annual adjustors for four years; otherwise, the block grant amounts stay constant through 2002 except for any adjustments due to bonuses or penalties. Under limited circumstances, a state experiencing an economic downturn may qualify for additional federal funding through a contingency fund.

The framework of an essentially fixed block grant was modified for a limited period of time when in 1997, Congress amended the TANF law to create a $3 billion funding stream for Welfare-to-Work (WtW) grants for FY 98 and FY 99. A state must contribute matching funds to receive its share of WtW funds. WtW funds must be expended for certain specified employment-related services for a population of "hard-to-employ individuals" and "individuals with long-term welfare dependence characteristics." Unless the Secretary of Labor approves another arrangement, WtW funds will be administered by local private industry councils rather than by TANF agencies.[10]

Broad State Discretion

States have extremely broad state discretion in deciding how to spend their TANF grants. The legislation sets forth a set of purposes, and states may spend their block grants in any manner reasonably calculated to accomplish these purposes. One permissible purpose is to provide assistance to needy families; the others are to end dependency on government benefits by promoting job preparation, work, and marriage; to discourage out-of-wedlock pregnancies; and to encourage the formation and maintenance of two-parent families.[11]

A Limited "Maintenance of Effort" Obligation

A state risks a reduction in its block grant if the state fails to spend state funds at a level reaching at least 80 percent (or in some circumstances, 75 percent) of the amount the state was spending in 1994 for a set of programs. A broad range of state programs and activities in relation to needy families can count toward satisfying the maintenance of effort requirement, and the amount will not be adjusted for inflation. Thus, in 2002, the required commitment of state resources will still be 75 percent or 80 percent of what the state was spending for AFDC-related programs in 1994.

No Entitlements to Assistance

The legislation ends entitlements to assistance under federal law. This means that there is no group that the state is legally required to assist with its TANF funds. Under prior law, states were legally obligated to assist those who were eligible under AFDC rules. Under TANF, states have broad discretion in deciding who will be eligible for assistance and once the state defines the groups eligible for assistance in its program, the state has no obligation under federal law to assist them.

Time Limits on Federally Funded Assistance

States are prohibited from using federal TANF funds to assist families in which an adult has received federal TANF assistance for sixty months, subject to allowable exceptions for up to 20 percent of a state's cases. States are free to use their own funds to assist families that have reached the federal time limits, and months in which a family is assisted with state funds (as opposed to federal TANF funds) do not count against the federal limit. A state is also free to impose time limits shorter than the federal sixty-month limit.

Federal Work and Participation Requirements

There are two principal work/participation requirements in the TANF structure. First, a state must describe how it will require all parents or caretakers receiving TANF assistance to "engage in work" within 24 months of beginning to receive TANF assistance. States have broad discretion in implementing this provision, as it appears to be largely up to states to determine what activities count as being "engaged in work" for purposes of the twenty-four-month requirement.

Second, states risk fiscal penalties if they do not meet federal TANF *participation rates*. A participation rate for all families receiving TANF assistance starts at 25 percent in FY 97 and reaches 50 percent in FY 2002; in addition, a higher rate is calculated for two-parent families receiving assistance. For each participation rate, a state risks a fiscal penalty if it does not ensure that the required percentage of families are engaged in activities that count toward the participation rate requirements. Involvement in work counts toward the participation rates; under limited circumstances, involvement in certain education or training programs can count, though the restrictions on when education and training can count are broadly viewed as an attempt to discourage states from extensively relying on such activities in their programs.

The participation-rate rules contain a strong incentive for states to reduce the number of families receiving assistance. A state's required participation rate can be adjusted downward if the state's caseload has declined since 1995 for reasons other than changes in the eligibility rules; for example, if the caseload fell by 10 percent from 1995 to 1996, the state's required participation rate could be adjusted downward by 10 percentage points (i.e., from 25 percent to 15 percent). Thus, a state's strategy for meeting the participation rate requirements might either involve increasing the number of recipients in countable work activities or simply reducing the number of families receiving assistance, or some combination of the two.

An Emphasis on Discouraging Out-of-Wedlock Pregnancies

Reduction of out-of-wedlock pregnancies is one of the express goals of TANF, and one of the permissible uses of TANF funds is expenditures seeking to reduce out-of-wedlock pregnancies. In addition, a state may qualify for a federal bonus payment if it is among the states that demonstrate the largest reductions in the share of out-of-wedlock births while reducing the number of abortions in the state.

TANF and the Child Care and Development Block Grant

TANF will interact in important ways with the other block grant created by the 1996 legislation, the Child Care and Development Block Grant (also known as the Child Care and Development Fund). The CCDBG consolidates four federal child care funding streams into a single block grant and allows states broad discretion in the design of state child care systems.

Before enactment of the 1996 legislation, one of the principal criticisms of federal child care funding was its fragmented nature: federal funding explicitly targeted for low-income child care was located within four different programs:

- AFDC Child Care provided open-ended federal matching funds for child care for AFDC recipients who needed child care to participate in education, training, or employment;
- Transitional Child Care provided open-ended federal matching funds for up to one year of child care assistance to families leaving AFDC due to employment;
- At-Risk Child Care was a capped federal matching funding stream providing limited funding for child care for non-AFDC low-income working families; and
- the Child Care and Development Block Grant was a capped block grant provided to states for child care, and could be used for both AFDC and non-AFDC families.

Child care was guaranteed for AFDC families (under the law, if not always in practice) and for families qualifying for transitional child care, but not for other families, and there were numerous large and small differences in rules among the varying funding streams.

The 1996 legislation essentially consolidated each of these funding streams into a single Child Care and Development Fund. States qualify for part of their funding without any state match requirement and can qualify for additional funds (up to a capped limit) by meeting a "maintenance of effort" requirement and contributing additional state funds. While the total amounts available are capped, the caps were set at a level above that which states were projected to reach under prior law.

Under the new child care structure, the previous federal guarantees were eliminated, so that no group of low-income families now has any assurance of child care assistance under federal law. States are, of course, free to develop their own guarantees and assurances if they choose to do so.

The fiscal interaction between the TANF block grant and the Child Care and Development Block Grant is a significant feature of the new structure. In relative terms, the TANF block grant is much larger: in 1997, federal spending for the TANF block grant was projected to be $16.4 billion, while federal spending for the Child Care and Development Block Grant would only reach $3 billion (if all states drew down available funds). However, the law permits states to transfer up to 30 percent of their TANF funds into the Child Care block grant, and also permits states to spend an unlimited share of their TANF funds for child care without transferring the funds.

Early State TANF Experience

The TANF legislation was enacted in August 1996. States electing to participate (as all states chose to do) were permitted to begin implementing their TANF Programs almost immediately and were required to begin implementation no later than July 1, 1997.

Two principal themes emerged early in the implementation of TANF. First, in establishing their program rules, most states continued and often accelerated the policy directions that had emerged in the years immediately before the law was enacted, with implementation of time limits, increasingly strong work-related requirements, and penalties against families who did not meet state requirements. Second, TANF implementation was accompanied by a dramatic reduction in the number of families receiving assistance across the country.

After having received broad discretion in the use of block-grant funds, most states initially opted for structures that looked like those that had been emerging from the waiver process in the last years of the AFDC system. As a result, the initial state TANF rules typically did not look very different from the rules that had been in place immediately before the law passed in 1996. However, because the waiver process had already resulted in radical change, the initial TANF rules were significantly different from, for example, the rules that had been in place in 1992. The key changes since 1992 which are evident in state TANF rules were the following:

- *Expanded work-related participation requirements:* In their TANF programs, states greatly expanded requirements to participate in work-related
  activities in return for receipt of assistance, moving from a structure where
  most families were exempt to one where most, or in some states, all families
  could be penalized for failure to participate in work-related activities.
- *More severe penalties:* Most states significantly expanded penalties for
  noncompliance with work-related requirements, moving from a structure
  where the penalty for noncompliance was a partial (typically about one-
  third) grant reduction to a structure where, in thirty-six states, all cash
  assistance could be terminated for a violation of program rules.
- *Time limits:* All but two states implemented policies under which family
  assistance would be terminated or reduced after a time limit of sixty
  months or less, with nineteen states imposing time limits shorter than
  sixty months for at least some families.

- *Continued assistance for recipient families who entered employment:* The majority of states modified their treatment of earnings so that families entering employment could maintain assistance for a longer period of time, though subject in almost all states to the program time limits on assistance.
- *Less restrictive treatment of assets:* Almost all states removed the most restrictive provisions affecting treatment of savings and other assets.
- *Broadening of eligibility for two-parent families:* Most states reduced or eliminated prior restrictions on two-parent family eligibility.[12]

Beyond any specific rule, however, TANF implementation was characterized by a shift to a philosophy generally known as "Work First." The guiding principle of the philosophy was that any job is better than no job and that wherever possible, programs should emphasize rapid connection to the labor force rather than allowing access to education, training, or other skill-building activities. As in the program rules, the shift to a Work First philosophy had also begun well before TANF was enacted, but appeared to accelerate in early TANF implementation.[13]

Initial press coverage of TANF implementation often focused on the fact that most states made little or no change in the basic benefit payments for families with no income, and that most states did not make new categories of families ineligible for assistance (beyond those made ineligible for federally-funded assistance through the TANF legislation). Thus, it was initially emphasized that there had not been a "race to the bottom" among states, at least in the sense that most states had not slashed benefits or sharply curtailed the categories of families eligible for assistance.

However, within a short period of time, it began to become evident that state caseloads were dropping more rapidly than ever before in program history. While the caseload had begun falling modestly in 1994, the nation's caseload dropped 27 percent in the first eighteen months of TANF implementation. The number of families receiving assistance fell from 4.4 million to 3.2 million, with all but four states experiencing at least a 10 percent caseload decline and with ten states reporting a decline of at least 40 percent.

The reasons for the caseload decline were sharply contested, in part because there was little national data regarding why families were leaving assistance or the circumstances of those no longer receiving assistance. Thus, it was unclear how much of the caseload decline was attributable to increased job entries and how much was attributable to other factors such as more rigid enforcement of program requirements and increased use of penalties and grant terminations that simply resulted in denial or elimination of assistance for needy families. Even for the part of the caseload decline attributable to increased job entries, it was unclear how much could appropriately be ascribed to state initiatives, how much might be attributable to other national initiatives (such as the expansion of the Earned Income Tax Credit, the raises in the minimum wage, and the expansions of Medicaid coverage and federally-funded child care assistance for poor families) and how much simply reflected the strength of the U.S. economy. It was also unclear how much of the decline was attributable to families leaving assistance and how much could be explained by fewer families entering assistance. In implementing their "work first" philosophies, a number of states had also implemented new "job search" requirements that applicants must satisfy in order to receive assistance. There were indications that in some states, fewer applicants were beginning to receive assistance, either because they had successfully found employment or because they were unable or unwilling to comply with new state application requirements.

Despite the array of uncertainties about the reasons for the caseload decline, there seemed little doubt that there had been an increase in employment entries among families applying for or receiving assistance.[14] As might be expected with a work-first philosophy, the jobs that such families entered frequently did not provide sufficient wages for families to reach the poverty line, even though the earnings were high enough to make the families ineligible for TANF assistance.[15]

As caseloads continued to fall, it became increasingly apparent that one consequence of the caseload decline was that substantial amounts of fiscal resources that had, until then, been used for cash assistance to needy families were now potentially available for an array of other uses. These funds became available because in the block grant structure, state block grants remain constant whether caseloads rise or fall. in fact, because caseloads had already begun declining before the 1996 law, and continued to decline further in 1997, the U.S. General Accounting Office estimated that states had access to an additional $4.7 billion in 1997 above the levels that they would have had under prior law. Only limited data were available about how states were expending these additional funds; based on voluntary state reporting, there were indications of a shift away from cash assistance and toward greater expenditures on child care, but only fragmentary information existed about how states were expending the additional funding.[16]

Accordingly, in the earliest stages of TANF implementation and in the context of a strong economy, TANF implementation resulted in sharply declining caseloads, increasing numbers of working poor families, and a significant level of state resources that could be directed in many different ways.

TANF Over Time: Risks and Opportunities in the Block Grant Structure

In considering the potential significance of TANF for national working poor family policy, one needs to distinguish between the short-run experience and the long-run possibilities for state responses to the block grant structure. The initial state choices only reflect a fraction of the alternatives available to states within TANF. Unless congress acts to modify it sooner, the basic block grant structure will be essentially fixed through 2002. So, it is important to appreciate the extent of both risks and opportunities presented by the TANF structure.

The Risks

For many, the greatest concerns about eventual state directions under TANF flow from the combination of the elimination of state responsibilities and the establishment of strong fiscal incentives to deny assistance. The elimination of state responsibilities creates the possibility of sharp restrictions on assistance to poor families; the fiscal incentives to states increase the likelihood that such restrictions occur.

While all states initially responded to TANF by maintaining some form of program of cash assistance to poor families, there is no requirement that a state do so or maintain such a program over time. Under the law, states have no responsibility to assist any family or group of families for any period of time, and in their initial TANF designs, nineteen states opted to impose time limits shorter than five years for at least some families. Apart from time limits, states wishing to do so are also free to impose new restrictions that make it more difficult for eligible families to establish or maintain eligibility for assistance.

States have no responsibility to process applications for assistance within a reasonable period of time or to provide assistance after a family is determined to be eligible. States are free to deny or terminate all assistance if a family fails to comply with work requirements, even if the family had good cause for its failure to comply; the only good cause exception states must allow is for the situation where a single parent of a child under age six is unable to comply due to lack of available child care. Otherwise, the authority of states to restrict the availability of assistance is virtually unlimited.

Further, under the law, a state has no obligation to operate a program of income assistance for low-income families. Thus, a state wishing to do so could opt to shift from a program of cash assistance to one of noncash assistance; it could shift the funding to social services rather than any form of assistance; it could opt to turn over the funding to counties and let each county design its own program; it could turn over some or virtually all funding to nonprofit organizations, religious groups, or for-profit organizations for an array of different approaches.

There are also significant "opportunities" for states to simply shift funds away from low-income assistance altogether. Most explicitly, states are only required to maintain a state spending level of 75 percent or 80 percent of what they were spending in 1994. The relevant state spending level in 1994 was $13.9 billion, and if all states were to drop to the 75 percent level, state spending could fall to $10.4 billion each year through 2002. However, the potential loss of low-income funding is even greater. Some of the allowable expenditures with block grant funds have little or no relationship to assisting low-income families. For example, an abstinence education program targeted at a high-income school district would appear to be an allowable use of TANF funds. Moreover, a state wishing to do so has substantial ability to use the block grant to supplant existing state spending, as the state may idendify current state spending for programs and activities allowable under TANF, substitute block grant funds for those purposes, and free up the equivalent state funding for any number of purposes that are wholly unrelated to the needs of low-income families. In short, one consequence of the new structure may simply be a substitution of federal for state funds, and an outflow of funds away from assistance to low-income families.

The concern about the outflow of state funds occurs both because it is permitted under TANF and because the structure results in strong fiscal incentives to shift funds away from low-income assistance. It is permitted for the reasons just noted: the limited maintenance of effort requirement, the lack of any requirement to assist needy families, and the permissible substitution of federal funds for state funds. The fiscal incentive operates because if a state generates caseload reduction—whether because more people have gone to work or because the state has simply made it more difficult to receive assistance—the state has significant ability to redirect the savings to other parts of the state budget.

The early experience of TANF implementation makes clear that the fiscal incentives of the block grant structure are not the only factor encouraging caseload reduction. States also face an indirect fiscal incentive and a strong political incentive because caseload reduction dramatically reduces the work participation rate requirements states would otherwise face. And, in a context where only minimal information about program outcomes is available, many people treat evidence of caseload decline as the best evidence of program effectiveness, creating a substantial political incentive on the part of states to generate further caseload decline.

The fundamental risk, then, is that over time, the combination of lack of state responsibilities and political and fiscal incentives to reduce the numbers of families receiving assistance will come together to sharply restrict the availability of income support for unemployed or minimally employed families. The constriction may occur through formal restrictions on eligibility for assistance or through an array of state practices that have the effect of making it difficult or impossible for needy families to receive assistance. In either case, the net result may be a dramatic curtailment in access to income assistance for the poorest families.

The Opportunities

The discussion until now has highlighted the risk side of TANF: that states may ultimately respond by implementing more stringent and restrictive programs and by shifting funds away from low-income assistance. The opportunity side of TANF flows less from its rules than from its fiscal structure and from the areas in which there are no rules. In particular, it may be easiest to identify the opportunities in three categories: opportunities to reinvest, to reallocate, and to rethink.

The reinvestment opportunity flows from the same feature of the block grant structure that may cause severe problems in times of economic downturn: the essentially fixed nature of state funding. While the legislation was pending, there was considerable discussion of the potential risks of a fixed block grant when an economic downturn occurs, because the federal funding would be unable to respond to increased need. While this concern remains, it is plainly not the principal concern in initial implementation. Rather, because block grants were set based upon 1994 caseloads, most states initially received funding well above what they would have received based on their current caseload levels. As caseloads continued to decline, the magnitude of these unobligated funds continued to grow. Thus, the fact that funding stays flat as caseloads decline makes it more possible for discussion in states to focus on how to reinvest funds that have been freed up by declining caseloads. In theory, a state always could have taken a similar approach to budgeting, and "reserved" savings from caseload declines for related purposes, but psychologically, the block grant structure may foster this way of thinking.

The reallocation opportunity also flows from another potentially destructive feature of the new structure: the lack of any requirement that states provide cash assistance to a defined population and, more fundamentally, the lack of any requirement that a state run a program of cash assistance for low-income families. While states may opt to reallocate resources in very troubling ways, they can also opt to reallocate them in ways that might better promote work force entry, or reentry, or stability. For example, TANF block grant dollars may be used for the funding of public employment, for wage subsidies for nonprofit (or for-profit) organizations, to promote microenterprise initiatives, and for other job creation strategies. Thus, a state might decide that, under certain circumstances, it would make available publicly funded employment opportunities, either in lieu of or in addition to income support assistance. A state can elect to rechannel funds that had previously been expended for income support to expand training programs, job development initiatives, and job retention support programs. In addition to promoting job retention, a state can use its block-grant funds in support of mobility strategies to promote expanded access to training and job development for low-wage working parents who have left (or never received) TANF assistance. One of the state initiatives that began in the waiver process was the use of diversion assistance, in which more intensive, short-term assistance was made available to families (e.g., car repair, special housing assistance) in order to respond to urgent needs that could help parents attain or retain employment. At a more structural level, the law fosters the ability to redirect funds toward child care assistance for low-income families, both because a state can transfer up to 30 percent of its TANF funding and because the state can expend block grant assistance directly for child care. It seems quite foreseeable that, over time, a group of states will increasingly ask whether there are circumstances in which increased public expenditures for low-income child care assistance would obviate the need for welfare assistance for some groups of low-income families.

In the broadest sense, the opportunity presented by the TANF structure is the opportunity to rethink social policy in an array of areas: family poverty policy, early childhood care and education policy, work force development policy, work-and-family policy. In many respects, the principal federal policy in relation to support for unemployed or minimally employed low-income families is now—with the notable exception of the EITC—the absence of federal policy. In the TANF structure, the federal government sends a set of signals, but it is largely up to states how they choose to respond to those signals. Some of the federal signals may be quite troubling (e.g., that states have no responsibility to assist poor families, that states have no responsibility to spend more than a percentage of what they were spending in 1994, that assistance should be time-limited rather than in reference to need), but the choices are still choices for states.

In this analysis, the central issue for states should not simply be how to modify particular rules of the welfare system, or even how to spend a block grant. Rather, the issue becomes how to construct social policy in an environment where fundamental decisions have been left to the states and where many prior federal mandates and constraints on resource allocation have been eliminated. In constructing policy, states can begin with two goals often articulated as central to welfare reform—expanding parental work force participation and enhancing the well-being of families with children—and ask whether, freed from prior federal constraints, there are better ways to advance those goals.

In exploring alternatives, the new environment provides not just the ability to revise welfare rules but to step back and consider which policies could reduce the need for welfare. Historically, families entered, and sometimes stayed, in the welfare system for an array of different reasons. In some instances, the principal problem a parent may have faced was the lack of affordable child care or health care or the inability to pay rent with wages from available jobs, or the lack of consistent reliable child support payments. In other instances, parents were forced to rely on welfare because of gaps in coverage of the unemployment system. In still other instances, parents were forced to rely on welfare because there was no other affordable way to pursue an education. And, for a significant group, welfare has functioned as the basic means of income support when labor force participation was difficult or impossible due to disability of a parent or child, mental health or substance abuse problems, domestic violence, severe basic skills deficits, or other barriers to consistent work force participation. In the new structure, a state can seek to address some or all of these issues as TANF issues, but it can also seek to reframe them as nonwelfare issues. And, by going beyond TANF, a state can both address the needs of a broader group of families and workers and can develop policy approaches that have the potential to reduce the need for TANF assistance over time.

The focus here on developing supports for working parents is not intended to suggest that every parent is capable of work or of consistent work force participation, and it is not intended to minimize the severity of the barriers faced by many families receiving assistance or the need for commitment of TANF and other resources to address the needs of those families. At the same time, it may be possible that the development of a better structure of support for families capable of work force participation could also result in better identification of situations where work is not a reasonable expectation or of the circumstances where far more comprehensive services are needed.

What are the components of an approach that could foster labor force participation, enhance the well-being of children, and reduce the need for welfare? Some of the components of this vision are clear and others are likely to emerge with experience over time. At the most basic level, it would seem clear that if there is a goal of increasing labor force participation without jeopardizing the well-being of children, it is essential to expand the availability of child care assistance. The new structure promotes the ability to expand child care funding, both by increasing available CCDBG funding and by allowing the transfer or expenditure of TANF funds for child care. In the new structure, there is no longer a mandated linkage between income support and child care assistance (i.e., states need not guarantee child care assistance for TANF recipients). The troubling aspect of the loss of linkage is that there is no longer any assurance that needy families receiving income support also receive needed child care. At the same time, the opportunity is the ability to expand the numbers receiving child care assistance, to move toward a unified child care system rather than one fragmented among its funding streams, and to move to a structure where families do not need to enter a welfare system in order to gain access to child care assistance.

A similar analysis applies to the relationship between welfare and health care coverage. In the prior structure, families receiving AFDC automatically qualified for Medicaid assistance. Young children in poverty automatically qualified for Medicaid even if they were not receiving AFDC (though in many instances, eligible children were not enrolled), but there might be no Medicaid coverage for older poor children or working-poor parents not receiving AFDC. As with child care, the categorical linkage between income support and Medicaid was terminated by enactment of TANF. States must now determine eligibility for Medicaid based on income and resources (rather than based on TANF receipt) for those parents and older children who do not otherwise qualify. Again, there is reason to fear that one result may be that some families do not learn about or are not able to maintain Medicaid coverage. At the same time, there is an increased potential to create statewide health coverage systems that do not depend on whether a family receives income support, so that no parent need ever be fearful that entering employment will mean jeopardizing access to health care coverage for herself or her children.

A third component of new support for working families could involve the restructuring of the child-support system to provide for back-up payments of child support in a child-support assurance system. For many years, it has been recognized that a principal difficulty facing a custodial parent when she enters employment is that she often has no way to know whether she can reliably depend on child-support as a source of income. Even after she has fully cooperated with the child-support enforcement system to the greatest extent possible, her income from child-support depends on factors beyond her control: whether the noncustodial parent chooses (or has the ability) to pay and whether government is effective in attaining compliance with support orders. The concept of a child-support assurance system is that when a parent has cooperated with child-support enforcement, the government assures (up to some specified level) that there will be a back-up payment made even in those months when the noncustodial parent does not or cannot meet his required obligation. The perceived policy advantage of child-support assurance is that a parent entering a low-wage job could reliably depend on child support to supplement wages and that the ability to count on regular receipt of child support could both foster job stability and reduce the poverty of such families.[17]

This set of policies—child care, health care, child support—can work in complement with the federal EITC, but a gap in support still remains. Provision of child care and health care coverage can lower the cost of working, but so long as the EITC typically remains a once-a-year lump sum, there is still a need for some mechanism for delivering income assistance over the course of the year for low-income families with low-wage workers. To date, the system many states have developed is a plainly unstable one: states have significantly expanded access to TANF cash assistance for working-poor families but in a context where the TANF assistance typically counts against the federal TANF time limits. The result, over time, may be that working families are actually hurt by receiving assistance they qualify to receive, because even those months in which minimal TANF assistance is received will count against the time limit and increase the risk of exhaustion of eligibility for any future TANF assistance.

There are several possible ways to address this problem. Ideally, there would be a restructuring of TANF rules so that TANF funds used for income supplements to working families need not be time-limited. Absent a federal law change, the time limits apply when federal TANF funds are used for income supplements, but not when state funds are used. To date, two states, Illinois and Maine, have developed a structure under which state-funded assistance is provided to working families to prevent their assistance from being subject to federal TANF time limits. Other states could choose to emulate this approach, or seek to explore other funding mechanisms for income assistance to working-poor families that do not implicate the TANF time limits on assistance.

While one cluster of policies can provide support to families while engaged in work, it is also necessary to address policy development for parents who would be in the work force but are not currently employed. Here, as discussed in Chapter 8 states could take advantage of the new framework to rethink the operation of their unemployment insurance systems. Just as the argument was made that the welfare system largely reflected the labor and family structures of an earlier time, much the same critique can be directed at state unemployment insurance structures, which have not effectively adapted to an economy with increased levels of part-time, contingent, and flexible employment, and to the circumstances of parents seeking to balance caretaking and employment responsibilities. It is possible to consider both a limited, but important, set of changes relating to eligibility qualification rules, and it is also possible to consider a more fundamental restructuring in which unemployment insurance and income support programs for low-wage and unemployed parent families were integrated into a single structure.

The new framework also allows new consideration of when publicly funded jobs should be available to employable but unemployed parents. Publicly funded jobs are a permissible use of block grant funding. A state can use TANF funding or state funds for a publicly funded jobs component, whether as a counter-cyclical measure in times of high unemployment, as a means of addressing areas of high unemployment, as part of a training program, or simply in recognition of the reality that some adults may be employable but are not likely to attain or maintain steady unsubsidized employment.

The focus on policies that would reduce the need for TANF assistance also suggests the potential to reframe the question of access to postsecondary education for low-income parents. Over time, families needing income assistance (or sometimes, child care assistance) to pursue postsecondary education have sought assistance through the welfare system. A state could provide such assistance in the TANF structure but faces strong federal pressure not to do so (largely because an individual's involvement in postsecondary education will often not count as 'participation' when a state seeks to meet required participation rates.) Moreover, the incentives to generate caseload declines will likely lead many states to further restrict access to postsecondary education. At the same time, the TANF structure allows states to reconceptualize the issue: low-income families may need financial aid to attend or complete school, but there is no reason why the financial aid needs to be provided in the form of welfare assistance. An expansion of financial aid for low-income families (which could be an allowable use of a state's maintenance of effort funds in the TANF structure) may have far more long-run viability as an approach to fostering access to postsecondary education.

Finally, going beyond the TANF structure in framing of supports for working families may also help to generate a broader discussion about the shaping of policies to better balance work and family expectations. While welfare initiatives in recent years have been driven by a focus on maximizing work force participation, it is by no means clear that there is a broad social consensus that all able-bodied parents should be in the work force on a full-time basis at all times. Many parents would wish to have greater opportunities to stay home with infants or very young children; many parents feel conflicted and dissatisfied about the stresses on family life resulting from their work hours or schedules; and many parents share concerns about the safety, health, and well-being of their children when they go to work. Each of these concerns suggests serious issues about how to balance work and family in a world of increased parental labor force participation. Yet each of these issues have been resolved in the most restrictive ways when framed as issues of welfare policy. Much of the public anger at welfare has been rooted in concerns about equity—if other parents must return to work when an infant is three months old, why should there be an exception for welfare recipients? If other parents have to go to work despite lack of affordable, quality child care, why should there be an exception for welfare recipients? In an important sense, the opportunity presented by the TANF structure is the opportunity to reframe the questions being asked. It allows one to not just ask what policies would foster work force participation, but what policies should be advanced for all workers to ensure that all workers have both the resources and the time to function as both workers and parents.[18]

In short, the TANF structure has the potential to generate significant change in social institutions that goes far beyond the curtailment of welfare assistance. It is possible that states will respond to the new structure by simply curtailing assistance and shifting funding away from low-income programs. It is also possible for states to use this as an opportunity to rethink and redesign antipoverty policy and design new nonwelfare supports, to move away from the often artificial line between welfare families and working families, and to put in place new visions of support for working families. While the initial public attention may focus on whether and how much caseloads decline, the longer-run question involves the nature and direction of the new framework.

Notes

1. The principal focus of this discussion is cash assistance; there are, of course, other significant programs of assistance to low-income families. For example, a family with little or no income would typically qualify for food vouchers from the food stamp program and for Medicaid assistance; such a family might also qualify for low-income housing assistance. In 1995, census data indicated that 97 percent of AFDC recipients also received Medicaid, 87 percent received food stamps, and 31 percent received public or subsidized rental housing. See Committee on Ways and Means, U.S. House of Representatives, *1996 Green Book, Background Materials and Data on Programs Within the Jurisdiction of the Committee on Ways and Means*, WMCP 104–14, at p. 856.

2. In 1996, the poverty guideline for a family of three in the 48 contiguous states was $12,980, or $1,082 per month.

3. A basic choice for any structure of means-tested assistance involves how to treat a family receiving assistance when the family has or attains other income, that is, at what rate should assistance be phased down or out based on the existence of other income. Before 1981, AFDC policy regarding treatment of earnings had been that when a family attained employment, the first $30 plus one-third of the remainder, along with all reasonable work-related expenses, would be "disregarded," that is, not counted in determining eligibility and assistance levels. The 1981 modification restricted the treatment of employ-

ment income, both by limiting the availability of work expense deductions and by providing that the principal earning disregard expired after four months. The result was a sharp decline in the number of working-poor families receiving assistance.

4. From 1950 to 1995, the rate of labor force participation by women increased from 22 percent to 70 percent; for those with children under age 6, labor force participation increased from 14 percent to 62 percent.

5. For more information on the policy directions taken by states in the waiver process, see *Setting the Baseline: A Report on State Welfare Waivers,* U.S. Department of Health and Human Services, June 1997; S. Savner and M. Greenberg, *The CLASP Guide to Welfare Waivers* (Washington, DC: Center for Law and Social Policy, 1995).

Before the 1996 federal legislation passed, the aspect of state directions for which there was the least consensus may have been that of time limits. While most states were moving in the direction of something called a time limit, there were—until the 1996 legislation passed—three distinct models of time limits: those in which a family's assistance would be terminated after reaching a time limit; those in which a family's assistance would be reduced after reaching a time limit; and those in which an adult would be required to participate in a work program as a condition of further assistance after a time limit. For an overview of state approaches to time limits before the 1996 legislation, *see* M. Greenberg, S. Savner, and R. Schwarz, *Limits on Limits: State and Federal Policies on Welfare Time Limits* (Washington, DC: Center for Law and Social Policy, 1996).

6. While EITC costs exceeded those of AFDC, the EITC did not provide more assistance to the poorest families than did AFDC. In 1997, only 21 percent of EITC benefits were provided to families with incomes below $10,000; an additional 48 percent of benefits were provided to families with incomes between $10,000 and $20,000; and the remaining share of EITC benefits were provided to families with incomes exceeding $20,000. See *1998 Green Book Materials on Programs within the Jurisdiction of the Committee on Ways and Means,* WMCP 105–7, Table 13–13, p. 871.

7. For a family with one child, the EITC provided a 34 percent tax credit of the first $8,890, up to a maximum credit of $2,152, with a phaseout rate of 16 percent after the family reached the $11,610 point.

8. Apart from the block grants, the most substantial changes resulting from the PRWORA were:

- a set of changes affecting the operation of the child-support enforcement structure;
- a set of reductions in the availability of assistance to legal immigrants in an array of programs;
- a set of reductions and restrictions affecting the food stamp program, with reductions in projected spending estimated in the range of $25 billion;
- a curtailment of the circumstances in which children could qualify for federal disability assistance.

For more information about the child-support provisions of the 1996 law, see P. Roberts, *Analysis of Child Support-Related Provisions of the Personal Responsibility and Work Opportunity Reconciliation Act of 1996* (Washington, DC: Center for Law and Social Policy, 1996); for a general overview of other provisions, see D. Super, S. Parrott, S. Steinmetz, and C. Mann, *The New Welfare Law* (Washington, DC: Center on Budget and Policy Priorities, 1996).

9. More detailed descriptions of these and additional TANF requirements can be attained by consulting the web site of the Center for Law and Social Policy, located at http://www.clasp.org.

10. For more information about the Welfare-to-Work grants, see M. Greenberg, *Welfare-to-Work Grants and Other TANF-Related Provisions in the Balanced Budget Act of 1997* (Washington, DC: Center for Law and Social Policy, 1997).

11. More precisely, states can, unless prohibited by the law, spend the funds in any manner that was previously permitted under AFDC and a set of AFDC-related programs (Emergency Assistance, the Job Opportunities and Basic Skills Training Program; and a set of child care programs). In addition, states can (unless prohibited by the law) spend the funds in any manner reasonably calculated to accomplish the goals of the law. The goals are defined as follows:

> [t]he purpose of this part is to increase the flexibility of States in operating a program designed to:
> (1) provide assistance to needy families so that the children may be cared for in their homes or in the homes of relatives;
> (2) end the dependency of needy parents on government benefits by promoting job preparation, work, and marriage;
> (3) prevent and reduce the incidence of out-of-wedlock pregnancies and establish annual numerical goals for preventing and reducing the incidence of these pregnancies; and
> (4) encourage the formation and maintenance of two-parent families.

12. The most detailed description of initial state choices in TANF implementation is contained in L. Gallagher, M. Gallagher, K. Perse, S. Schreiber, and K. Watson, *One Year after Federal Welfare Reform: A Description of State Temporary Assistance for Needy Families (TANF) Decisions as of October 1997* (Washington, DC: The Urban Institute, 1998).

13. For a description of the Work First framework, see United States General Accounting Office, *Welfare Reform: States Are Restructuring Programs to Reduce Welfare Dependence* (GAO/HEHS 98–109, June 1998) and P. Holcomb, L. Pavetti, C. Ratcliffe, and S. Riedinger, *Building and Employment Focus Welfare System: Work First and Other Work-Oriented Strategies in Five States* (Washington, DC: Urban Institute, 1998).

14. The GAO found that five of seven case study states reported significant increases in the rates at which people in their programs found jobs between 1994 and 1997. United States General Accounting Office, *Welfare Reform*, pp. 98–99.

15. See S. Parrott, *Welfare Recipients Who Find Jobs: What Do We Know About Their Employment and Earnings?* (Washington, DC: Center on Budget and Policy Priorities, November 1998); see also, Staff of National Governors' Association, National Conference of State Legislators, American Public Welfare Association, *Tracing Recipients After They Leave Welfare: Summaries of State Follow-Up Studies*, (July 1998).

16. See National Governor's Association and National Association of State Budget Officers, *The Fiscal Survey of the States* (May 1998).

17. For an overview of the potential advantages of a child-support assurance system, see Roberts, *Ending Poverty as We Know It* (Washington, DC: Center for Law and Social Policy, 1994); for a discussion of the process by which a child-support assurance structure could be funded in the block grant framework, *see* Greenberg, Roberts, Savner, and

Turetsky, *Child Support Assurance: A New Opportunity in the Block Grant Framework* (Washington, DC: Center for Law and Social Policy, 1997).

18. For an extended discussion of the importance of time for parenting and of policies that might promote it, see S. Kammerman and A. Kahn, *Starting Right: How America Neglects its Youngest Children and What We Can Do About It* (New York: Oxford University Press, 1995).

3

Julia R. Henly

BARRIERS TO FINDING AND MAINTAINING JOBS

THE PERSPECTIVES OF WORKERS AND EMPLOYERS IN THE LOW-WAGE LABOR MARKET

The 1996 Personal Responsibility and Work Opportunity Reconciliation Act (PRWORA)[1] fundamentally alters our nation's system of public assistance to poor families without threatening long-standing American beliefs about economic mobility and self-sufficiency. Whereas the new law reflects a major change in public policy (with the repeal of the entitlement provision of public cash assistance to poor families), it is quite familiar both in terms of its conceptualization of the problem and in the overarching policy prescriptions it advances. Reminiscent of prior reforms, an underlying assumption of the PRWORA is that a recipient's employment difficulties are the result of moral and behavioral problems that have been normalized by bureaucratic welfare practices. It is suggested that by changing the climate of the welfare office and by sending a clear message to welfare recipients that work is an expectation of citizenship, economic independence will eventually follow.

Specifically, PRWORA purports a goal of self-sufficiency through employment. The bill attempts to accomplish this goal by time-limiting welfare and by involving welfare recipients in mandatory work activities, with an emphasis on job placement over education and training.[2] Additional funds have been directed for child care assistance, however client participation in mandated work activities is not necessarily linked to the availability of child care, as it was with the Job Opportunities and Basic Skills Training (JOBS) program—the employment and training provided under the Family Support Act.[3]

Thus, the new welfare law is designed to address primarily moral and behavioral deficits, with less emphasis on social-contextual and structural factors that also operate to facilitate or hinder labor market success. In this chapter, I consider the importance of these latter factors in the lives of low-income mothers who work in relatively low-skilled jobs. In addition to drawing from previous research in the welfare and labor market domains, I report findings from an interview study conducted with welfare recipients, other low-income mothers, and employers in Los Angeles County prior to the implementation of the new welfare law. In doing so, I attempt to develop a picture of low-wage work as understood by workers and supervisors in a variety of low-skilled employment settings. Findings from the interview study underscore the tenuous nature of jobs available to low-skilled workers, as these jobs typically provide low pay, few benefits, limited hours, and are particularly susceptible to economic fluctuations. Although seldom addressed in public policy debates, I argue, on the basis of these interviews, that informal social networks and the resources and connections they confer to their members are critical to our understanding of labor market experiences. Consistent with past research, findings from this study suggest that employers recruit new workers largely via social network referrals, rather than through direct applications and job training and placement agencies. The type and quality of connections available through one's social contacts are, therefore, of particular relevance in efforts to move people from welfare to work. Moreover, once employed, social network members are often enlisted to provide a variety of supports to working parents, especially in low-wage jobs with limited financial rewards that could otherwise be directed toward the purchase of formal support services. Yet, findings from this study also suggest that a system that relies so heavily on informal networks of support appears to be impractical for many low-income women who are embedded in informal networks with members who are themselves struggling to make ends meet in the low-wage labor market. I conclude, then, by arguing that if we expect women to successfully fulfill the dual—and often conflicting—roles of mother and worker, the workplace itself might benefit from significant reform, and a formal, more adequate system of support should be adopted. Attention to individual-level interventions alone would seem to fall short as a primary policy measure.

The Workplace Environment Study

The following discussion is based in part on findings from the Workplace Environment Study. The Workplace Environment Study was designed to collect information regarding the workplace experiences of employees and employers in low-paying occupations. Employees—both with and without welfare histories— were interviewed about their workplace experiences; and employers who supervised the occupations represented by the employee respondents were interviewed about their own experiences managing this segment of the work force. Through these semi-structured interviews—which were carried out between July 1996 and July 1997—information was collected on a variety of issues related to basic job characteristics, the quality of workplace interactions, and the demands and responsibilities outside of work that have the potential to spill-over into the workplace. Although this study is exploratory in nature, it expands our understanding of the potential barriers to economic security facing welfare recipients, as well as other low-income parents.

Methodological Approach and Sample Characteristics

A semi-structured interview schedule was followed for both the employer and employee interviews. Although the interview schedule included some standard questionnaire items and response choices, it also included several less structured items to which respondents provided open-ended, in-depth responses. The open-ended items were designed to elicit information about specific participant "stories," to gain access to participants' subjective understanding of their workplace experiences, and to allow respondents the opportunity to clarify and expand their responses to closed-ended items. A semi-structured interview protocol that combined standard survey items with less structured qualitative approaches, was viewed as appropriate for the purposes of this study because the research questions of interest were often most amenable to one or the other approach. Whereas closed-ended survey data have been gathered about concrete events, behaviors, and demographic characteristics for which quantitative methods are well-suited, there was also specific interest in uncovering the meaning and importance of such events and behaviors to the study participants, and the strategies they use to negotiate their work and family responsibilities. This latter goal is better met through the use of qualitative approaches that allow for a richer picture of social interactions as perceived by the multiple actors within the workplace setting.

The employee interview was structured so that respondents answered questions about their current job if they were currently working and their most recent job if they were not currently working. If a respondent held more than one job, she was asked about the job that she worked the most hours per week or, if the respondent held two jobs and worked the same number of hours, she was instructed to respond according to the job that was subjectively most important to her.

The interview was administered to a sample of 44 welfare recipients with work experience (the welfare sample), a sample of 30 women without welfare experience but who held comparable jobs to the welfare recipient sample (the coworker sample), and a sample of 30 employers who held supervisory positions over workers in jobs represented by the welfare and coworker samples (the employer sample). The employer sample was drawn from the Dun and Bradstreet 1995 database of firms located in areas of Los Angeles County that have a 20 percent or greater poverty rate. Firms were selected within certain industries that are typically known to employ welfare recipients. Specifically, the Census Bureau's Standard Industrial Codes (SIC) that represent the following industries were selected: retail eating and drinking establishments, retail trade, health care services, social services, and schools. The majority of firms included in the final sample were small, employing 25 or fewer employees. The employer interviews were carried out with the employer in a firm who held a supervisory function over one of the occupations of interest.[4]

Access to the welfare sample was granted by the California Department of Social Services (CDSS), utilizing case records from their California Work Pays Demonstration Project database. A convenience sample was selected based on "first come-first served" responses to a letter requesting participation that was mailed to a random list of recipients who: (1) resided in Los Angeles County, (2) demonstrated some work experience in the previous two years, (3) were female, and (4) spoke either English or Spanish. Because of the study's emphasis on employment experiences, only welfare recipients with work experience were selected, and the least employable recipients, therefore, were purposely excluded.

In order to draw the coworker sample, representative employers from a list of firms from the 1995 Dun and Bradstreet database were asked to provide a list of workers employed in similar job categories as our welfare sample. From the pooled list, coworkers were selected and screened to ensure no previous welfare history, that the woman was a parent, and to document English or Spanish proficiency. Because many employers were reluctant to provide names of employees, snowball sampling techniques (referrals from welfare and coworker respondents) and convenience sampling through canvassing firms that were not identified on the original list were used as well.

This sampling process resulted in interviews with a non-representative and non-random sample of employers and employees in a variety of industries and occupations, which were collapsed into four broad industrial and occupational categories (see Tables 3.1 and 3.2). There is a relatively good match of occupations and industries across the welfare and coworker samples, with a few exceptions. No health care workers were identified for the coworker sample, and only two of the coworkers worked in food service jobs. The remaining occupations are distributed relatively evenly across the welfare and coworker groups. By design, the employer interviews are concentrated in health, social services, and education, and in retail, food, and hotel industries.[5] In addition, administrative occupations are underrepresented in the employer sample.

In total, 30 employers and 74 employees (welfare and coworker) were interviewed. Of the welfare and coworker samples, over three-fourths ($n = 58$) had children under thirteen years of age living in their households. The employees are diverse in respect to ethnicity and marital status: 38.4% ($n = 28$) described themselves as African American, 12.3% ($n = 9$) described themselves as white, and 47.9% ($n = 36$) described themselves as Latina or Hispanic; the remainder identified themselves as Asian/Pacific Islander ($n = 3$) or Native American ($n = 5$).[6] The marital status of the employee respondents varied such that 38.9% ($n = 29$) reported being either married or living with a partner; 26.4% ($n = 20$) were divorced, separated, or widowed; and 34.7% ($n = 25$) were never married. The employee respondents reported a median of two children, with a parity range from 1 to 7.[7] Employee respondents ranged in age from 21 to 66, with 80% falling between the ages of 26 and 43. The mean age was 34.7 years. Less than a high school education was reported by 28.4%, either a high school degree or GED but no further education by 29.7%, a high school degree or equivalent plus some postsecondary education (either courses in a vocational training school, a community college, or four-year college) by 29.7 %, and a postsecondary degree by 12.2 %.

Table 3.1

Industries

Industries	Employees						Employers (N = 30)	
	Total (N = 74)		Welfare sample (N = 44)		Coworker sample (N = 30)			
	n	%	n	%	n	%	n	%
Health, social services, and education	35	47.3	21	47.7	14	46.7	16	53.3
Retail, food, and hotel	21	28.4	12	27.3	9	30.0	14	46.7
Public service/manufacturing	8	10.8	3	6.8	5	16.7	—	—
Financial, business, and real estate	10	13.5	8	18.2	2	6.7	—	—

Table 3.2

Occupations

Occupations	Employees						Employers (N = 30)	
	Total (N = 74)		Welfare sample (N = 44)		Coworker sample (N = 30)			
	n	%	n	%	n	%	n	%
Teachers aides, child care, social service, and health aides	19	25.7	14	31.8	5	16.7	11	36.7
Retail, food and beverage workers	20	27	12	27.3	8	26.7	14	46.7
Public service/production and construction/cleaning	14	18.9	7	15.9	7	23.3	3	10.0
Office/administration	21	28.4	11	25.0	10	33.3	2	6.7

Table 3.3

Sample Demographics

	Total	Welfare sample	Coworker sample
Sample size	74	44	30
Age (in years)			
Mean	34.7	34.6	34.8
SD	7.6	6.5	9.1
Race/Ethnicity %*			
Latina/Hispanic	47.9	30.2	73.3
African American	38.4	53.5	16.7
White	12.3	16.3	6.7
Asian/Pacific Islander	4.1	4.7	3.3
Native American	6.8	9.3	3.3
Marital Status %			
Married/cohabitating	38.9	21.4	63.3
Divorced/separated/widowed	26.4	28.5	23.3
Never married	34.7	50.0	13.3
Education %			
Less than high school/No degree	28.4	31.8	23.3
High school degree or GED/No further	29.7	29.5	30.0
Some vocational or college	29.7	34.1	23.3
College or vocational degree	12.2	4.5	23.3

*Race/Ethnicity categories are not mutually exclusive. Because some respondents classified themselves in more than one category percentages add up to more than 100 percent.

Of the 74 employees interviewed, 44 reported some prior AFDC experience in the previous five years (the welfare sample). While the welfare and non-welfare (i.e. "coworker") subgroups are comparable in terms of the kinds of jobs held, there are important demographic differences between the welfare and co-worker samples (see Table 3.3). The mean age for both groups is approximately thirty-five years; however, the coworker sample tends to be Latina and married, whereas the welfare recipient sample is more likely to be African American and residing without a partner. Specifically, the welfare sample is 53.5% African American, whereas the coworker sample is only 16.7% African American. Co-workers, on the other hand, are predominantly Latina (73.3% compared to 30.2% of the welfare sample). Almost two-thirds (63.3%) of the coworker sample is either married or cohabiting, yet only about one-fifth (21.4%) of the welfare sample is living in one of these arrangements. The disproportionate number of African Americans represented in the welfare sample does not accurately reflect Los Angeles County's welfare population, which is approximately one-fourth African American. Whereas the coworker sample on average has reached a

Table 3.4

Employment and Welfare Status of Welfare Sample

	n	%
On welfare, working	15	34.9
On welfare, not working	12	27.9
Not on welfare, working	12	27.9
Not on welfare, not working	4	9.3
Total	43	100.0

Note: Data on the current welfare status for one respondent in the welfare sample is missing.

higher educational level than the welfare sample, the major educational differ-ence appears to be in the completion of a college or associate's degree. That is, 46.6% of the coworkers and 38.6% of the welfare recipients have at least some post–high school education, however only two of the welfare recipients (4.5% of the sample) hold a college or associate's degree compared to almost one-fourth of the coworker sample (23.3%).

Fifty-five employee respondents (74.3%) were working at the time we inter-viewed them, and nineteen (25.7%) were recently unemployed.[8] The welfare sample was more likely than the coworker sample to be unemployed at the time of the interview. This is an artifact of the sampling strategy used for the coworker sample (i.e., the sample was found through employers and interviewee referrals and by canvassing businesses) and therefore should not be interpreted as informa-tion regarding the overall employment stability or instability of either sample. As a result of this sampling, however, it should be kept in mind that those respon-dents not working at the time of the interview were almost exclusively in the welfare sample (all but three of them had welfare experience). Most survey items referred to the period of time in which the respondent was employed.

Table 3.4 reports the welfare and work status at the time of the interview of only the 44 respondents in the welfare sample. Almost all of the respondents in the welfare sample (90.7%) were receiving some income (either from welfare benefits, or earnings, or both) at the time of the interview; 34.9% of the welfare sample was combining welfare and employment, and another 27.9% were work-ing but no longer receiving welfare benefits.

Method and Sample Limitations

The Workplace Environment Study provides a rich set of data drawn from three unique samples of individuals. These data are analyzed and interpreted in an effort to develop a richer and more complex understanding of how low-income workers experience paid labor and how they manage the role demands and situational constraints of parenting and working outside the home. Because the findings are based on interview data from small, nonrepresentative, nonrandom samples of three distinct groups of individuals they cannot be safely generalized to the larger population of low-wage employers, welfare recipients, or low-wage workers. Moreover, given the study's emphasis on the experiences of *working* low-income mothers, data were gathered from a select group of low-income mothers—those with recent employment experience. This permits access to information about the experiences of mothers who combine paid labor with motherhood, but does not allow for the comparison of these experiences with those of mothers who either choose not to work or who have been unsuccessful at finding employment. Moreover, the employer sample is made up primarily of small retail and service employers in moderate- to high-poverty areas, and therefore tells us nothing about the attitudes and experiences of larger employers, or of employers in non-sampled industrial sectors. Finally, whereas the employee respondents were selected on the basis of their shared experience in low-wage, low-skilled jobs and their dissimilar experience with public assistance, the two groups differ in ways other than welfare status. In particular, single parenting is more common among the welfare sample, and the two samples differ by racial and ethnic composition, with the welfare sample being disproportionately African American and the coworker sample being disproportionately Latina.

Thus, comparisons across the samples must be made with appropriate caution. Still, such an exploration provides for a more in-depth look at the employment experience than large survey data allow. Moreover, as the following discussion suggests, despite the heterogeneity within and between samples, there are commonalities across these unique samples in the experiences, strategies, and challenges described. These commonalities, especially when viewed together with related findings from previous research, suggest similarities in the everyday management (and complications) of parenting and working in low-skilled, low-wage jobs.

Getting Jobs: The Importance of Referrals

Previous studies have documented the importance of informal networks to the hiring process.[9] This literature suggests that, especially for low-skilled positions, employers prefer hiring through an informal referral process rather than by advertising in newspapers or relying on formal employment agencies. This may be especially true for small employers who have few positions to fill at any one time.

Consistent with this prior research, 88% of the employers who were interviewed in the Workplace Environment Study stated that they used referrals to recruit workers, and 64% of employers stated that this was their primary hiring strategy. In some instances the recruitment of new employees was almost entirely carried out by the firm's current employees, who would either recommend a replacement for themselves before leaving a job or provide referrals when new positions opened.

The importance of informal networks to the hiring process was also noted by the employees interviewed, both those with and without welfare experience.

Slightly less than half (45.9%) of employee respondents had found their current or most recent job through a referral, and this was most frequently through a friend or family member. About one-fifth reported finding their job through door-to-door walk-ins and coincidences, such as getting a job offer from a child's day care center or a restaurant they frequented. Advertisements (17.6%) and job placement agencies (16.2%) were relatively less common entrees into the labor market for the employees interviewed.[10]

Whereas the importance of informal referrals for job search and recruitment has been documented previously in numerous studies, less research has explored why employers rely so heavily on referrals. Thus, employers were asked to discuss their reasons for preferring certain recruitment strategies over others. An analysis of their responses suggests that the reliance on referrals serves two primary functions for employers. First, it is a timesaving strategy, especially when the number of applicants outpaces the number of positions; and second, referrals serve as a proxy for ambiguous job qualifications.

Timesaving strategy. Several studies investigating the availability of jobs for low-skilled workers, even in the growing service sector industries, have concluded that there are not enough jobs to accommodate the number of workers looking for work.[11] This is evidenced by the fact that the unemployment rate of less-skilled workers continues to be significantly higher than overall unemployment figures. At a more micro-level, Kathryn Newman's study of fast-food establishments in New York City's Harlem found fourteen applicants for every position; and Carol Stack reports a 4.5 to 1 ratio of applicants to positions in a new fast-food restaurant that she studied in Oakland, California.[12]

Although the study discussed herein did not attempt to measure the actual ratio of jobs to applicants, several of the employers interviewed indicated that hiring through referrals represented one method to ease the process of wading through numerous applications. For example, the owner of a small grocery store in South Central Los Angeles noted that he no longer advertises openings because the one time he did so (by putting a sign in the window) he had over 200 applicants for his small store. Now, he states that he "keeps it more contained" by relying on referrals from existing employees. Thus, as his comment suggests, some employers relied heavily on informal networks as a recruitment strategy in part because the ratio of applicants to jobs can be an uneven one. Reliance on referrals facilitated the hiring process in a market that employers said provided them with more job seekers than openings.

Proxy for ambiguous job qualifications. There has been a great deal of attention, both popular and academic, to the importance of "soft skills" to employers in low-skilled jobs. Employers, it is argued, give a disproportionate amount of attention to interpersonal skills and motivational factors when recruiting workers, with relatively less attention to objective skills tests or education credentials. Because the low-skilled labor market is increasingly dependent on workers whose primary job is to interact with customers,[13] it is argued that employers

Table 3.5

Importance of Worker Qualifications to Employers
(1 = not important at all; 7 = extremely important)

Qualities	N	Mean	Standard deviation
Past experience	28	4.68	1.98
Ability to relate to customers	29	6.38	1.08
Getting along with coworkers	29	6.45	.95
Willingness to take orders from supervisors	29	6.38	.78
Physical appearance	28	5.39	1.17
Educational credentials	28	3.89	2.13
Language skills	27	5.56	1.58

need workers who possess a strong aptitude for "getting along" with others. Whether or not the possession of strong soft skills predicts actual work performance or job stability is an open question; however, there is a growing body of literature documenting the influence of employers' expectations regarding the possession of soft skills on hiring practices.[14] The concern over soft skills has been mentioned with increasing frequency in post-PRWORA discussions about the "new" problems that may arise as welfare recipients enter the workplace. Consistent with popular views about welfare recipients, there is a concern expressed by employers, welfare caseworkers, and others that welfare recipients will fall short on the necessary interpersonal skills and work-related values to be integrated successfully into the workplace.

In interviews with employers, this focus on soft skills over education and work experience was apparent. When asked to rate the importance of several different worker qualifications, the employers interviewed consistently rated educational credentials below such skills as the ability to relate to customers, the ability to get along with coworkers, a willingness to take orders from a supervisor, presenting a pleasing physical appearance, and using proper grammar and vocabulary (see Table 3.5). Education was rated more highly for some occupations, in particular teacher's aides and licensed nurse's aides; however, even supervisors of these occupations rated soft-skills at least as high or of greater importance. Thus, of primary importance to employers was a work force that would "get along" or "fit in" with other employees and customers, that would consist of "team players," and that would display the right attitude and personality to carry out the job well.[16]

However, by focusing on soft skills, in contrast to human capital skills, the employment decision becomes particularly subjective because testing for such intangible qualities is difficult. In such situations of ambiguity, employers necessarily search for cues that will serve as a proxy for the existence of the unmeasurable quality. The referral appears to serve this very function for many of the employers interviewed. Thus, in part because there is no clear measure of the qualifications necessary for a particular job (e.g., how does one measure an applicant's ability to get along with coworkers a priori?), employers may rely on existing employees to recommend candidates. *The recommendation, in effect, replaces the skills test.*

The employers in the study herein gave several reasons for their confidence in the employee referral. First, several employers stated that the familiarity an employee has both to the job and the person being referred puts him or her in a unique situation to evaluate the "fit" of an employee with a workplace. As the manager of a small fast-food restaurant stated, "you know them, they know what you want." Moreover, employers assumed that it was in an employee's own self-interest to refer qualified individuals. Employers trusted their workers to make good referrals because the referral would ultimately reflect either positively or negatively on the employee himself or herself. Whereas the incentive to recommend good job candidates was generally assumed, in at least one case a formal incentive structure was introduced into the organization to ensure that self-interest would be operating. In this case, the employer offered a bonus of $100 to any employee whose referral stayed on the job for at least ninety days.

In addition to familiarity and self-interest, employers often expressed the belief that their best workers were likely to be embedded in social networks with other qualified workers. In the words of one employer,

> Have you heard of the phrase, "Birds of a feather flock together"? I try to make a functional work environment that will promote good referrals. This is a culture they are very proud of, and [employees] will make good referrals.

Moreover, it is believed that hiring friends and family members of existing employees increases the likelihood that the work force will form a cohesive working group—one that will get along well, with minimal conflict. The comments of the manager of a franchise restaurant were typical. In response to a question about the challenges he faced keeping good workers, this manager indicated that, by in large, he did not have these difficulties, because new hires most frequently were friends of existing employees who got along well with one another. In his words, "Quite frankly, I've been lucky. They either stay or replace themselves . . . we hire from within and people get along." Although a few employers expressed some concern about workers who were too friendly with one another, even these employers were likely to rely on employee referrals and were generally satisfied with this approach. For example, the owner of a small grocery store stated,

> From my experience, referrals are better. Although you don't want them to be too much friends with each other or the work slows down. But in general it works fine. If someone works here they know what I expect.

Thus, employers expressed satisfaction with the informal referral process. Given this preference, however, job seekers without network ties to jobs may be disadvantaged in the job search process. Past research has suggested that inner-city African Americans, in particular, are likely to experience the negative side of this reliance on job networks.[16] Although this past work has not directly examined the effect of the referral process on welfare recipients, there is reason to believe that welfare recipients may be negatively affected by such a system because they are disproportionately nonwhite and because they may have fewer direct contacts to employment through their social networks. Because this study selected welfare recipients who had successfully found jobs, the extent to which the networks of welfare recipients without employment experience exclude them from being referred to jobs cannot be adequately assessed with these data. But it is important to keep in mind that the work requirements and time limits in the new welfare legislation are applied uniformly to all welfare recipients with children over age six (and for mothers of much younger children in many states). Because the extent to which the friends and family members of welfare recipients are themselves employed is likely to vary, we might expect variation across welfare recipients in their ability to rely on these networks for job entry.

This potential problem of job access has not gone unnoticed among policymakers. There are several new initiatives designed to encourage employers to hire welfare recipients. These include employer subsidy programs and programs that attempt to link employers to welfare-to-work programs. The success of these initiatives is predicated on a willingness, from the side of the employer, to change existing hiring practices. In this study, however, employers were generally satisfied with their hiring strategies. Reliance on referrals appeared to work well, especially for small employers who had few openings at any one time. Moreover, few employees had taken advantage of wage subsidy programs in the past, in part because they were unaware of existing programs, but also because they were sometimes skeptical of what was viewed by many as too much government involvement in the hiring of their work force.

All the employers were asked whether or not they would be interested in a program that provided incentives for hiring welfare recipients. There was an overarching concern expressed by many employers that such a program would not be "worth it" economically, given the time constraints and demands that were assumed to be part of participation. Several employers reserved judgment—stating that their interest would depend on the specifics of the program—but also indicated that in order for them to be interested, they would want full control over the hiring process,[17] participation would need to involve a minimum of hassles, and most stated that they would only consider candidates who were already qualified for the job. For example, the manager of a cleaning service for residential care facilities, who spoke about her experiences with office assistants, stated, "Yes [indicating she would be interested in a subsidy] if the person has the same qualifications, why not? But if it means taking someone just for the subsidy, No." This same respondent went on to state that although she was not opposed to hiring qualified welfare recipients, she doubted that they would have the right skills for the job.

It is this last point that may be a particularly difficult one for the success of employer initiatives. That is, although the employers that we interviewed reported little actual knowledge of the welfare status of their current job applicants and employees, many expressed doubt that their current employees had any experience with welfare and questioned whether welfare recipients were likely to make good employees. In effect, employers expressed many of the same opinions about welfare recipients as those held by other Americans. That is, many authors have noted that there is a public perception that individuals collecting welfare do not work, lack a strong work ethic, are lazy, and are taking advantage of the public welfare system.[18] These same concerns were expressed by many of the employers we interviewed. For example, the director of a community recreation center, who had not hired welfare recipients in the past as far as she knew, stated that she had concerns about the attitudes and motivation of many welfare recipients. To be a Recreation Assistant,

> they have to have a positive attitude and be responsible and I don't think most welfare recipients would have that. There is a difference between welfare recipients who are on welfare for a short time and those on it for ten years. I'm thinking of those welfare workers on a long time. I really wouldn't want them around. I worked at a rec center in [a different location] and there was a woman on welfare, and her fourteen-year-old daughter got pregnant. She was glad because her daughter could get welfare too. It's that welfare mentality.

Later in the interview, when this employer was asked about whether she would face different challenges as a result of legislation that would encourage employers to take a more active role in the hiring of welfare recipients, her same concern over the motivation of welfare recipients was expressed. She added to this an overall concern with what she identified as the honesty, punctuality, and self-motivation of recipients. The respondent stated,

> R: On a scale from 1 to 10, I think it would be a 5 [concerning whether welfare recipients have these traits]. Our gardener gets welfare workers and they don't work well. He lets people work off their ticketed community service and several of those will be on welfare.
>
> IW: What do you think are the major issues facing the private sector if they employed welfare recipients?
>
> R: Finding people that will be capable of doing the jobs they are hired to do. People that will keep their work schedule. Well, you can say honesty.

There were, of course, some employers that did not elicit attitudes that reflected presumed motivational or value deficits on the part of recipients. These employers, however, often expressed concerns about the extra time that they expected it would take to integrate new workers into the work force. For example, the director of a convalescent hospital remarked that welfare recipients would need to be educated for the job. She continued,

> If the person had been out of work for a long time, I would expect what I call transfer trauma for 90 days. An employer needs to do more hand holding in this period. . . . I think the transition would be the most difficult. I imagine that the employee would be nervous.

Moreover, several respondents wondered why welfare recipients would want to work, given the disincentives they believed were part of the system. The head teacher at a child care center, for example, replied when asked why she thought it was that welfare recipients were not hired as child care providers at her center: "Well, some people don't feel they need to be employed when they get something for nothing. I can't be judgmental. Maybe some of them have the need." Similarly, the supervisor of a fast-food restaurant stated, "to my point of view, they receive money without working, why should they sweat it out?"

What do these opinions mean for the employment prospects of welfare recipients who come to the attention of employers through, for example, a welfare-to-work program? Earlier, it was argued that in jobs available to less-skilled workers, employers are generally searching for candidates who possess strong interpersonal skills and positive attitudes, and that these soft skills are inherently difficult to measure. In such situations of ambiguity, it was argued that employers necessarily search for cues that will serve as a proxy for the existence of the unmeasurable quality, and reliance on employee referrals is one method that employers have used. However, when employers hire outside of an informal employee network, they may rely on their expectations and beliefs about particular groups as the cue to whether or not an individual group member is a qualified applicant. Preconceived views about group members have been found to be particularly relevant under situations of uncertainty,[19] suggesting that employers may utilize these group-level beliefs to infer whether or not an individual job candidate possesses the necessary skills for a job. A similar argument has been made regarding the barriers that African Americans face in the job market. Specifically, Kirschenman and Neckerman argue that employer decisions are heavily influenced by stereotypic beliefs that can signal the degree to which a worker is perceived as having the attitude and interpersonal skills necessary for a job. Being African American, coming from the inner city, and being poor puts a prospective employee at a distinct disadvantage in the hiring process.[20]

Given that welfare recipients disproportionately fall into many of these same categories (e.g., they are overrepresented in nonwhite racial groups, they are poor and may come from highly disadvantaged areas), and they carry with them the additional stigma of being a welfare recipient, it is possible that making welfare status salient to employers (i.e., through an employer subsidy program) may have unintended negative consequences.

The employers interviewed for this study had little actual knowledge of the welfare histories of their employees and gave no indication that they searched for such information during the hiring process. If the stigma hypothesis is accurate, this finding may, in fact, be a blessing for a welfare recipient who is looking for work. However, once a job candidate comes to the attention of a prospective employer *because* she is a welfare recipient (i.e., as the result of a subsidy initiative) an employer's preexisting attitudes about the abilities and motivation of welfare recipients might negatively affect the hiring decision or the subsequent performance evaluations of a recipient once hired. For example, the manager of the franchise restaurant stated his beliefs about welfare in this way. In response to a question about why he felt welfare recipients did not work at his establishment, he replied,

> R: Um . . . I have no idea. In my opinion, most welfare recipients either can't work or don't want to work. I had a restaurant across from a welfare office. I don't have any sympathy for them.
> IW: Would you be willing to hire a welfare recipient?
> R: I can't say no to that. I wouldn't not hire because they received welfare. I'll hire anyone who is willing to work.
> IW: Would you expect different challenges by hiring welfare recipients?
> R: I'm so unfamiliar with welfare recipients. I would expect they would have trouble adjusting to working with the public. (P: what about skill level?) Not skill level other than people skills. I would expect they wouldn't be quality workers.

Thus, while not categorically excluding welfare recipients, the substantial degree of apprehension expressed by this employer may affect his judgment of the actual qualifications of an individual job candidate on welfare who comes to his attention and his evaluation of her performance once hired. Because this apprehension was widespread among the employers interviewed, there is reason to be concerned about the success of policies that increase the salience of stigmatized category memberships, such as welfare, especially under conditions of uncertainty when individuating information that might counter the stereotype is unavailable.

Keeping Jobs: Job-Related versus Worker-Related Characteristics

Despite the barriers to finding jobs, many welfare recipients are active participants in the labor market. While estimates vary, studies find that somewhere between 25 and 65 percent of welfare recipients either leave welfare for formal sector work or combine welfare with employment.[21] A substantial proportion of welfare recipients that enter the work force, however, eventually return to welfare. For example, Kathleen Harris finds that slightly over 40 percent of women who leave welfare return at some point during the following two years. Seventy-five percent of these women exit welfare again shortly after returning.[22] Thus, Harris finds that while many women leave welfare as a consequence of finding a job in the paid labor force, the employment is relatively unstable, and "lead(s) to a revolving door pattern of welfare dependency."[23] This "cycling"[24] between welfare and employment, indicates that at least for a significant subgroup of welfare recipients, efforts to achieve economic independence through employment are unsuccessful.

In attempting to understand these welfare dynamics, researchers have traditionally focused on characteristics of welfare recipients that might explain work behavior. As such, the "welfare debate" has been largely individually focused, centering around the values of welfare recipients, on the one hand,[25] and their human capital deficiencies on the other.[26] Thus, Lawrence Mead argues that we are experiencing a crisis of values, exemplified by the entitlement approach that poor people are presumed to take toward welfare (e.g., welfare is thought to be a right of citizenship without a corresponding social obligation to work); whereas, from a human capital perspective, the problem of welfare dependency is one of inadequate investment in education and training.[27] Despite the popularity of the value argument, there is, in fact, little evidence that would suggest welfare recipients are less oriented toward work or prefer welfare over employment.[28]

Overall, the human capital hypothesis has received more empirical support.[29] Recipients with higher skill-levels have shorter average stays on welfare and are less likely to return after a welfare exit. Moreover, there is an extensive literature documenting the increased importance of postsecondary education and training for jobs that pay above the poverty line.

Yet, there is a growing consensus among economists that demand-side factors are important to explaining the declining position of low-skilled workers as well.[30] Factors such as declining wages within industrial sectors, increases in part-time and contingent employment, the rise of service sector jobs, the decline of unionized jobs, and the movement of manufacturing jobs outside of central cities have all contributed to the declining position of low-skilled workers.[31] The landscape of this low-wage work is diverse: Waitstaff, servers, and dishwashers in restaurants; line-cooks and cashiers in fast-food establishments; health care aides, orderlies, and housekeeping staff in hospitals, hotels, and nursing care facilities; cashiers and sales clerks in a variety of retail firms; and office assistants who are employed in financial, health, retail, and service industries. These are exactly the jobs welfare recipients disproportionately find; and these occupations are those that are most frequently represented by the employees that were interviewed as well.

National studies find that low-skilled nonmanufacturing jobs such as these just mentioned pay on average less than $8 an hour, and there continues to be a relative disadvantage to being nonwhite and female even in this low-skilled sector of the labor market.[32] The wages of low-skilled workers generally reflect

Table 3.6

Employment Characteristics of Employees by Educational Level (N = 74)

| | Educational Level | | | |
	Less than high school (n = 21)	High school degree (n = 22)	Some postsecondary education (n = 22)	Post-secondary degree (n = 9)
Currently working (% yes)*	52.4	81.8	86.4	77.8
Wages (mean)	$7.09	$7.67	$8.79	$9.70
Standard deviation	2.7	3.1	3.7	5.1
Wage categories (%)				
$6 or less	42.9	40.9	22.7	22.3
$6.01–9	38.1	36.4	45.5	44.4
over $9	19.0	22.7	31.8	33.3
Total	100	100	100	100

*Chi-square of education level by currently working = 7.67, $p < .05$.

the wages of welfare recipients who find employment as well. Specifically, using data from the National Longitudinal Survey of Youth, Burtless finds that women who received welfare at some point in time between 1979 and 1981 were earning $7.77 an hour in 1990 (in 1996 dollars).[33] Harris finds comparable figures using the Panel Study of Income Dynamics and examining a sample of women who left welfare at some point between 1983 and 1988.[34] Importantly, Harris's work also demonstrates that the wages of welfare recipients who leave the roles show negligible increases one ($7.78), two ($7.74), and three ($8.04) years after a welfare exit.

The importance of both supply- and demand-side factors in explaining job insecurity and work instability is exemplified by the experiences of the employers and the employees in the Workplace Environment Study. On the supply side, respondents' wages varied with educational level, and the unemployed respondents were more likely to have less than a high school education (see Table 3.6).[35] However, the variation in wages within educational level was great, especially among those with a postsecondary education, as illustrated by the fact that our lowest-paid respondent was a live-in nurse's aide with an associate's degree, and our highest-paid respondent was a college-educated woman who worked as a medical records technician for a large home health care organization.[36] Thus, although investments in human capital are clearly associated with improved employment opportunities, a range of employee skill levels are represented across the jobs examined in the current study. These jobs may themselves be tenuous regardless of the characteristics of individual workers.

As Table 3.7 indicates, welfare respondents earned on average less than the coworker respondents, were less likely to have jobs with health insurance, and

Table 3.7

Job Characteristics by Sample Subgroups

	Currently working			Not currently working*	Welfare sample	Coworker sample
	Total	Welfare	Coworker	Total	Total	Total
Sample size	55	27	26	19	44	30
Number of jobs (%)						
1	81.8	77.8	92.3	—	—	—
2	14.8	22.2	7.7	—	—	—
Hours per week (%)						
30 or less	25.5	37.0	18.5	44.4	38.1	23.3
31–40	52.7	44.4	59.3	44.4	45.2	56.7
41 or more	20.0	18.5	22.2	11.2	16.7	20.0
Mean	37.3	35.9	38.0	33.2	35.4	37.0
Standard deviation	12.5	15.0	10.0	11.1	13.5	10.7
Pay per hour (%)						
$6.00 or less	29.1	32.1	25.9	47.4	38.6	30.0
$6.01–$9.00	40.0	39.3	40.7	42.1	40.9	36.7
$9.01 or more	30.9	28.6	33.3	10.5	20.5	33.3
Mean	8.38	7.69	9.08	7.20	7.35	9.12
Standard deviation	3.4	2.5	4.0	3.8	2.4	4.5
Health insurance (%)						
Yes	32.7	21.4	44.4	10.5	15.9	43.3

*The job characteristics of respondents not currently working are not reported separately by welfare states as all but three respondents in this subgroup are in the welfare sample.

Note: Chi-square and *t*-tests significant at *p* < .05 are shown with asterisks.

were more likely to work part-time (and more likely to hold multiple jobs simultaneously as a result). This is true for the subgroup of respondents currently working, as well as the sample overall. But, importantly, across the two samples, these job characteristics were poor. That is, the wages of the welfare and coworker samples mirrored the wages of less-skilled workers generally, with slightly less than one-third of the total earning $6 or less an hour, and more than two-thirds earning $9 or less an hour. Overall, about two-thirds of all respondents were in jobs that did not provide health insurance, and one-fourth were working 30 hours a week or less. Not surprisingly, respondents with the lowest paying jobs ($6 or less) reported feeling more insecure about the stability of their jobs and reported thinking more often about quitting, as compared to respondents in the higher wage groups.

Even respondents whose employment appeared on the surface to be of better quality were faced with job-related barriers that had consequences for job security. For example, Sylvia, a 41-year-old Latina with an eleventh-grade education and a General Education Development (GED) certificate worked as a customer service representative for a temporary agency. She found the job through a friend, and was paid $11.50 per hour and worked full-time. In this job, Sylvia interviewed prospective temporary workers for specific jobs, conducted initial interviews with businesses that were considering using the temporary services, and was responsible for ongoing communications with temporary workers and business clients. Sylvia received health benefits; however, she stated that the cost of the benefit, at $300 dollars a month to cover both herself and her children, almost outweighed its usefulness to her. In her words, "it's not a benefit if you have to pay for it," referring to the fact that her health payments absorbed a significant portion of her monthly check. Still, this job was a better job than those held by most of the respondents, in that the pay was significantly higher, work was full-time, and a series of additional benefits were provided (e.g., life insurance, paid sick leave and vacation time, bonuses). Sylvia liked her job, stating that she learned a lot, did not find it boring, and got along well with coworkers and supervisors. Rather than this case being an example of a "success," however, Sylvia was terminated ten months after beginning because the job itself was eliminated. In fact, all of the regional sales positions at this agency were cut as a result of an organizational restructuring.

Although Sylvia's job was far superior to those held by most of the respondents, job-related factors that were beyond her control prevented her from staying employed. In fact, almost two-thirds (63%) of the respondents who were unemployed at the time they were interviewed stated that they had lost their most recent job due to such job-related factors. For example, a part-time office assistant was let go when her job was eliminated due to funding reductions, a claims representative at an insurance company lost her job when the company she worked for went out of business, and the position of a medical records technician was eliminated when her employer contracted with a different agency to carry out administrative services. Moreover, both employed and unemployed respondents stated that job-related barriers such as inflexible hours, low pay, and few advancement possibilities were common barriers to keeping prior jobs and led to complications at work that sometimes threatened job security.

The employers interviewed corroborated the employee data regarding the importance of job-related characteristics to understanding employment instability. In fact, the majority of the employers noted that economic conditions and job characteristics were their primary concerns—more relevant than finding qualified workers. These factors, rather than worker qualities, seemed to drive decisions to terminate employment. Thus, whereas most employers had devised successful strategies for recruiting good workers, they felt less capable of influencing workplace conditions. That is, employers recognized that low-wages and limited hours made their jobs unfavorable to workers, and also believed that broader economic conditions prevented them from improving these workplace conditions. For example, the owner of a small grocery store stated that cashiers tended to stay on the job for about 6 to 12 months. Whereas sometimes cashiers left for higher paying jobs, the "main reason . . . is that I cannot keep them. When business is slow my wife or me can do the cashier work."

The Importance of Informal Networks for Job Stability

In addition to demand-side factors that limit a job's quality and stability, workers in these jobs must often manage multiple demands that further complicate workplace success. Whereas some of the demands imposed by motherhood are shared by all workers (e.g., child-caring responsibilities), poverty itself can produce such psychological and physical stressors as insecure housing arrangements, impractical transportation arrangements, poor health, inadequate health care, and worries over unpaid bills and other economic concerns. These stressors were commonplace among the employees interviewed in the Workplace Environment Study. Over half (56.3%) of the total employee sample reported being behind on their bills, many reported housing problems such as being in arrears on rent (25.7%) or inadequate housing arrangements (25.7%), and slightly less than one-third reported having children with serious health problems (29.0%) or school-related problems (31.9%). Moreover, transportation was often difficult, as 40 percent of respondents did not own a car and relied instead on public transportation, friends, or relatives to get to and from work. Whatever one's regular mode of transportation, a significant minority of respondents (43.7%) reported that they did not have an *alternative* means of getting to work in the event that their usual arrangement fell through. All of these stressors can result in workplace interferences, especially for jobs in which workplace arrangements are inflexible and workers have little autonomy or control over the manner in which they complete their job tasks. Among the employees that were interviewed, job interferences were especially great for those respondents who reported having children with health and school behavior problems and for those employees with inadequate transportation and child care arrangements.

Of the multiple stressors facing respondents, child care demands represented the most significant barrier. Child care responsibilities, which all parents must juggle, are disproportionately burdensome for low-income workers who are less able to purchase formal child care services or other support services to help with family caregiving needs. In this study, over two-thirds of the women who reported having a regular child care provider during their current or most recent job (19% did not have regular care) relied on informal providers, usually care delivered by a female relative or friend. As expected, the respondents who had secured regular care were paying significantly less than the market rate. The median cost of child care was approximately $50 a week for both welfare and coworker samples. Several respondents noted that they traded child care responsibilities with other mothers, shared food stamps, or provided meals in return for care.[37] Most respondents reported using the arrangements they did for both financial and safety reasons; however, for many respondents it was the only option available to them. Over 40 percent of the respondents did not have an alternative source of child care, and stated that it would be either very unlikely or unlikely that they could find a child care replacement in the event that their current situation fell through. Moreover, 15 percent of respondents reported that their current child care arrangements were not safe, and most of this group (70%) reported that these safety concerns interfered with their job performance. Importantly, child care problems were equally frequent for single and cohabiting/married women.

The extent of reliance on informal care arrangements illustrates the importance of informal network relationships for the welfare and coworker samples alike. Just as these informal networks can provide an entree into the workplace, as evidenced by the significance of employee referrals to the hiring process, these friends and family members also subsidize the cost of working by providing necessary supports to working mothers that neither low-wage jobs nor government programs are likely to deliver. Thus, for many mothers, in order to find and keep jobs in the low-skilled segment of the labor market, it may be crucial to have access to an informal network of support that includes both individuals who are attached to the labor force and individuals who are not—the employed providing a connection to the labor market and the unemployed assuming responsibilities that one is unable to fulfill while working.

These data suggest, however, that a system that relies so heavily on the role of informal support, can have negative consequences for many low-income parents. Several of the women interviewed found themselves in precarious situations because their informal networks could not provide the supports necessary for them to maintain their jobs. The experience of Cheryl, a 36-year-old woman who worked part-time for four years as a food service worker at a stadium concession stand, helps to illustrate the limits of these informal network arrangements. Cheryl did not own a car and relied solely on public transportation to get to and from her job, which was about ten miles from her home. She estimated that it took her a little under two hours a day to get to and from work and indicated that she was late for work a few times a month because of transportation problems. Cheryl faced the additional barrier of inconsistent child care. Her 18-year-old son (who lived with her), or a neighbor, or relative, usually took care of her children; but she reported that it varied and that "it was hard all the time" to find a baby-sitter. In fact, Cheryl reported being late for work or missing work weekly because of child care problems. During the four years that she worked, she changed child care arrangements frequently—"constantly" in her words. She would pay her providers between $12 and $20 a day, depending on what she received in tips, and needed care about three days a week. Cheryl's child care problems were exacerbated by the fact that her work schedule was not consistent or predictable. Although there were formal rules and procedures for dealing with late employees (being docked pay or not being called back to work a shift), Cheryl stated that "the people I worked with loved me," so she felt fortunate that she had escaped these normal sanctions faced by other employees. Given that one-third of the respondents reported having lost prior jobs because of child care problems, it seems that Cheryl was, in fact, fortunate.

As the example of Cheryl illustrates, the workplace itself may be more or less flexible in accommodating external demands when they do spill over into the workplace. One's relationship with an employer becomes particularly important in these situations. In Cheryl's case, for example, her positive relationship with her supervisor undoubtedly saved her job. Yet, the employees interviewed generally preferred to keep personal matters, including child care and other family issues, outside of the view of employers. Although the reasons for this varied, their low-status positions contributed to their desire to not "rock the boat" with employers. In an effort to maintain smooth workplace relationships and keep a "professional relationship" with supervisors, respondents tried to work around external demands such as child care problems and chose only to discuss them with employers as a last resort.[38]

Employers themselves varied greatly in the extent to which they recognized child care and transportation problems as significant barriers. Several employers stated that they tried to accommodate the needs of their workers and felt that to some degree transportation and child care problems were "inevitable" given the low wages of the work and the fact that they employed women with children. Informal practices were sometimes put in place to deal with these problems so long as external demands did not routinely compromise an employee's ability to fulfill her work duties in a timely fashion. The most common employer responses to such situations included having other employees cover the missed shifts, working the job on their own until the employee arrived, or, more rarely, rescheduling an employee's hours for another day. In a few cases, employers stated that they would send an employee out to pick up another worker with a transportation problem or would leave work and pick up the stranded employee himself or herself. Some employers allowed employees to bring children to work in the event of a child care problem; however, these were exceptional cases. If problems became too significant or routine, many employers stated that they would either dock pay, limit future shifts, or terminate an employee.

In reviewing the employer responses to the multiple demands facing workers outside of the workplace, it is important to keep in mind the reluctance expressed by employee respondents to discuss these problems with employers. As a result, employers were potentially unaware of the efforts expended by employees in keeping these demands from spilling over into the workplace. For some respondents these efforts even compromised a child's safety in order to fulfill workplace duties. For example, one of the respondents, Gretchen, worked as a neighborhood patrol officer for a private security company. When she took this job, Gretchen lost her welfare benefits and the child care subsidy that had accompanied them. Because Gretchen did not have family or friends nearby who could provide child care, she reported leaving her 10-year-old son at home during her evening shifts, rehearsing with him a set of instructions that she hoped would keep him safe before locking the door behind her. Gretchen patrolled in a car by herself, a situation that allowed her the freedom to drive home periodically and check on her son (outside of her boss' awareness). But this arrangement was not one that left Gretchen satisfied; both for fear of her son's safety and because she preferred spending time with him during the evenings when he was not at school.

Gretchen's experience, as well as that of Cheryl's, both illustrate the incompatibility of work and family responsibilities in instances when neither informal networks nor formal policies are in place and functioning smoothly. The low wages paid to low-skilled workers prevent them from purchasing high quality and consistent formal services; yet, for a variety of reasons, informal networks often cannot provide the level of support necessary to maintain stable employment.

Conclusion

Low-income workers face a labor market that provides few opportunities for economic security. Their jobs are low paying, offer limited benefits, and are frequently part-time and temporary in nature. Moreover, finding work in this labor market can be difficult because many firms report more job seekers than jobs and because employers utilize hiring strategies that may benefit some workers but clearly work to the detriment of others. This chapter has argued that in order to maintain a cohesive and productive workplace, employers often rely on what they view as an efficient and effective strategy of recruiting workers based primarily on employee referrals. Referrals ease the hiring process and also help employers screen for difficult to measure, but highly valued, worker qualities. Unfortunately, qualified candidates who do not come to the attention of employers, or who are perceived by employers as coming from less qualified social groups, will have a difficult time getting hired. It is for this reason that the goals of policies that draw attention to the welfare status of a job applicant may fall short. Given that employers are likely to view welfare recipients as less qualified than other workers, they may be less willing to take risks with an individual job candidate if her welfare status has been emphasized.

Moreover, the role demands imposed by parenthood often conflict with the demands of the workplace. Managing these multiple and often conflicting demands is difficult for all working parents, but low-income parents face greater challenges because they have fewer resources to purchase support and because their jobs provide them less independence, authority, and flexibility to respond to competing demands. Despite these difficulties, there is little in the recent welfare reform law that addresses the unique problems of low-income working mothers. While there are funds available to help with child care and transportation needs, these are viewed largely as temporary supports. But the dual role of parent and worker is a long-term one, and without permanent supports as well as a flexible workplace, these conflicting demands will continue to pose problems for workers, especially those with the fewest resources.

Rather than addressing the fundamental barriers presented by low-wage work, the new welfare reform law attempts to address attitudinal and behavioral deficits that are presumed to affect the economic well-being of welfare recipients. However, welfare recipients often find themselves in the same poor quality jobs as other low-income individuals and have a similar set of family demands as well. A more fruitful approach to understanding and changing the behavior of welfare recipients might be to intervene on the side of the workplace and to increase the formal supports available to low-income parents. By proposing an approach that views the problem as resulting from structural constraints and role demands rather than one endemic to the worker, we begin to recognize challenges external to the individual that affect her ability to become economically independent. Moreover, successful interventions that would function to change the quality of the low-wage labor market, in general, would affect the economic well-being of not just welfare recipients but all poor working families.

Notes

Portions of this chapter were presented by the author, Yeheskel Hasenfeld, and Joel F. Handler, at the nineteenth Annual Research Conference of the Association for Public Policy Analysis and Management, Washington, D.C., November 6–8, 1997. This chapter was also included in the 1997–1998 Working Paper Series of the Center for American Politics and Public Policy at UCLA. The project was supported primarily through funds provided by the Urban Institute Small Grants Program to the author, Yeheskel Hasenfeld, and Joel F. Handler. The author also received support from the Lois and Samuel Silberman Fund, the UCLA Center for American Politics and Public Policy, and the UCLA Institute of Industrial Relations. Some of the research reported herein was performed with the permission of the California Department of Social Services. The author wishes to thank all of these parties for their tremendous support. Special thanks to Yeheskel Hasenfeld, Joel F. Handler, Demetra Nightingale, Margaret Rosenheim, Jens Ludwig, and Sandra Lyons for their comments and suggestions, and Megan Meyer, Martina Acevedo, and Christine Coho for research assistance. Thanks also to the many employees and employers who took the time to be interviewed for this study. The opinions and conclusions expressed herein are solely those of the author and should not be considered as representing the policy of any agency of the California state government, the Urban Institute, or UCLA. All errors in the reporting and interpretation of study findings are the responsibility of the author. Please address all correspondence to Julia Henly, University of Chicago, School of Social Service Administration, 969 E. 60th Street, Chicago, IL 60637, Email: jhenly@midway.uchicago.edu.

1. Personal Responsibility and Work Opportunity Reconciliation Act of 1996, P.L., 104–193.

2. There are several specific measures in the bill, but time limits on the receipt of welfare and a series of measures designed to increase work activities are most relevant for the present discussion.

3. In the 1988 welfare legislation (the Family Support Act) work requirements were strengthened, but states were prohibited from mandating participation in work programs unless child care was made available to recipients.

4. The Dun and Bradstreet data were made available from Rebuild LA, Los Angeles, CA.

5. As Table 3.1 indicates, several welfare recipients were employed in the financial, business, and real estate industrial sector. Most of these respondents held administrative/office occupations. Less common, but also represented among welfare recipients, was

public service/manufacturing. This included occupations such as mail carrier (public service) and light production (manufacturing). Because these industrial sectors were not selected a priori from the Dun and Bradstreet database for the employer and coworker samples, we did not interview any employers from these industries. Through referrals from the welfare sample, however, we were able to conduct interviews with a small number of coworkers employed in these two industrial sectors.

6. Percentages do not add up to 100 because several respondents identified membership in more than one ethnic or racial category.

7. One respondent did not have any children; however, she was caring for a relative's child at the time we interviewed her so she was included in the study.

8. Those not currently working had been out of the work force a median of 11 months. Only two respondents had been unemployed for more than two years. Differences in recall between those currently and not currently working might be expected; however, given the recency of employment for the unemployed group, this is unlikely to be a serious problem. No recipients, in fact, reported difficulties recollecting information about their past jobs.

9. R. Waldinger, "Black/Immigrant Competition Re-assessed: New Evidence from Los Angeles." UCLA Department of Sociology, Unpublished Monograph, 1995; H.J. Holzer, *What Employers Want: Job Prospects for Less-Educated Workers* (New York: Russell Sage Foundation, 1996); J. Kirschenman and K.M. Neckerman, " 'We'd Love to Hire Them, But . . .': The Meaning of Race for Employers," in *The Urban Underclass,* ed. C. Jencks and P.E. Peterson (Washington, DC: Brookings Institution, 1991), pp. 203–34.

10. The welfare recipients in our sample relied to an equal extent as our coworkers on these strategies for finding work. Also of note, only three respondents had been placed in their current or most recent jobs by a job-training program.

11. See for example, Holzer, *What Employers Want;* K. Abraham, "Structural-Frictional v. Demand-Deficient Unemployment," *American Economic Review* 73 (1983): 708–24; R.M. Blank, *It Takes a Nation: A New Agenda for Fighting Poverty* (New York: Russell Sage Foundation, 1997); for alternative view see D.P. McMurrer, I.V. Sawhill and R.I. Lerman, "Welfare Reform and Opportunity in the Low-Wage Labor Market," Discussion Paper No. 5, Urban Institute, July 1997.

12. See C.B. Stack, "Beyond What Are Given as Givens: Ethnography and Critical Policy Studies," *Ethos* 25, no. 2 (1997): 191–207; K. Newman and C. Lennon, "The Job Ghetto," *The American Prospect,* Summer 1995.

13. Holzer, *What Employers Want.*

14. See Waldinger, "Black/Immigrant Competition Re-Assessed"; Kirschenman and Neckerman, " 'We'd Love to Hire Them, But . . .'."

15. Although he also emphasizes the importance of these soft skills to employers, Holzer finds that even in these low-skilled jobs, employers have a preference for workers with stronger educational credentials and experience. Our own data lead us to believe that education mattered relatively little to the employers we interviewed.

16. W.J. Wilson, *The Truly Disadvantaged* (Chicago: University of Chicago Press, 1987); W.J. Wilson, *When Work Disappears: The World of the New Urban Poor.* (New York: Alfred A. Knopf, 1996); Waldinger, "Black/Immigrant Competition Re-assessed"; Kirschenman and Neckerman, " 'We'd Love to Hire Them, But . . .'."

17. In most instances, the issue of control over hiring was in reference to a candidate's job qualifications. That is, employers had a concern that a subsidy program might include incentives or mandates to hire unqualified candidates, and this was something few employers were willing to consider. In one case, however, an employer feared that she would be "harassed" both by program personnel and employees if she tried to fire an employee that was not working out. She stated, "I think we could get stuck with harassment. . . .

Most employers are good about knowing the qualifications needed for a job. They need to be able to fire people with a bad attitude."

18. See, for example, M.R. Rank, *Living on the Edge: The Realities of Welfare in America* (New York: Columbia University Press, 1994); M. Katz, *The Undeserving Poor: From the War on Poverty to the War on Welfare.* (New York: Pantheon, 1989); J.F. Handler and Y. Hasenfeld, *The Moral Construction of Poverty* (Newbury Park, CA: Sage Publications, 1991).

19. See L. Ross and R.E. Nisbett, *The Person and the Situation: Perspectives of Social Psychology* (New York: McGraw-Hill, 1991).

20. Kirschenman and Neckerman, " 'We'd Love to Hire Them, But . . .'." That employers rely on category membership as a proxy for the possession of social skills (which are inherently difficult to measure) is consistent with the social psychological literature that suggests that beliefs about social groups are most likely to influence our evaluations of individual group members in ambiguous situations when more objective individuating information is unavailable. Nisbett and Ross, *The Person and the Situation.*

21. K.M. Harris, "Work and Welfare among Single Mothers in Poverty," *American Journal of Sociology* 99, no. 2 (1993): 317–52; K.M. Harris, "Life After Welfare: Women, Work, and Repeat Dependency." Paper presented at the American Sociological Association Meetings, Los Angeles, CA, 1994); L.A. Pavetti, "The Dynamics of Welfare and Work: Exploring the Process by Which Women Work Their Way Off Welfare," Malcolm Wiener Center for Social Policy Working Papers: Dissertation Series, Harvard University, 1993; M.J. Bane and D.T. Ellwood, *Welfare Realities: From Rhetoric to Reform* (Cambridge, MA: Harvard University Press, 1994); L. Parker, "The Role of Workplace Support in Facilitating Self-Sufficiency among Single Mothers on Welfare," *Family Relations* 43 (1994): 168–73. Different techniques for measuring exits and the use of different types of longitudinal data (some based on monthly and some on annual records) account for the variation in findings. Studies that use monthly records estimate greater numbers of work exits. See Bane and Ellwood, *Welfare Realities,* for review of these methodological variations.

22. Harris, "Life After Welfare."

23. Ibid., p. 36.

24. Bane and Ellwood, *Welfare Realities.*

25. For example, G. Gilder, *Wealth and Poverty* (New York: Basic Books, 1981); L.M. Mead, *Beyond Entitlement: The Social Obligations of Citizenship* (New York: Free Press, 1986); C. Murray, *Losing Ground: American Social Policy 1950–1980.* (New York: Basic Books, 1984).

26. For example, Bane and Ellwood, *Welfare Realities;* LaDonna Pavetti, *Against The Odds: Steady Employment Among Low-Skilled Women,* A Report to the Annie E. Casey Foundation, July 1997 (Washington, DC: Urban Institute Press).

27. Mead, *Beyond Entitlement.*

28. L. Goodwin, *The Causes and Cures of Welfare: New Evidence on the Social Psychology of the Poor.* (Lexington, MA: Lexington Books, 1983); J. Henly and S.K. Danziger, "Confronting Welfare Stereotypes: Characteristics of General Assistance Recipients and Post-Assistance Employment," *Social Work Research* (1996): 217–27; Rank, *Living on the Edge;* K. Edin, "Surviving the Welfare System: How AFDC Recipients Make Ends Meet in Chicago," *Social Problems* 38, no. 4 (1991): 462–75. In the study reported herein standard measures of work ethic were included (Irwin Katz and R. Glen Hass, "Racial Ambivalence and American Value Conflict: Correlational and Priming Studies of Dual Cognitive Structures," *Journal of Personality and Social Psychology* 55, no. 6 [1988]: 893–905) as well as a mastery scale (L. Pearlin and C. Schooler, "The Structure Of Coping," *Journal of Health and Social Behavior* 19 (1978): 2–21). Both

consist of several agree-disagree statements that are designed to measure one's commitment to the American work ethic (Katz and Haas, "Racial Ambivalence") and one's sense of control over her own environment (Pearlin and Schooler, "The Structure of Coping"). Both of these scales are commonly used in psychological research. Results show no evidence at all that these two groups hold different values toward work, in fact the mean scores for the two groups are identical (3.76 for coworkers, 3.73 for welfare recipients on a 5–point scale). Similarly, the two groups do not differ significantly on their Mastery scores, with welfare recipients reporting a mean Mastery score of 3.14 and coworkers reporting a mean score of 3.08.

29. Bane and Ellwood, *Welfare Realities;* Pavetti, "The Dynamics of Welfare and Work"; Pavetti, *Against the Odds;* Harris, "Life After Welfare."

30. See, for example, Blank, *It Takes a Nation;* S.H. Danziger and Gottschalk, *America Unequal* (Cambridge, MA: Harvard University Press, 1995); see also Chapter 1 of this volume.

31. The decline has been greatest for men because they had further to fall. Blank, *It Takes a Nation.* That is, whereas low-skilled women have historically had limited opportunities in the labor market, the opportunities of low-skilled men have deteriorated in the last two decades. Lawrence Mishel and Jared Bernstein, *The State of Working America 1994–1995* (Armonk, NY: M.E. Sharpe, Economic Policy Institute, 1994); R.B. Freeman, "How Much Has De-Unionization Contributed to the Rise in Male Earnings Inequality?" in *Uneven Tides: Rising Inequality in America,* ed. S. Danziger and P. Gottschalk (New York: Russell Sage Foundation, 1994), pp. 133–64; S.H. Danziger and D.H. Weinberg, "The Historical Record: Trends In Family Income, Inequality, and Poverty," in *Confronting Poverty: Prescriptions for Change,* ed. S.H. Danziger, G.D. Sandefur, and D.H. Weinberg (Cambridge, MA: Harvard University Press, 1994), pp. 18–50; Wilson, *The Truly Disadvantaged;* Wilson, *When Work Disappears.*

32. For example, Harry Holzer finds that whereas the jobs available to less-educated workers are of poor quality regardless of the race or gender of the worker, the return to work continues to be lower for nonwhites and for women. White females with a high school education or less earn an average of $7.91/hour in nonmanufacturing sectors, Black females earn $6.79/hour, Hispanic females earn $7.52/hour; in contrast, white males with a high school degree or less in nonmanufacturing jobs earn $8.20/hour. Thus, there continues to be a significant wage advantage to being a white male over both white females and nonwhite females and males; but Holzer also finds that white women with a high school degree or less actually earn more on average in nonmanufacturing jobs than both black males and females and Hispanic males and females with comparable skills in comparable jobs. Holzer's findings call into question purely skill-based (supply side) arguments of income inequality, as his findings show wage inequalities within a sample of similarly skilled workers. Holzer argues that these income disparities by race and gender can more reasonably be understood as the result of employment discrimination. Holzer, *What Employers Want.*

33. G. Burtless, "Employment Prospects of Welfare Recipients," in *The Work Alternative: Welfare Reform and the Realities of the Job Market,* ed. D.S. Nightingale and R. Haveman (Washington, DC: Urban Institute Press, 1995).

34. K.M. Harris, "Life After Welfare: Women, Work And Repeat Dependency," *American Sociological Review* 61 (1996): 407–26.

35. It is important to keep in mind that the welfare sample was screened for prior employment; thus, to the extent that education and employment vary together, our welfare sample will be biased upward in terms of education. This "creaming" was intentional, given that, for the employee interviews, our central interest was to learn more about experiences in jobs, rather than experiences looking for work.

36. As we discuss later, even these relatively high paying jobs were often insecure. In the case of this respondent, she was unemployed at the time of the interview her because the organization she worked for had contracted out the services that she provided to another company.

37. See C. Stack, *All Our Kin: Strategies for Survival in a Black Community* (New York: Harper & Row, 1974); K. Edin and L. Lein, *Making Ends Meet: How Single Mothers Survive Welfare and Low-Wage Work* (New York: Russell Sage Foundation, 1997); R.J. Taylor, L.M. Chatters, M.B. Tucker, and E. Lewis, "Developments in Research on Black Families: A Decade Review," *Journal of Marriage and the Family* 52 (1990): 993–1014 for other examples of the importance of in-kind reciprocal support among low-income families.

38. Although beyond the scope of this chapter, the employees spoke in depth about the atmosphere of their jobs. Whereas overall employees described relatively benign workplace interactions, the lack of power and control respondents felt they had over their workday was a theme in the majority of interviews. This included perceived gender discrimination and sexual harassment, being treated with a lack of respect, and not being taken seriously by employers. Conflict with coworkers and supervisors was relatively uncommon; however, when it occurred, it was seldom resolved on the side of the employee. A combination of these factors can lead to an insecure workplace environment where open communication with one's boss about external demands or workplace problems is generally avoided by employees.

4

Susan R. Jones

SELF-EMPLOYMENT

Possibilities and Problems

Self-employment as a route to economic self-sufficiency for low-income people is receiving increased national attention.[1] One manifestation of this is microenterprise development, a community economic development (CED), and antipoverty strategy in which small loans, peer support, and/or technical assistance are made available to persons starting very small businesses.[2] While the need for neighborhood small businesses to complement affordable housing and other CED initiatives is well recognized, the notion that low-income people can own them is relatively new.[3]

Witness for example, Dorothy Wallace, separated from her husband, with two teenagers, and on welfare, who used an $800 loan from the Chicago-based microenterprise program, Women's Self-Employment Project (WSEP), to start the fragrance vending business of which she dreamed. Founded in 1986 to assist low-income women interested in self-employment as a way out of poverty, WSEP required Dorothy to participate in a five-member borrowing circle of women who also wanted to be self-employed. The five-member group chose the first two members to receive a loan. As one of the first two borrowers, Dorothy had to keep her loan current for six weeks and all five members had to attend three meetings in a row before a third member was eligible for a loan. These requirements created peer pressure, or "moral collateral," to ensure timely repayment.[4]

With the assistance of microenterprise development programs, low-wage workers and other targeted populations are receiving small-business loans to start a wide range of microbusinesses, from beauty shops to word processing services. This chapter discusses how self-employment can play a beneficial role in helping low-income people enhance their income and in the process facilitate development of human capital, the term social scientists use to describe the positive externalities that accrue when individuals take control of their lives, develop self-esteem, and succeed in the economic marketplace.[5] The chapter also contends that serious consideration of microenterprise development as a public policy option is both timely and bipartisan, given the recent passage of the Personal Responsibility and Work Opportunity Reconciliation Act (PRWORA) of 1996, with its emphasis on individual responsibility, and the relationship between an individual's place of work and personal dignity.[6]

Most traditional efforts to help low-income people escape poverty and eliminate reliance on welfare have focused on job placement. In some regions, however, few businesses are hiring because of depressed local economies. Some of those that are hiring are reluctant to engage recipients of public assistance because they see them as lacking basic work skills, a work ethic, and education. As noted in Chapter 1, local studies consistently show a job shortage; there are many more applicants seeking work than there are available jobs. The number of job seekers per job can be as high as 6 to 14 persons for one low-wage job. Thus, the future is not promising for the less-skilled worker for this and other reasons, including the decline in union membership, race discrimination, the overall decline in real wages, the increasing demand for higher levels of education and skills (beyond a high school diploma) for better jobs, and increasing low-wage and part-time jobs without benefits.[7]

The traditional focus on job placement is inadequate also because poverty entails more than having insufficient money. Family and life issues, such as child care, housing, employment, and health, are exacerbated for low-income people. Employment thus addresses the economic aspect of poverty but not the other issues that hinder employment.

Self-employment for low-income people may offer a partial antidote to these vexing problems. Self-employment often allows for flexibility, which is particularly critical for low-wage workers because of child care, health care, and transportation time and costs. These realities for low-wage workers suggest that self-employment (particularly home- and neighborhood-based) offers an increasingly important option for welfare policymakers. Self-employment may be the sole source of employment, serve as a bridge to a job, or supplement low-wage work.[8] Proponents of microenterprise development also believe that entrepreneurial education, teaching people to create jobs, is as productive as basic education in the new American economy, and, as such, deserves sustained public investment. They argue that, given the current economy and low-wage work trends, "training people to simply fill jobs is an anachronism."[9]

Microenterprise Development in the United States

By providing small loans, training, and technical assistance to microbusinesses as diverse as home-based child care, fashion designers, street vendors, massage therapists, automobile mechanics, and carpenters, U.S. microenterprise development programs have successfully helped to raise the family incomes of many low-income people and minorities, as well as other targeted populations such as displaced workers and disabled people.[10] Moreover, the industry's involvement in CED efforts is evidenced by contributions to economic enfranchisement, human capital, and leadership development.

Microenterprise is an important subcategory of a larger, diverse, U.S. small business sector. The definition of a small business varies according to the industry and number of employees. The U.S. Small Business Administration (SBA), for example, defines a small business as one that has "fewer than 100 employees, is independently owned, locally operated . . . not dominant in its field of operation and grosses less than three million dollars annually."[11] The fact that small businesses are creating most of the new jobs in the country (54 percent of the private work force and 62 percent of the 3.3 million new jobs created in 1994)[12] is a primary reason for examining self-employment as an option for welfare recipients and low-wage workers.

The development of the microenterprise subsector in the United States began in the early 1980s. Initially, microenterprise development programs in the United States were often modeled on their counterparts in Latin America, Asia, and Africa. One of the most successful of these models is the Grameen Bank, started by Muhammad Yunus, an economist from Bangladesh. Yunus, who is considered to be the world's leading proponent of "trickle up" development, believes that access to credit can provide a lifeline to rescuing many people from poverty. Founded in 1983, the Grameen Bank lends over $6 million a month to more than 690,000 members (92 percent of whom are women) in 14,000 villages throughout Bangladesh.[13]

U.S. microenterprise practitioners are quick to distinguish the successful and impressive international examples from the American models because the U.S. economy is more sophisticated and the society is more heterogeneous than the countries where microenterprises have traditionally flourished. For example, while Bangladesh has a long history of self-employment, less than one in ten Americans work for themselves. As a result, the American microenterprise movement has to be customized to different populations, regions, and communities. To this end, the U.S. microenterprise community is undergoing continuous self-study and analysis of the best practices.[14]

Today there is no standard definition of microenterprise in the United States. It is often defined as a sole proprietorship, partnership, or family business that has fewer than five employees, does not generally have access to the commercial banking sector, can initially utilize a loan of under $15,000[15] to start or expand a business that usually grosses less than $250,000 per year, and employs fewer than five people.[16] A microenterprise has also been defined as a business, often home-based, comprised of one to five people, with less than $5,000 in start-up capital.[17]

Currently, there are over 500 microenterprise programs in forty-six states and the District of Columbia, reflecting a wide range of purposes, goals, values, and program designs.[18] A majority of these programs target low-income people as part of their mission.[19] Over one-half serve welfare recipients.[20] In 1995, 15,957 low-income individuals were served by microenterprise practitioners.[21] Programs encouraging microenterprise in the United States generally provide three services: microloans, which range from $500 to $25,000; training; and technical assistance in business planning, accounting, and accessing markets. These services go primarily to low-income persons, women, minorities, and other targeted populations, such as farm or Native American communities, dislocated workers, disabled persons, and refugees.

The Good Faith Fund (GFF) in Pine Bluff, Arkansas, is one of the early microenterprise programs that has received much national attention. Since 1988, GFF has made over 200 business loans of more than $800,000 and provided training and technical assistance to 600 entrepreneurs.[22]

The microenterprise industry boasts impressive statistics. Since the inception of the first U.S. microenterprise program in 1983, 328 U.S. microenterprise programs served 171,555 participants and dispersed $126 million in loans.[23] In 1995 alone, 36,211 businesses were assisted; 13,787 of these were start-up companies. Programs loaned $35,508,657 to microentrepreneurs; the average loan size for group loans was $1,597 and $9,248 for individual loans.[24] Loan repayment rates are as high as 100 percent.[25]

Because a large percentage of the programs are under three years old,[26] microenterprise development essentially is still at a fledgling stage. Nevertheless, microenterprise development today has developed into an industry, complete with a national trade organization founded in 1991,[27] statewide networks, and a newly established financial intermediary called the Fund for Innovation, Effectiveness, Learning and Dissemination (FIELD), designed to "develop, document, and disseminate the best practices in developing antipoverty microenterprise programs."[28] The importance of microenterprise development has not gone unnoticed, and it is being supported by a number of government programs and nonprofit groups, such as the SBA's Microloan Program, the Corporation for Enterprise Development (CFED),[29] and the Mott Foundation.[30]

The Opportunity Presented by the Work Requirements of the Personal Responsibility and Work Opportunity Reconciliation Act (PRWORA) of 1996

Congress recently brought about the most dramatic change in the treatment of low-income people in the previous 63 years with the passage of the PRWORA. The PRWORA was signed by President Clinton in August 1996, instituting a five-year lifetime limit on welfare benefits for adults.[31] The statute also requires states to have 50 percent of their caseload working at least thirty hours per week by the year 2002.[32] Microenterprise development programs, through microloans and business training, provide another policy option for states as they identify employment strategies.

One of the PRWORA's goals was to decentralize the federal welfare program, encouraging the states to act as public policy laboratories. This was achieved by authorizing them to arrive at their own solutions to the problems presented by unemployment. The new PRWORA's emphasis on work requirements, community groups' interests in fostering long-term economic independence, and the need for job creation in low-income communities suggest that microenterprise development could be used to satisfy a portion of the PRWORA's work requirement. States, by more fully incorporating microenterprise into their welfare policies, can facilitate the self-sufficiency of low-income people instead of merely castigating them for failing to find a job.[33]

One of the changes related to microenterprise development made by the PRWORA was the repeal of Aid to Families with Dependent Children (AFDC). The PRWORA replaced AFDC with a federal-state formula for matching monies entitled Temporary Assistance for Needy Families (TANF).[34] Under TANF, states must meet certain requirements that fall into two categories: work and participation. Under the two-year work requirement, the PRWORA directs states to require individual parents or caretakers on welfare to be "engaged in work" once it is determined she is "ready" to do so, or when she has received assistance for 24 months, whichever is sooner.[35] States can require recipients to engage in work before 24 months.[36] Meanwhile, the definition of work is subject to state interpretation; states can consider participation in training or employment as work if they choose.[37]

The second category is the PRWORA's participation section. To satisfy this facet of the law, states must ensure that a specified percentage of families receiving welfare participate in specified work or work-related activities for 20 hours per week in 1997 and for 30 hours by 2000.[38] A range of activities (with certain limitations) count as 'participation,' such as on-the-job training and providing child care to an individual participating in a community service program.[39] To facilitate microenterprise development, states should define operation of a microbusiness as work to meet their participation requirements.

Although policymakers may be more inclined to view work more favorably than self-employment, the reality is that there are simply not enough low-wage jobs to meet the existing demand for them. Moreover, low-wage jobs often do not have the long-range benefits that accrue from self-employment training, such as the accompanying sense of hope and opportunity.

Another change suggesting an enhanced role for microenterprise is the PRWORA's basic maintenance of effort (MOE) requirement.[40] Under this stipulation, states must spend 75 percent to 85 percent of their historic state welfare expenditures (also known as qualifying expenditures) in cash outlays, child care assistance, and educational activities to facilitate increased self-sufficiency, job training, and work.[41] A state has several options for satisfying its MOE spending requirement, each choice bringing with it varying degrees of limitations.[42]

Microenterprise proponents argue that states should arrange their welfare spending in order to leverage the benefits microenterprise development programs offer. The best means to do this, they posit, is by structuring their spending to implicate as few TANF restrictions as possible. They advocate narrow definitions of work and training and broad legal interpretations to preserve the applicability of time limits so that self-employment training time, ideally ranging from three to nine months, is not included in the running of the five-year time limit. TANF restrictions, microenterprise practitioners point out, may hinder microenterprise development and other long-term human investment strategies.

The Self-Employment Investment Demonstration (SEID) Study: Is Self-Employment an Option for Welfare Recipients and Low-Wage Workers?

The PRWORA's passage begged the question of the relevance of self-employment and its viability as a welfare policy option. Only five years after the first microenterprise program was started in the United States,[43] a project known as the Self-Employment Investment Demonstration (SEID) helped answer this very inquiry. The 1987 SEID study published findings on the feasibility of operating a program to encourage self-employment among AFDC recipients.[44] Funded by the CFED, the SEID demonstration project began by recruiting a small proportion of the eligible AFDC population in its local area.[45] A total of 1,082 interested AFDC recipients attended the program orientation, approximately 1 percent of the AFDC caseload in urban areas and 6 to 7 percent of the AFDC caseload in rural areas.[46] Participants in the SEID program numbered two to three times those of highly selective, voluntary employment programs for welfare recipients, evidence of a special interest in self-employment as opposed to job training.[47]

Program operators modified their programs as they gained experience with the special needs of AFDC recipients. The reformulated program focused on addressing clients' unfamiliarity with the traditional business world, weak self-esteem and the lack of life-management skills, as well as an early assessment of the proposed business idea, the clients' capacity to implement it, and obstacles to successful small business development.[48]

Several key findings of the SEID study demonstrate the role self-employment can play for facilitating self-sufficiency and poverty alleviation for welfare recipients and low-wage workers. Most of SEID enrollees (between 44 and 74 percent) had been receiving welfare for more than two years. Close to 90 percent of the participants had a high school diploma or General Educational Development (GED) certificate; 83 percent had worked full-time; and most SEID clients were over 30 years old, older that the typical welfare recipient in the areas served by the demonstration project. The higher age factor meant that these SEID clients had a longer period of time to go to work, to school, and to receive welfare.

The second finding was that a significant proportion of the SEID enrollees, about 34 percent, reported that they had been self-employed either in the past or at the time they applied for the program. This fact suggests that an important function of SEID's study of self-employment training and the microloans may be to help microentrepreneurs make marginal enterprises more profitable, resuscitate failed businesses, or legitimize an underground business.

At the conclusion of the SEID study in 1993, CFED observed:

> The importance of self-employment lies not in the number who take advantage
> of it—1 to 10 percent of welfare recipients—but in the whole new approach to
> combating poverty: one that recognizes and builds on the talents and efforts of
> low-income people; one that invests in the expansion of low-income econo-
> mies rather than simply maintaining consumption; one that builds assets—sav-
> ings, skills, businesses, homes—rather than simply maintaining income.[49]

The SEID study verified that microenterprise development and self-employment are viable alternatives for some welfare recipients. It also began to
answer the next question in the post-PRWORA era: under what circumstances does self-employment work best? It is now up to states and federal
agencies charged with reinventing welfare policy to seriously consider the
self-employment option.

The Benefits of Self-Employment

> *Give someone a fish and they're fed for a day. Teach someone to*
> *fish and they're fed for a lifetime.*[50]
> *In the U.S. you sit down and fold your hands and say I don't have a*
> *job. You can make your own job.—Muhammad Yunus*[51]

Short-term practical benefits of self-employment abound. First, self-employment
does not depend on traditional educational credentials,[52] opening the field to
those lacking formal education. Second, as explained in Chapter 1, low-income
women with children need available and affordable day care to be able to leave
home to seek employment and to go to work. Self-employment often allows
low-income women to work out of their homes, potentially obviating the need
for child care.[53] Alternatively, self-employment may render child care more
accessible by locating the workplace closer to child care.

The child care example demonstrates how critical transportation issues can be
to helping welfare recipients and low-wage workers find and keep jobs. The
problem is that workers are far from potential jobs, a phenomenon researchers
call *spatial mismatch*. One study has shown that "only 8–15 percent of entry-
level jobs were accessible to welfare recipients within 37 minutes via public
transportation. Thirty-nine to forty-four percent of the entry level jobs were
accessible within 80 minutes, and no matter how much time was allowed for
transportation, welfare recipients could never reach fifty percent of the jobs."[54]
Most entry-level jobs are simply inaccessible for welfare recipients. About 56
percent of present AFDC welfare recipients live in central urban areas, only 6
percent of them own an automobile, and the majority of new jobs are in the
suburbs.[55]

One middle-term benefit of microenterprise development is the revival of communities, which depends on neighborhood small businesses. Heretofore, the major
emphasis in community economic development has been on affordable housing,

however, CED practitioners are now urging the creation of local businesses to complement housing, job creation, and other community building efforts.[56] There are a variety of service jobs and commercial niches available in low-income neighborhoods, such as barbershops and beauty parlors, home repair, painting, electrical services, plumbing, carpentry, small appliance repair, child and elder care, computers and information services, and catering.[57] Neighborhood small businesses can provide essential goods and services, supply larger industries such as manufacturing, and serve as important role models for neighborhood residents.[58]

The longer-term goal of microenterprise development is the success of the participants, measured by positive personal outcomes, such as improved self-esteem, exercising control over one's life and household income, taking advantage of educational opportunities or alternative employment, and the overall ability to exercise personal and economic choices.

Over time, self-employment has the potential to generate income that far exceeds the minimum wage and helps to break the cycle of isolation, dependency, and hopelessness by restoring responsibility, dignity, self-esteem, initiative, and other personal assets, such as leadership ability, personal and business confidence, and economic literacy.[59] Connie Evans, director of WSEP, believes that the value of such programs lies in "economic enfranchisement," the capacity to dig people out of the isolating experiences of poverty and to develop a sense of self by connecting with other people whose experiences they share.[60] The children (who are the majority of people on welfare) of self-employed microentrepreneurs are also exposed to positive entrepreneurial role models.[61] This process is known as the development of human capital. For example, Judy, one of WSEP's welfare-mother participants, began selling shoes door-to-door with a $600 loan and business training from WSEP. She has now repaid her loan, borrowed more money, and purchased her own store. A significant feature of microenterprise programs such as WSEP is education and training, often provided as part of a peer-lending or circle-lending model. Participants undergo a set number of hours (e.g., 30 hours) of business training, during which they are taught marketing, record keeping, accounting, and other business skills. After completion of the training, program participants are eligible for an initial loan, often as low as $500. Loans are made on a "stepped up" basis, increasing to a maximum amount (e.g., of $2,000 to $7,000) with a six-month to one-year repayment schedule per loan.[62]

WSEP participants organize themselves into loan groups, or "borrowing communities," comprised of five persons each. Borrowing community members have their own business and agree to provide mutual support and responsibility for other members in case of trouble with loan repayment. The microenterprise program certifies that members of the borrowing community have learned borrowing and repayment rules. A person desiring to receive a loan makes a presentation to the group. The group establishes "moral collateral" by becoming responsible for the loan, if it deems the project viable and worthwhile. The peer-lending group then meets every two weeks to give each other personal and business support, review new loan applications, make weekly loan payments, and to contribute to a "rainy day" fund, which is a savings account to be used for loan repayment in an emergency or in the event of a default.

Jubilee Jobs, another nonprofit organization dedicated to fomenting microentrepreneurship, illustrates how microenterprise can help inner-city families supplement their income. Jubilee primarily locates entry-level jobs for the inner-city poor, the homeless, recovering substance abusers, ex-offenders, and recent immigrants. Since 1981, Jubilee Jobs has placed over 6,000 persons in permanent employment. Nevertheless, most of these jobs pay only minimum wage. In 1994, hoping to facilitate economic self-sufficiency for their clients who were low-wage workers, Jubilee founded the Barnabas Self-Employment Fund, to help inner-city families supplement their income by providing limited credit, business training, and moral collateral. Operating on a trial basis as a pilot project, Barnabas assisted 25 microentrepreneurs in starting or improving their businesses. It offered eight business cycles to 156 persons, 107 of whom completed five weeks of training.[63] Barnabas highlights the current funding challenge of many microenterprise programs. The absence of sustained funding makes it difficult to analyze and evaluate the positive externalities evidenced by many mature programs. The social and personal development components of microenterprise development raise myriad questions, such as how does self-employment impact child care, transportation, and health care? Would low-income workers be more inclined to consider self-employment if they knew the short-term and long-term benefits?

A third group that demonstrates the human capital possibilities for self-employment is the "e.villages" (short for electronic villages). Recognizing that the new economy is driven by telecommunications and digital technology, e.villages, located in a low-income housing project in Washington, D.C., provides a ten-week intensive training program to community residents to improve basic competence, literacy, and advanced data management skills.

The group's founding companies recognized the community's needs and developed a pilot project to establish a Learning and Training Center to help graduates create and market their own technology-based, computer-related companies.[64] These companies will provide services to the financial, corporate, and government sectors.

The creators of e.villages believe that innovations in telecommunications and computer industries will soon change the face of conventional urban development. They have identified four trends that can make cities competitive and move people from welfare to work. First, there is a growing need for semiskilled labor. Just as the drill press was the tool of the industrial era, a computer is the tool of the information age. The notion that computer personnel require advanced degrees is a misconception. Advanced software (point and click technology) allows persons with limited education to perform specialized tasks without having to understand the underlying programming. Today, there is a whole class of semiskilled tasks that pay in the $15 to $25 per hour range. Second, because of technological advances, persons who are less formally educated will be able to play a greater economic role in today's world. For example, because of computers, a clerical worker can now process a bank loan, whereas twenty years ago, a more educated, full-service banker was needed. Third, jobs—which can be beamed anywhere by videoconferencing or the Internet—are more mobile than people. In some instances, "If you have a telephone (and a computer) you have a job." Fourth, digital jobs are less expensive to create than the capital-intensive factories and distribution centers on which the inner city used to depend. Today, it is often too expensive to bring this sort of new job to the cities.[65]

E.villages has very likely tapped into a progressive and timely solution to the problem of job creation for the inner-city poor. If cities are to remain competitive and move persons from welfare to work, emphasis must be placed on developing information-age skills, including problem solving, computer literacy, information management, and basic reading.

Overcoming Obstacles to Self-Employment:
Relaxing Unduly Burdensome Government Regulation

Two main obstacles to self-employment for women moving from welfare to work are unduly burdensome and sometimes conflicting government regulations and a general lack of access to capital. Relaxation of some business regulations and streamlining bureaucratic legal and regulatory procedures would facilitate microbusiness development.[66] An illustration of the problem of bureaucratic hurdles is found in a study of microbusiness development in public housing in Knoxville, Tennessee, which identified the plethora of state agencies that issue licenses and permits and the multiple government agencies that regulate home-based businesses. For example, a child care provider must demonstrate that he or she has 35 feet of outdoor space to comply with local zoning requirements but must prove that he or she has 50 square feet of space to comply with state Department of Human Services regulations. Moreover, within departments, individual inspectors who seemingly have unlimited discretion, interpret identical regulations differently.[67] Microbusiness development can be promoted only if conflicting regulations are reconciled. While most government regulations protect consumers and result in high-quality industry standards, the requirements must be rational, and state and local government should institute systems—such as one-stop shops—which streamline and facilitate regulatory compliance.

One means of addressing the lack of access to capital, beyond microloans, discussed herein, and federal and state support for health care for a business's early stages, is through a concept called Individual Development Accounts (IDAs). Like traditional Individual Retirement Accounts (IRAs), IDAs are investment accounts held in the name of one person at accredited financial institutions. IDAs provide the capital accumulation essential to self-employment and poverty alleviation. Instead of tax breaks to encourage savings, as with IRAs, however, IDAs use matching deposits from philanthropic organizations. IDA accounts are dedicated to high return investments in homeownership, business capitalization and higher education. At present, 15 states and 30 community groups are sponsoring IDA initiatives.[68]

Criticisms of Microenterprise Programs

Opponents (and some supporters) of microenterprise programs level several criticisms. The first set of complaints are valid, and point to areas where microenterprise programs need to focus their efforts, including (1) the programs are expensive to maintain and thus have to be subsidized because small loans involve higher operating costs; (2) unlike their international counterparts, domestic microbusinesses encounter a maze of legal, tax, and business regulations, which make the prospects of running a small business daunting; (3) microenterprise development faces geographic and societal impediments; and (4) there is only a small percentage of potential entrepreneurs.[69]

Proponents, on the other hand, point out that higher operating costs for loans channeled to low-income people should be expected, due to a heightened need to screen, and, if necessary, repair the credit of potential applicants.[70] With respect to regulatory barriers, as this chapter has argued, states and local governments can streamline unduly burdensome laws and regulations. Such efforts could form part of states' implementation of the PRWORA. Microenterprise development programs are actively involved in this legislative and regulatory reform process. Finally, geographical, societal, and demographic impediments, such as those resulting from diverse urban communities and isolated rural ones, require microenterprise development programs to target markets to create heterogeneous groups of participants.

A second set of arguments are demonstrably contrary to or unsupported by statistical evidence. For example, some claim that microbusinesses are more likely to fail than mainstream businesses.[71] Others warn that industry-specific microbusiness, operated by those less able to protect themselves, may become sweatshops, especially in the garment industry.[72] This latter concern has no evidentiary support.[73]

A final group of critics fail to recognize a more comprehensive understanding of the nature and benefits of microenterprise development. First, they contend that the risk associated with entrepreneurship places an undue economic burden on low-income persons least able to bear it.[74] Entrepreneurship is inherently fraught with risk, however, low-income people have had to cope with survival and risk before.[75] Furthermore, unlike a middle-class or upper-class entrepreneur who gives up a secure job to start a business, many low-income people never had a secure job in the first place. When they do, it is often unchallenging and lacks the opportunity for advancement. Microenterprise development programs challenge the rigidity of low-wage work, offering business and leadership training, as well as improved credit ratings.[76] The moral support in a peer-lending environment also results in the "safe space" discussed by Professor Kathleen Sullivan in Chapter 10.

Second, the critics allege the "creaming" argument: that microbusinesses do not really create jobs, they merely help a more highly educated microentrepreneur than the typical welfare recipient. They also contend that those who ultimately take advantage of the opportunities presented by microenterprise programs are sufficiently ambitious that they would find a job anyway. These same critics complain that although microenterprise loans do create some jobs, the loans are not large enough nor are there enough of them to revitalize poor communities.[77] The "no net job creation" argument is simply unfounded. A comparison between microenterprise development programs and traditional welfare-to-work programs suggests that welfare-to-work programs are unlikely to create jobs, especially when the training is inadequate. Microenterprise development programs create jobs for the participant and potentially for others in the future. Further, a low-income entrepreneur is more likely to employ others similarly situated. And, even if the "creaming" argument holds true, the individual is removed from the top of the welfare job applicant pool, leaving space for someone else to accept a job.

More important, though, microenterprise programs must be evaluated in terms of long-term, as opposed to short-term, traditional economic benefits. Bottom-line figures, such as expenditures to support microloans to low-income people, do not capture the hope generated within the recipients themselves and their family, friends, and communities around them. Microenterprise is about more than a job—it also is about alleviating poverty by inspiring dignity, pride, and motivation in individuals and communities—the creation of which only the most cold-hearted would leave to the unfettered market.

Legal and Policy Changes that Will Support Microenterprise Development

To maximize the effect of microenterprise development on the problems facing low-wage workers outlined in this book (poverty, access to child care, health care, transportation and capital), microenterprise advocates set forth the following recommendations:[78]

1. That states should recognize microenterprise development as an important, legitimate, and promising welfare-to-work strategy that is too real to ignore. Microenterprise development offers important opportunities to reduce welfare receipt, boost income and assets of the poor, build economic literacy and human capacity skills, create jobs, and generate tax revenues.

2. States should open microenterprise opportunities for welfare recipients so that they do not count against federal or state limits on receipt of assistance.

Advocates acknowledge that microenterprise development is a high-risk, high-return strategy; therefore, states should not penalize recipients willing to try self-employment by restricting their eligibility for assistance.

3. Regarding the treatment of assets and income, states should set reasonable auto, business and Individual Development Account (IDA), and personal asset limits, as well as ensure the protection of home ownership for all recipients. At a minimum, states should allow for $8,000 in business assets, $2,000 in personal assets, $10,000 in an IDA, and ownership of a serviceable car.

4. Only business income actually drawn from the business for personal use should be considered by the state in determining monthly levels of assistance.

5. States should raise disregards for earned income, including business income, which would increase work incentives and reduce average caseloads. The reason that welfare has often paid better than work is because benefit reduction formulae usually confiscate a new business' earnings. Microentrepreneurs who are supporting a family and working their way off of welfare should not be penalized as their earnings increase.

6. States should ensure access to health insurance programs or Medicaid that are not tied to an income support system. Many low-income people, including entrepreneurs, continue to receive public assistance longer than they need to in order to retain health benefits for themselves and their children.

7. States should provide child care training for participants and for a specified period of time consider providing child care subsidies for business start-ups.

8. A minimum of six months of training and two years of business operations should be allowed for welfare recipients to develop viable businesses.

9. States should recognize that microenterprise development is an "income patching" strategy for some as well as a "full income" strategy for others. Therefore, states should design microenterprise programs to augment income and full economic independence. Both income patching and full income self-sufficiency produce positive outcomes for welfare recipients, the state, and taxpayers.

10. States should provide assistance that is not subject to time limits for the eligible working poor. One example of this model is the "Bridges" demonstration project in Illinois, which provided counseling and support, help with Medicaid and child care benefits, job search assistance, and a program to help low-income families threatened with the loss of sustained employment.

11. States should consider the development of a funding system for monthly stipends for microenterprise development outside of the welfare system or, alternatively, dedicate a percentage of nonfederal MOE funds for microenterprise development. Separate or segregated state funds could be used to support a range of microenterprise development activities and satisfy MOE requirements. For example, a grant could be provided from different state agencies to cover training, marketing, outreach, access to credit, and so forth. This model would relieve states of the "caseworker" responsibility. Moreover, states could also dedicate a percentage of their MOE funds to a state-funded nonassistance program to pro-

vide the microenterprise development industry with flexibility to develop appropriate policies and programs to support its work.

12. Reflecting a recognition of the myriad benefits of microenterprise development, states should develop interagency task forces to link job creation, skill building, education, economic, and work force development strategies into microenterprise programs that could also assist nonwelfare low-income populations. Examples of these types of linkages can be found in five states (Michigan, New Jersey, South Dakota, Texas, and Vermont), which have developed "work force investment boards."

13. Microenterprise programs and microentrepreneurs should attempt to secure loan capital, seed capital, and/or IDA monies from sources outside of TANF. Using federally funded TANF monies to provide cash assistance during business development, or seed capital to start a microbusiness, will count against the five-year lifetime limit on assistance; assistance will be interpreted as providing a "direct monetary value" to a family. Therefore, states should establish as many linkages among welfare, work force, job creation, and job development strategy. Seven states (Delaware, Georgia, Hawaii, Iowa, Kentucky, New Hampshire, and Pennsylvania) have developed exemplary linkages in the form of "interagency task forces" to, among other things, integrate microenterprise development into state welfare-to-work strategies.

14. Microenterprise programs and microentrepreneurs should try to secure loan capital, seed capital, and/or IDAs from sources outside of TANF. Such sources include loans from the SBA, traditional financial institutions, or community development financial institutions, or IDAS.[79]

Conclusion

Self-employment for welfare recipients and low-wage workers is an important component of a larger CED strategy. While self-employment may not work for all—often the most educated or persons who have already been self-employed are the best suited—it does represent an important opportunity for developing human capital, reducing welfare dependency, and supplementing low-wage work. Because microenterprise development is a new CED strategy that has already shown significant promise, additional private, federal, and state resources should be developed to support it.

Notes

The author thanks her research assistant Brett Grosko for his excellent assistance in researching and editing this chapter. She is also grateful to her research assistant Joann Lee for helping to finalize the work. Finally, the author extends special thanks to Christine M. Benuzzi, executive director of the Association for Enterprise Opportunity, for commenting on earlier drafts of this chapter. The author is also deeply appreciative of the work of microenterprise practitioners and the entire microenterprise community.

1. According to the U.S. Department of Labor, self-employed persons are those who work for profit or fees ten hours or more a week in their own business, profession, or trade. See *1996 Directory of U.S. Microenterprise Programs,* ed. C. Alexander Severens and Amy J. Kays (Washington, DC: Aspen Institute, Self-Employment Learning Project, 1996) [hereinafter *1996 Microenterprise Directory*], xii.

2. See Susan R. Jones, "Small Business and Community Economic Development: Transactional Lawyering For Social Change and Economic Justice," *Clinical Law Review* 4 (1997): 195–234.

3. Very small businesses, also known as microenterprises or microbusinesses, are by no means new. They have formed an important sector of the economy since the inception of capitalism. See Brad Caftel, "Helping Microenterprise Programs Succeed," *CED Exchange* (June 1993): 1. On the other hand, most microenterprise development programs (which support microenterprises) were started in the mid to late 1980s. See Peggy Clark and Amy J. Keys, *Enabling Entrepreneurship: Microenterprise Development in the United States: Baseline Year Report of the Self-Employment Learning Project* (Washington, DC, 1995). See generally Susan R. Jones, *Battling Poverty Through Self-Employment: A Legal Guide to Microenterprise Development* (American Bar Association Commission on Homelessness and Poverty, 1998) [hereinafter *Battling Poverty*]. The evolution of the microenterprise development movement was recently evidenced by the first Presidential Awards for Excellence in Microenterprise Development. These nonmonetary awards recognized several long-standing microenterprise programs with the goal of bringing wider public attention to the field.

4. David Wessell, "Doing Business in the Inner City—Small Victories: Two Unusual Lenders Show How 'Bad Risks' Can Be Good Business," *Wall Street Journal,* June 23, 1992, p. A1. The Women's Self-Employment Project (WSEP) is a recent recipient of the 1996 Presidential Awards for Excellence in Microenterprise Development.

5. For several scholarly definitions of human capital, see Theodore Hershberg, "Human Capital Development: America's Greatest Challenge," *The Annals of the American Academy* 544 (1996): 43–51; Robert E. Suggs, "Bringing Small Business Development to Urban Neighborhoods," *Harvard Civil Rights–Civil Liberties Law Review* 30 (1995): 493.

6. See generally, Personal Responsibility and Work Opportunity Reconciliation Act of 1996 (PRWORA), Pub. L. No. 104–193, 110 Stat. 2105 (1996); James W. Fox, Jr., "Liberalism, Democratic Citizenship, and Welfare Reform: The Troubling Case of Workfare," *Washington University Law Quarterly* 74 (1996): 103.

7. See Chapter 1.

8. One study found that microenterprise program enrollment often led to further education or employment. Robert Friedman and Puchka Sahay, "Six Steps Forward for Microenterprise Development," in *Entrepreneurial Economy Review: Strategies for Economic Well-Being* (Washington, DC: Corporation for Enterprise Development, 1996), p. 36; see also Cynthia A. Guy, Fred Doolittle, and Barbara L. Fink, *Self-Employment for Welfare Recipients: Implementation of the SEID Program* (New York: Manpower Demonstration Research Corporation, 1991) [hereinafter *SEID Study*].

9. Friedman and Sahay, "Six Steps Forward," p. 37.

10. See generally Jones, *Battling Poverty.*

11. 13 C.F.R. 121.501 (1996).

12. See the White House Conference on Small Business Commission. *Foundation for a New Century: A Report to the President and Congress.* (Washington, DC: The Commission, 1995). [hereinafter *The White House Conference Report*].

13. See Alex Counts, *Give Us Credit* (New York: Time Books, 1996).

14. See Friedman and Sahay, "Six Steps Forward," pp. 32, 34–5.

15. See *1996 Microenterprise Directory*, p. xii.

16. Ibid.

17. See Lewis D. Solomon, "Microenterprise: Human Reconstruction in America's Inner Cities," *Harvard Journal of Law and Public Policy* 15 (1992): 191, 192.

18. See Friedman and Sahay, "Six Steps Forward," p. 32. For example, some microenterprise programs work with refugees, dislocated workers, disabled persons, or the homeless.

19. See *1996 Microenterprise Directory*, p. xvii.

20. Ibid.

21. Ibid, p. xvii.

22. See "Association for Enterprise Opportunity," Association of Enterprise Opportunity Policy Paper 10, May 1997 (available from the Association for Enterprise Opportunity, 70 East Lake Street, Suite 1120, Chicago, IL 60601) [hereinafter AEO Policy Paper].

23. Fifty-one of the 328 programs have been in business longer than ten years, while 69 began providing services in 1994. See *1996 Microenterprise Directory*, p. xvii.

24. Ibid., pp. xv–xvii.

25. Linda Burstyn, "Microlending Gains as Way Out of Welfare," *Christian Science Monitor*, December 29, 1995, available in 1995 WL 6398978.

26. See *1996 Microenterprise Directory*, p. xvii.

27. The trade organization is the Association for Enterprise Opportunity (AEO).

28. The Association for Enterprise Opportunity (AEO), founded in 1991, is a national trade association of organizations committed to microenterprise development. For more information, contact AEO, 70 East Lake Street, Suite 620, Chicago, IL 60601, Tel: 312/357–0177 or Fax: 312/357–0180.

29. For more information, see the Corporation for Enterprise Development (visited September 19, 1997) http://www.cfed.org.

30. See Small Business Act 7(m), 15 U.S.C. 636(m) (1994), as amended by Small Business Reauthorization Act of 1997, Pub. L. No. 105–135, 201(c), 111 Stat. 2592, 2598 (codified as amended at 15 U.S.C.A. 631 note (1997)). Implemented in 1992, The Microloan Program is a program of the Small Business Administration designed to make loans through intermediaries to very small businesses, many of which are located in poor communities. The program also offers grant monies to qualifying entities that offer technical assistance in areas such as marketing and management. For more information, see Office of Advocacy, U.S. Small Business Administration, *The White House Conference on Small Business Commission: Issues Handbook, Foundation for a New Century* (Washington, DC: U.S. Small Business Administration, 1994) [hereinafter *The White House Conference Issues Handbook*].

Other government programs supporting microenterprise are the U.S. Department of Housing and Urban Development's (HUD) Community Development Block Grant Program (CDBG), Community Development Banks, Community Development Credit Unions (CDCU), Community Development Loan Funds (CDLF), the program set out in the Community Reinvestment Act (CRA) and Empowerment Zones and Enterprise Communities. Regarding HUD's CDBG, see 42 U.S.C. 5302(a) (1994) and the Community Development Block Grant Program Economic Development Guidelines, as found at 24 C.F.R. 570 (1996). For more information on CDBs, CDCUs, and CDLFs, see Rochelle E. Lento, "Community Development Banking Strategy for Revitalizing Our Urban Communities," *University of Michigan Journal of Law Reform* 27 (1994): 773, 776. The Community Reinvestment Act (CRA) requires the federal bank regulatory agencies to encourage banks to meet the credit needs of low- and moderate-income people. See Richard Marsico, "Fighting Poverty Through Community Empowerment and Economic Development: The Role of the Community Reinvestment and Home Mortgage Disclosure

Acts," *New York Law School Journal of Human Rights* 12 (1995): 281, 283; Richard
Marsico, "A Guide to Enforcing the Community Reinvestment Act," *Fordham Urban
Law Journal* 20 (1993): 165; Richard Marsico, "The New Community Reinvestment Act
Regulations: An Attempt to Implement Performance-Based Standards," *Clearinghouse
Review,* March 1996, p. 1021; Lisa Maslow, "Is the Community Reinvestment Act Worth
Saving?" *J. Affordable Housing* 6 (1996): 65. Finally, for an extensive discussion of
empowerment zones, see Audrey G. McFarlane, "Empowerment Zones: Urban Revital-
ization Through Collaborative Enterprise," *J. Affordable Housing and Community Dev. L.*
5 (1995): 35.

  31. See PRWORA 103, 110 Stat., p. 2137.

  32. Ibid., p. 2129.

  33. See Ray Boshara, Robert E. Friedman, and Barbara Anderson, "Realizing the
Promise of Microenterprise Development in Welfare Reform," (Corporation for Enter-
prise Development [CFED], April 1997), p. 10 [hereinafter "Realizing the Promise"]).
Available from the Corporation for Enterprise Development.

  34. See PRWORA 103, 110 Stat., p. 2113.

  35. Ibid.

  36. Ibid.

  37. Ibid.

  38. Ibid., p. 2131. The percentages are 25 percent in 1997, rising to 50 percent in
2002. There is a higher percentage for two-parent families (75 percent in 1997 rising to
90 percent in 1999). Ibid., p. 2129.

  39. Ibid., p. 2113.

  40. Ibid. Also, informal economic activity—that which is not recorded in the national
accounts, nor subject to formal rules of contract, licensing, labor-inspection, reporting and
taxation—may also present an opportunity for states to take advantage of the microenterprise development policy option. Although some microbusinesses may have been underground (for example, a home-based seamstress), the PRWORA, by limiting the time that a
person can spend on public assistance and microloans, may present in some states new
reasons to formalize informal business activity. Microloans give the business owners access
to formal credit sources and government support that are not otherwise available. Unfortunately, there is insufficient literature on the informal underground economy, and this area
deserves further study, especially in light of the PRWORA. See generally Michael H.
Morris and Leyland F. Pitt, "Informal Sector Activity as Entrepreneurship: Insights from a
South African Township," *Journal of Small Business Management* 33 (1995): 78; Kathryn
Edin, "Surviving the Welfare State: How AFDC Recipients Make Ends Meet in Chicago,"
Social Problems (November 1991): 462, 468–69 (describing how AFDC recipients supple-
mented welfare checks by participating in informal economic activity).

  41. See PRWORA 103, 110 Stat. p. 2124.

  42. Ibid.

  43. The first microenterprise program, Women Venture (formerly known as
CHART/WEDCO) in St. Paul, Minnesota, was started in 1983. See Self-Employment
Learning Project of the Aspen Institute, *1993 Microenterprise Briefing Packet: Facts and
Figures on Seven U.S. Microenterprise Development Programs* (Aspen Institute, 1993).

  44. See Guy, Doolittle, and Fink, *SEID Study.* The sites for SEID were selected based
on the states' willingness to invest the effort to administer the program. Service providers
were required to develop curricula, recruit and orient clients, develop workshops, conduct
group training on business plan development and financing, and provide ongoing technical assistance for business operations.

  45. The demonstration project included Iowa, Michigan, Mississippi, Minnesota, and
Maryland. Maryland was added to the project in 1990.

46. After screening and self-selection, fewer than half of the SEID orientation participants (490) enrolled in the business training and technical assistance services program. Full implementation of the program was achieved by four of the six participating agencies. These were the Institute for Social and Economic Development in Waterloo, Iowa; Women's Economic Development Corporation in St. Paul, Minnesota; Mid-Minnesota Business Concepts in St. Paul, Minnesota; and Friends of Children of Mississippi in Canton, Mississippi. See Guy, Doolittle, and Fink, *SEID Study*, p. xv.

47. Enrollment at the sites varied from seven participants (at Meridian Community College, Mississippi, which in the end did not successfully implement the program) to 116 (at WEDCO).

48. A total of 64 participants, 30 percent, completed a business plan within 13 to 20 months; the average time for completion of the business plan was four months. Fifty participants were able to obtain start-up financing, as needed, and began operating businesses.

SEID clients had varied business ideas, including desktop publishing, take-out restaurants, office cleaning services, retail sales, custom clothing, and jewelry. Most start up loans were $5,000. In the period covered by the report, 1988–92, most SEID participants operated their business alone.

As a condition to granting the waivers of standard welfare regulations (e.g., pertaining to asset limits), the Office of Family Assistance (OFA) required business start-up goals that ranged from 100 to 202 new businesses over three or four years, depending on the state.

49. The SEID study also concluded that:

- The participants who succeed with their microbusinesses tended to be older, longer-term welfare recipients with larger families, higher than average educational levels, and more extensive work histories than the general caseload, but they are limited by lack of opportunity, not lack of capability.
- There were 1,316 welfare recipients who participated in SEID, 408 of whom started businesses by the end of the demonstration project in 1992. Seventy-nine percent of SEID businesses surveyed were still operating an average of 2.6 years later, creating 1.5 full- or part-time jobs per business.
- The microenterprises earned an average accumulation of $4,867 in net business assets and $8,738 in gross personal assets.
- Six times as many businesses in the demonstration project derived their primary income from their business after participation in SEID than before (55 and 9 percent, respectively).
- There was a 65 percent decline in reliance on AFDC and a 62 percent decline in reliance on food stamps among those starting microenterprises.
- Participants who enrolled in SEID often later sought further education or employment. The success of self-employment is more than business starts-ups; even failure to start or succeed in business often produced positive results in increased human capital, such as business skills, confidence, and initiative.
- A wide variety of nonprofit groups can run effective self-employment programs for welfare recipients—the program elements and determinants are known.
- Policy changes are needed to take advantage of microenterprise development as a route to self-sufficiency. The most significant immediate policy change required was waivers to the existing welfare law to allow welfare recipients to pursue self-employment. See Boshara, Friedman, and Anderson, "Realizing the Promise."

50. *The Attitude Treasury: 101 Inspiring Quotations,* ed. Marty Maskall, 4th ed. (Fair Oaks, CA: Attitude Works, 1993), p. 86.

51. *The MacNeil/Lehrer News Hour* (PBS television broadcast, February 17, 1994).

52. See Counts, *Give Us Credit;* Suggs, "Bringing Small Business Development to Urban Neighborhoods."

53. The author is well aware that for some microbusinesses, child care needs will still exist.

54. "Research Shows Transportation a Major Factor in Moving AFDC Recipients Off Welfare," *Transportation Link* (April 1997), p. 1.

55. Ibid.

56. See John J. Accordino, *Community-Based Development: An Idea Whose Time Has Come* (Richmond: Federal Reserve Bank of Richmond, Community Affairs Office, April 1997).

57. See Solomon, "Microenterprise: Human Reconstruction in America's Inner Cities," p. 208.

58. See Accordino, *Community-Based Development,* p. 6. With respect to neighborhood small business development, see Suggs, "Bringing Small Business Development to Urban Neighborhoods," p. 489.

59. See Solomon, "Microenterprise: Human Reconstruction in America's Inner Cities," p. 207.

60. Edward O. Welles, "It's Not the Same America (How the Demise of Achieving the American Dream and Over-Regulation of Business Prevented Minorities From Achieving Economic Success," *Inc.,* May 1, 1994, p. 82, available in 1994 WL 2811539.

61. See Regina Austin, "An Honest Living: Street Vendors, Municipal Regulations and the Black Public Sphere," *Yale Law Journal* 103 (1994): 2119, 2120.

62. Wessell, "Doing Business in the Inner City," p. A1.

63. See 1995 Annual Report available from Jubilee Jobs or from the author. Barnabas ceased operating when its founding coordinator left the program.

64. The founding companies were Hamilton Securities Group of Washington, DC, and Adelson Entertainment of Los Angeles.

65. See e.villages (visited Sept. 19, 1997) http://www.evillages.com/wire/russcty.html.

66. See Solomon, "Microenterprise: Human Reconstruction in America's Inner Cities," pp. 213–4.

67. See Margaret Bebee Held, "Developing Microbusinesses in Public Housing: Notes from the Field," *Harvard Civil Rights–Civil Liberties Law Review* 31 (1996): 473, 487.

68. For more information about IDAs, see Michael W. Sherraden, *Assets and the Poor: A New American Welfare Policy* (Armonk, NY: M.E. Sharpe, 1991); Robert Friedman, "Individual Development Accounts: From Local Experiment to National Impact," in *Entrepreneurial Economic Review: Strategies For Economic Well-Being* (Washington, DC: Corporation for Enterprise Development, 1996), p. 16; and materials from the First International Conference on Individual Development Accounts, held November 13–15, 1995 (on file with the Center for Social Development, Corporation for Enterprise Development, and the author); see also Friedman and Sahay, "Six Steps Forward," p. 37; AEO Policy Paper, p. 6.

69. See Solomon, "Microenterprise: Human Reconstruction in America's Inner Cities," pp. 206–9.

70. The average microenterprise program operating budget is $332,941; see *1996 Microenterprise Directory,* p. xvii. To illustrate the fact that microenterprise programs are costly to administer, WSEP, discussed earlier, estimates that about $280,000 of its $700,000 a year budget goes to running two loan programs; some of the rest goes for administrative costs. Ibid.; see also Wessell, "Doing Business in the Inner City," p. A1.

71. Microenterprise development programs help microentrepreneurs write business plans and carefully screen participants before making loans. Statistics do not show that microbusinesses fail at a higher rate than any other kind of business.

72. See Solomon, "Microenterprise: Human Reconstruction in America's Inner Cities," p. 207.

73. For a more extensive look at exploitation in the garment industry and innovative techniques community groups are using to combat the abuse and empower workers, see Laura Ho, Catherine Powell, and Leti Volpp, "(Dis)assembling Rights of Women Workers Along the Global Assembly Line: Human Rights and the Garment Industry," *Harvard Civil Rights–Civil Liberties Law Review* 31 (1996): 383.

74. The author would like to acknowledge the comments made by Professor Jonathan Simon (University of Miami) on May 29, 1997, at the Roundtable: Getting Real About "Work" for Low Income Women, part of the 1997 Law and Society Annual Meeting in St. Louis, Missouri. Professor Simon cautioned that self-employment through microbusiness development may place an undue burden on some low-income people. The author acknowledges that self-employment is not an option for a vast majority of low-income people.

75. Entrepreneurship offers low-income women a chance to utilize their resourcefulness to its maximum potential. Studies have shown that women on welfare are extremely resourceful. The small monetary amount of a welfare check forces many women to find outside work, although it is infrequently reported. Using false identities to obtain jobs with different social security numbers, and sometimes working in the underground economy, low-income women manage to make the money needed to feed their families and stay afloat. Many of these women blamed the lack of quality child care as a reason for staying on welfare and taking on odd, and sometimes illegal, employment. See Edin, "Surviving the Welfare State," pp. 467–68, 471–72.

76. Solomon, "Microenterprise: Human Reconstruction in America's Inner Cities," pp. 202–7.

77. Microenterprise programs have never pretended that they alone can revitalize communities. Even incremental steps are positive developments in areas lacking basic businesses. For an example of the kinds of problems these communities face, see Sari Horwitz, "The Missing Ingredient: In Washington's Mostly African American Neighborhoods, Finding a Sit-Down Restaurant Isn't Easy," *Washington Post,* August 11, 1997, p. B1.

78. See Boshara, Friedman, and Anderson, "Realizing the Promise," pp. 32–7.

79. Ibid.

5

Peter Pitegoff

SHAPING REGIONAL ECONOMIES TO SUSTAIN QUALITY WORK

THE COOPERATIVE HEALTH CARE NETWORK

As stock offerings go, this was no standard Wall Street fare. The offerees were home health care aides—workers, and now shareholders as well, at Cooperative Home Care of Boston, Inc. (CHCB). Their employer is the offeror, a home health care company founded in 1995 in inner-city Boston. CHCB has provided its employees with focused training, quality jobs, ongoing support, and, in the summer of 1997, an ownership stake and further control over their work lives.

Eventually, as the business grows and achieves sufficient stability, the worker-owners will increase their role in governance and elect a majority of the company's board of directors. Profits, although quite limited, will continue to be reinvested to ensure decent pay and benefits and will be allocated among the workers when possible. This focus on the quality of work is in sharp contrast to typical home care jobs, characterized by inadequate wages and benefits, inconsistent hours, no job security, and too little respect.

The home health care work force typifies the world of low-wage labor markets, where so-called welfare reform in the late 1990s promises to make a difficult situation even worse. While experiencing daily the stress and turmoil of living at the economic margin, many of CHCB's employees are working hard to distance themselves from welfare. Yet, unlike many others among the working poor or unemployed, they work in an institution that provides them a relatively safe and supportive space for the ongoing transition—or transitions—from welfare to work.

This chapter chronicles a creative response to social retrenchment, a saga of strategic deployment of accessible resources and a reshaping of regional economic forces for the benefit of targeted labor markets. While charting its own course, CHCB is part of a mutually supportive network of health care employers and trainers, including successful home care companies in Philadelphia and the South Bronx. Together, these three corporations form the core of the Cooperative Health Care Network and employ over 500 home health aides. About 80 percent of the employees were formerly dependent on public assistance. The network reflects a worker-centered model of enterprise development and employment training, offering sustained job opportunities for a predominantly female work force, most of whom are African American or Latina. The model expressly links the quality of health care services with the quality of paraprofessional home care work—where a stable work force strengthens the enterprise in the health care market and better jobs are created in a growing low-wage labor market.

The network strategy involves women in the transition from welfare to work and provides them with ongoing training, counseling, career upgrading, and an opportunity for participation in ownership and governance of the home health care enterprises. An inspiring case study in its own right, the home care example gives rise to lessons for employers, low-wage workers, advocates, and federal and state policymakers at a fluid moment in welfare policy. The network experience is not easily replicated, certainly not in its entirety, and may be of limited relevance to strategies for the most distressed and least employable populations. But for the working poor and for unemployed people seeking work, it is an evolving strategy that will help inform public policy and private initiatives in the years to come.

One clear lesson from the home care experience is that the successful transition from welfare to work, rather than a single event, is a complex process that occurs over a period of time and that requires carefully crafted systems for ongoing support. Employers of low-wage workers can adapt selected elements of the network's employment and training model to their own industries. Over time, government policies can reinforce these successful elements through effective public support to low-wage workers in transition from welfare. With respect to home health care workers, in particular, wage and benefit standards can be tied to a public health care finance system that has helped to create and maintain effective demand for a low-paid home care work force.

Integration of sophisticated economic development and corporate finance with an underlying strategy to bolster a targeted labor market distinguishes the Cooperative Health Care Network from most welfare-to-work initiatives. As social entrepreneurs, theirs is a sectoral approach, aiming to upgrade the status of the home care work force and achieving a leadership role as employers in regional markets for the home health care industry. That employer role and stature contributes to their credibility with businesses and policymakers and their ability to affect industry practice beyond their own enterprises. Add to this mix the worker ownership of network affiliates and the central role their employees play in corporate decision making, and the network's collective voice includes the critical perspective of former welfare recipients and low-wage women workers.

This chapter begins with a brief examination of the home health care labor market, particularly in the context of welfare reform and work initiatives. It then describes the Cooperative Health Care Network as an employer-based strategy for employment training, job creation, and strategic intervention to reshape a wider economic sector. The chapter concludes with lessons learned from the network experience and their applicability to other employer initiatives or to broader public policy.

Home Health Care Workers

As growing numbers of the elderly and disabled depend on paid workers for daily assistance, home health aides battle at the front line of health care delivery. They are paraprofessionals who operate near the bottom of a service hierarchy of physicians, nurses, social workers, and therapists. Most home health aides are women, many of them minorities, working for low wages and few benefits— contingent workers with no job security and few career opportunities. At the same time, they constitute a critical component of the expanding home health care industry.[1]

Paraprofessional home care services are fragmented among a variety of job categories, including personal care workers and home attendants, as well as homemakers who receive little training and provide nonmedical services such as cleaning, cooking, and laundry. The network's focus is instead on home health aides, who are required in most states to complete between 75 and 120 hours of training and to work under a nurse's supervision. Home health aides provide, in addition to homemaker services, certain medical services defined by Medicare, such as bathing, wound dressing, monitoring of vital signs, and assistance with patient mobility. Much of the clientele is elderly, with acute or chronic care needs that can be addressed at home.[2]

As a strategic matter, the Cooperative Health Care Network works to organize within and transform a targeted labor market of home health aides, one of the fastest-growing groups of low-wage workers. In an expanding home health care industry, home care aides constitute the largest group of workers, and despite variations among different local labor markets, the overall number of home care workers is projected to increase substantially in the coming years.[3] Moreover, in many urban areas, home health care is one of the few sources of paid work available to women with limited schooling or job experience.

A number of factors have led to an increased demand for home health care services, including the growing elderly population, the AIDS epidemic, increasing limitations on families' ability to provide informal care to family members, and advances in technology. A leading factor is the rapidly escalating expense of institutional health care, driving hospitals to release patients as early as possible to reduce in-patient costs. Substantial government support for health care also helps to drive the industry. Public financing, especially through the Medicare system, accounts for roughly half of all expenditures for home health care services.[4] The growth in home health care is attributable in part to revision of Medicare coverage guidelines following the 1988 federal court decision in *Duggan v. Bowen,*[5] which resulted in Medicare payments for part-time or daily home health services for as long as an eligible patient requires such care.

Yet, such massive public subsidy for home health care has not generally translated into good jobs for home care workers. The typical home care aide is poorly paid and ineligible for employee benefits, such as health insurance. The work is often part-time and episodic, as many home care employers act as temporary help agencies, contracting with individuals from a pool of available aides and preferring flexible workers who can adapt to changing client caseloads. The work force is further atomized by the nature of the work, with individual aides traveling to patients' homes and apartments and spending minimal time at the employer agency. Limited contact with co-workers, nurses, and service coordinators can lead to a sense of isolation, compounded by the physical and emotional strain of the work. These factors, combined with few opportunities for career advancement, contribute to high turnover and inconsistent quality of service in the home care industry. Clearly, from a managerial perspective, many home care employers have an interest in work-life improvements that would alleviate recruitment and retention problems, and "quality of work life programs" have been documented in a number of home health care companies.[6] But, the structure of the political economy and underlying societal values reinforce the marginal status of the home care work force.

Our society views home health care as women's work, and most home care workers are women. As in other gender-segregated labor markets, such as child care, employment growth at the bottom of the occupational hierarchy has channeled women into caregiving jobs deemed unskilled and underpaid. Yet, with circular reasoning, the "unskilled" label is often applied to such employment because of the predominance of women in the field—work that in fact requires skill and demands responsibility.[7]

The worker-centered companies in the Cooperative Health Care Network provide a direct challenge to society's marginal view of gendered work. Rather than accepting caregiving as marginal, the network enterprises place home health care workers at the center of sophisticated economic activity. Not only does this approach help to make women's traditionally invisible work visible, but it bolsters the stability and status of home health aides and the quality of their collaborative enterprise. Despite all the characteristics of home care work that typify low-wage labor markets, home care can be a motivating job as well. When coupled with an adequate support system, the upside of isolation can be autonomy, and the flip side of the emotional strain can be personal involvement and immediate feedback on the job. The network enterprises reinforce these motivating job characteristics with better pay, benefits, career opportunities, communication, and organizational support, along with worker involvement in decision making—all contributing to respect and a valued status for home care workers.

The network experience suggests expanded possibilities for poor women in transition from welfare to work and also counters common stereotypes of welfare recipients. The myth that welfare policies caused female-headed households to remain poor ignores real barriers to ongoing employment of the working poor. In the rush to welfare reform, the assumption that dismantling the federal welfare system would lead to personal responsibility and work opportunity failed to account for lack of available jobs with adequate pay and benefits, huge gaps in health insurance and child care assistance, transportation barriers, continuing challenges of domestic turmoil, and other realities of life at the economic margin.

Changes in the welfare system, including new work requirements, will continue to strain already overcrowded low-wage labor markets. A flood of new workers competing for limited jobs, combined with workfare programs that place welfare recipients in jobs as a quid pro quo for their public assistance, creates downward pressure on wages and increased vulnerability of low-wage workers to economic downturns. The resulting demand for creative welfare-to-work solutions is giving rise to a wide range of private sector and nonprofit initiatives in employment training and placement.[8] The most successful of these programs involve support services and extended involvement with participants beyond initial training and are closely coordinated with industries that hire low-wage workers. Evolving federal and state policies provide financial support for these programs, and with encouragement from the Clinton administration a number of large private employers have announced plans for hiring welfare recipients.

But despite notable successes, many efforts are unfocused and ineffective at placing people in decent and lasting employment. A counterproductive ramification of the 1996 changes in federal welfare law is a disincentive for state governments to support effective training programs. With pressure to reduce their welfare rolls, the incentive for states is to push as many public assistance recipients as possible, as quickly as possible, into quick-fix positions—workfare, work readiness courses, and part-time jobs at minimum wage—instead of more indepth training programs that might lead to stable jobs. It is in this context that the network example sounds a useful counterpoint, with elements that could be instructive for public policy and private industry.

The Network and Enterprise Development

The Cooperative Health Care Network stands out as an unusually successful welfare-to-work initiative. As an employer-based strategy, the network's approach combines sophisticated economic development with express social goals of creating quality jobs for workers and providing quality home health care for clients. The network currently consists of a nonprofit training and development corporation, three worker cooperative home health care companies, and a new managed care organization at a formative stage.

The network enterprises are profitable businesses that were carefully planned and developed with strong management, targeted market demand, and long-term equity capital. This alone is a concrete measure of success, particularly in the competitive and fluid health care market environment. From the outset, though, the business success was explicitly a vehicle to create better and more stable jobs in a growing low-wage labor market—to build a career ladder that enabled inner-city women to climb, rung by rung, from poverty to job training to a stable job and ultimately to lasting employment at a livable wage. The ladder extends even further, beyond the reach of most home care aides elsewhere, with the option of employee ownership and the potential for work in training, management, or other skilled jobs in health care. The network's success in sustaining employment is built in part on a careful process of screening and training, consistent standards for worker performance, a substantial investment in ongoing support, and a worker-centered organizational culture.

The initial member enterprise, Cooperative Home Care Associates, Inc. (CHCA), began operations in the South Bronx in 1985. As a licensed paraprofessional home health care company, CHCA positioned itself in the market as a subcontractor of services to Medicare-certified home health agencies. It was founded as a community economic development project of the Community Service Society (CSS), a large nonprofit social service organization in New York City. CSS played an entrepreneurial role in the difficult start-up years, providing needed equity and management expertise. Two former CSS employees who conceived of the home care enterprise strategy stepped into key management roles early on, became employees and members of CHCA, and today help to lead a work force of over 350.[9]

In terms of bridging welfare and work, one CHCA innovation was to place the training program at the site of the employer, offering industry-specific training to women on public assistance and the promise of a job to successful graduates. This on-site training model enables CHCA, as the employer, to control a structured process of recruitment, selection, and training—critical for building its desired work force, although clearly screening out many potential workers who cannot meet threshold standards for becoming quality caregivers. The training program, typically 4–6 weeks in length, embodies goals and expectations that are consistent with the host enterprise, and also contributes to a continuing corporate culture that provides in-service training and ongoing support to its employees.

In 1991, CHCA strengthened its training component by spinning off the Paraprofessional Healthcare Institute, Inc., a nonprofit organization that focused initially on CHCA's entry-level training program. In short order, the institute supplemented this internal role with an external initiative to replicate CHCA's success with start-ups in other urban areas. This led to the start-up of Home Care Associates of Philadelphia, Inc. (HCA) in 1993 and Cooperative Home Care of Boston, Inc. (CHCB) in 1995, both now operating as successful worker-cooperative enterprises and providing over 150 jobs for former welfare recipients. With foundation support, the institute acted as initial sponsor and developer in both start-ups—guiding local entrepreneurs in feasibility assessment, business planning, management recruitment and orientation, equity investment, and support for work force training. It continues to consult nationally to other home health care enterprises, some of which will join the network in years to come.

The institute, later renamed the Paraprofessional Healthcare Institute, Inc. (PHI), also serves as a site for exchange of ideas and mutual support among the three core home care enterprises, each operating in a different market and all of which are represented on the PHI's governing board. PHI will continue to nurture the emerging Cooperative Health Care Network as a broader association of home care companies, welfare-to-work trainers, and public policy advocates who share the goal of quality work for paraprofessionals in the health care industry.

The network's success at enterprise development distinguishes it from many other efforts at job training or at promoting transition from welfare to work. It has integrated its training program with a capacity to create and sustain employment opportunities and its social goals with savvy business planning and management skills. In terms of finance, the network has combined philanthropic support for its charitable and educational work with more conventional health care financing and revenue for its component business operations. The health care context was an early and strategic choice, not simply because of a growing low-wage labor market but also due to the huge cash flow of federal Medicare expenditures and the opportunity to apply those funds to worker and community development. The philanthropic support is in part a factor of the policy potential of such an innovative approach.

The network's sectoral employment strategy and labor-based model represent advances beyond conventional approaches to community-based economic development. In recent decades, much of the economic activity of community development corporations has concentrated on creating affordable housing, with substantial subsidized financing available. Community efforts to create employment for the urban poor have tended toward neighborhood-based resource-delivery strategies—channeling finance and other resources into a narrowly defined geographic area and among a variety of industries and small businesses. In contrast, the network's approach identifies the problem of urban joblessness not simply as a lack of resources but as the absence of marketplace relationships as well. Thus, with sophisticated business planning and management expertise, it has penetrated deeply within a single industry, selected in terms of a regionally defined labor market rather than a narrow geographic neighborhood.[10]

This sectoral strategy has targeted a particular labor market that employs many low-wage women, with the concrete objective of reshaping that market in selected regions. In order to influence the quality of entry-level jobs accessible to inner-city women, the network's enterprises have intervened as employers inside the home care industry, competing on the basis of quality and helping to raise employment standards in local markets. Characterizing themselves as "yardstick corporations" against which other companies can measure their employment practices, the network enterprises provide better pay and benefits than most of their competitors and have achieved a rate of employee turnover that is roughly half the 40 percent industry average. The companies' "investment" in the front line work force, rather than weakening their competitive position, has contributed to a reputation for high-quality service. They have nurtured a worker-centered corporate culture, instead of viewing workers as fungible employees, and thus have equated better working conditions with an improved bottom line. By building on the connection between the quality of work for home care aides and the quality of care for their clients, the network enterprises have translated individual responsibility and self-worth into organizational strengths.

A critical component of this sectoral approach is that each of the core enterprises is engaged in a web of regional relationships, in the marketplace as well as the political arena. Early on, for instance, CHCB staff conducted orientation presentations to caseworkers at all six Boston welfare offices, stressing job opportunities and high selection standards. The company continues to work with these public agencies and with community-based organizations, both for recruitment and as advocates for employees in transition from welfare to work. Similarly, CHCA leadership worked with historically antagonistic players in the New York home care industry—other providers, unions, legislators, regulatory authorities, and consumer advocates—to boost Medicaid reimbursement rates in 1989, arguing and demonstrating that better work conditions can lead to greater reliability and quality of care. A year later, this unlikely coalition produced a report calling for standardized job titles for home care workers, uniform training and certification, reforms in government oversight, and a client complaint system.

This external strategy, defined with reference to a selected low-wage labor market, is complemented by a worker-centered internal culture and legal structure. Each of the three network home care companies is a worker cooperative, a for-profit corporation owned and controlled by its employees.[11] In a worker cooperative corporation, each worker has the opportunity to obtain a membership share for an affordable fee, ordinarily paid in modest installments after completion of an initial trial period of employment. Share ownership gives each member the right to one vote in shareholder voting, including election of the board of directors, and a right to a portion of corporate profits allocated to members on the basis of their work in the cooperative. When a member leaves the job for whatever reason, the company redeems her membership share in exchange for her original fee, plus any accrued but unpaid dividends and, in some cases, reduced by corporate losses allocated to equity shares.

The worker-elected board makes organizational policy decisions and oversees management. Senior managers retain substantial discretion to make day-to-day operational and personnel decisions, and to guide the board in longer-term planning. But, the worker participation in governance helps to reinforce a corporate culture that respects all workers, wherever they may be in the management hierarchy. It encourages greater psychological ownership and job commitment and creates a safer space for the difficult transition from welfare to work. This worker-centered organizational culture includes a range of informal or ad hoc supports—a supervisor helping an employee resolve a problem with her welfare caseworker, peer group encouragement to maintain work standards, constructive responses to breakdowns in child care or transportation, and so on.

The network affiliation provides some shelter from the harsh market environment for health care enterprise. The Paraprofessional Healthcare Institute, systematizing the entrepreneurial function, was the controlling owner of the Philadelphia and Boston home care companies during the difficult start-up years, playing much the same role as the Community Service Society played a decade earlier in start-up of the Bronx cooperative. This trusteeship period allows the institute to take much of the financial investment risk in the early years, extending ownership to the workers after the enterprise has achieved some stability and value in the home care market. Majority control shifts to the worker-owners over the course of several years, after which the institute retains a minority equity stake and continues to participate in governance.

This balance between enterprise self-management and mutual support among network affiliates has enabled the enterprises to build on their common experience while responding to different local market conditions. Health care finance is substantially subsidized through Medicare for the elderly, and the network's collective experience has helped to build relatively stable enterprises within this finance and regulatory system. At the same time, the regulatory environment and the health care industry are changing rapidly and driving many health care providers toward managed care, including mergers and consolidations of numerous institutions. Medicare cuts and other regulatory changes, combined with private sector adjustments to managed care, are causing upheaval in home health care labor markets. The near-term result is growth in some regional markets and no growth or even shrinkage in others. Bureaucratic changes associated with welfare reform, meanwhile, have disrupted recruitment networks for home care workers. Each of the three network cooperatives has responded to these changes, with strategies tailored to its local market.

In Boston, for instance, saturation of the inner-city market suggests that CHCB might need to expand its regional base in order to continue its growth and job creation. This presents a challenge to the cooperative culture of the organization, as CHCB explores affiliation with other home care providers and faces a more scattered work force from neighboring cities. CHCB is also exploring diversification of its training component—training health care paraprofessionals other than home health aides, such as certified nursing assistants, and coordinating the placement of these successful trainees in jobs at hospitals and nursing homes. In planning, CHCB is drawing in part from the Philadelphia experience of HCA, which already has established an external placement program.

In response to home care market limitations in Philadelphia, HCA diversified its services to include training and placement of some workers at other institutions. Its Trial Placement Program combines up-front job training with job placement that includes three months of intensive job coaching. Trainees must complete an eight-week job-readiness program focused on workplace comportment, problem-solving skills, and job-specific health and clinical skills, resulting in certification as home health aides or certified nurse assistants. Successful trainees are then placed temporarily in full-time positions at a mental health facility, nursing home, hospital, or clinic. The first three months of employment are a trial period during which the worker is employed by HCA, with HCA in turn paid by the host company and the worker receiving intensive job coaching and guidance from HCA. After the trial period, either the host company makes a permanent job offer or HCA places the worker at another company or back at HCA as a home health aide. As in Boston, this program has the potential to disperse the workers and thus undermine the cooperative culture of HCA, but it has increased the company's ability to promise decent jobs for its trainees.

In the Bronx, CHCA and the institute are confronting the health care industry changes head-on by forming a specialized managed care organization for chronic and severely disabled residents of New York City. The broader health care market is in an unprecedented period of turmoil and restructuring, with health care providers attempting to reduce costs through consolidation and new managed care groupings. Government budget cutting and changes in Medicaid and Medicare funding are helping to accelerate the rush to managed care, a model that enables providers to contain their risk of open-ended and costly services.

Massive consolidation in the industry is placing far greater power into far fewer hands and buffeting the less powerful players who are unable to join forces and compete. With the shape of managed care networks driven by hospitals, physicians, health maintenance organizations, national service providers, the federal Health Care Finance Agency, and private insurance plans, home health care providers stand on shifting ground and face an uncertain future. In response, many home health care organizations are consolidating or forming alliances to gain leverage in negotiating larger volume contracts, and mergers and acquisitions in the home care industry reached record numbers in 1996.[12]

The newest network affiliate, Independence Care System, Inc. (ICS),[13] takes that response a step further by shaping the home care market environment more directly and essentially building an institution that assures a flow of quality work for CHCA. ICS is a managed care group, with a management team assembled by the institute and core participation by three New York–area health care organizations—the Institute for Urban Family Health as the lead provider for primary care physicians, the Visiting Nurse Service of New York as the provider of professional home nursing, and CHCA as the paraprofessional home care service provider. Additional organizational relationships will strengthen and expand the capacity of ICS—Concepts of Independence assisting clients in consumer-directed personal care planning, five major hospitals (Montefiore, Bronx Lebanon, Beth Israel, Mt. Sinai, and Lenox Hill) available for in-patient services, a number of social work organizations (including the Independent Living Centers, the Brookdale Center on the Aging, and the International Center for the Disabled) providing specialized services, and other service providers for such matters as substance abuse treatment, dental care, pharmacy, and adult day care.

This vertical integration will increase stability of CHCA's home care enterprise at such a fluid moment in the health care industry, securing a market for a projected 1,000 home health aides. In a comprehensive and flexible manner, ICS intends to integrate the full range of primary care, specialty care, hospital care, nursing home care, home care, and social support services for a targeted clientele with severe disabilities throughout New York City. With paraprofessional home care aides in a central role, ICS furthers the goal of redefining the relationship of home care workers with other health care professionals, particularly with doctors and nurses. The result will be a managed care initiative that values the paraprofessional role and presents more career advancement opportunities for low-income women. This stands in dramatic contrast to the relatively weak position of home care providers that contract with integrated vertical systems organized by hospitals, with physician groups, or with national companies emerging in the new era of managed care.

Policy Implications

The network's move into managed care signals a bold strategic turn and a new phase of an inspiring saga. Yet, since its inception in 1985, Cooperative Home Care Associates and its progeny have appeared in profiles and reports as somehow unattainable or inapplicable to other community development settings. The elements of success—visionary leadership, skilled business management, institutional and philanthropic support, a burgeoning and federally subsidized labor market, democratic worker ownership, a worker-centered organizational culture, a mutually supportive network, and intense collaborative work for over a decade—presumably would all need to be part of a successful replication. Transposing particular elements of the enterprise model without others arguably would have limited results in different circumstances. One of the founders likened CHCA in the past to a gem, significantly valuable while intact but of considerably less value in smaller pieces chipped away.

But context is critical, and the convergence of welfare reform and health care reform has made the network experience more relevant to other employers and more timely with respect to public policy than ever before. Moreover, the network enterprises have evolved as respected and seasoned employers in the home health care industry. They can draw valuable lessons from their experience, for welfare-to-work policies and for employers of low-wage workers.

Fueled by election year politics in 1996, Congress enacted the Personal Responsibility and Work Opportunity Reconciliation Act. This version of welfare reform eliminated Aid to Families with Dependent Children (AFDC), the longstanding federal guarantee of minimal cash benefits to poor families with children. The Act shifted responsibility to the states for assisting the poor by replacing AFDC with a capped block grant program known as Temporary Assistance for Needy Families (TANF). Of particular relevance to employers of low-wage workers, the Act directs states to require adult TANF recipients to work after two years on public assistance (with a five-year lifetime limit) and to meet overall work participation rates for TANF recipients—provisions likely to cause severe crowding in already strained low-wage labor markets. Nothing in the Act, however, addresses the paucity of quality jobs available to those on public assistance and the obstacles faced by the working poor in sustaining employment.[14]

The Cooperative Health Care Network can speak first-hand about the role that an employer plays in helping people move from welfare to work and about how to respond to increasing pressure to hire former welfare recipients.[15] The network experience underscores the need for an effective welfare-to-work training program to be in a marketplace position to guarantee a decent job for successful training graduates. The training itself must be linked to job-specific skills and knowledge, while also helping people to become socialized to the world of work and to develop problem-solving and communication skills. The transition from welfare to work may require a realignment of an individual's social system, which is more likely to succeed with a cohort of peers in the workplace making that change in concert and with some training and supervision by others who have succeeded in their own similar transition. Ongoing support for employees in the network enterprises is customized by those who know first-hand what type of support is required.

The success of the network as trainers and employers also depends upon careful initial screening and high standards for training and work performance. Some of those recruited never make it past the initial interview, for reasons ranging from drug abuse problems to an inability to show up when scheduled. Others may fail the training or the initial on-the-job trial period for lack of the required sensitivity, maturity, judgment, and caring required of a good home health aide. Still others drop out of the training or the job for personal reasons or crises at home. The bottom line, then, is that only a fraction of those who express an interest in working in one of the cooperative enterprises will become permanent members. Thus, while lessons from the network experience are applicable in other settings, its model targets a particular and more employable band of the working-poor spectrum, leaving to others the question of how to craft policies and initiatives that support more distressed and troubled people.[16] To survive as employers, the enterprises demand that workers continue to meet well-defined rules and standards in exchange for the guarantee of a decent job. Exceptional efforts at communication and support help to nurture an organizational culture that reinforces this exchange and where peer enforcement of standards may even be more pronounced than management dictates.

If the transition from welfare to work requires the availability of decent work, then employers are essential to any policy prescription for welfare reform. The network has demonstrated the advantage of tying training programs directly to the ultimate employer or at least to an industry-specific intermediary in tune with the needs of employers. Thus, a public policy to move people permanently from welfare to work should reward certain employer-based transition programs— providing subsidies to companies that guarantee a decent job for all successful training participants and that maintain those jobs for a defined period of time.

A public policy for subsidies to employers dances dangerously close to the "corporate welfare" so widely criticized in other contexts. Employer subsidies for hiring low-wage workers, in fact, have been roundly criticized in recent years. The Targeted Jobs Tax Credit (TJTC) provided federal tax incentives to employers of low-wage and disadvantaged workers from its enactment in 1978 until it expired in 1994. Preceding the TJTC program's termination, the Inspector General's Office of the Department of Labor conducted a program audit, concluding that employers who took advantage of the tax credit in hiring low-wage workers would have hired most of these workers even without the tax incentive.[17] Retroactive certification that employees were part of the targeted group, for instance, led many employers to identify and certify workers already on their payroll. The audit also confirmed that most jobs obtained with TJTC incentives were near minimum wage, part-time, and without benefits.

Nonetheless, after a two-year hiatus, Congress enacted the Work Opportunity Tax Credit (WOTC), essentially reinstating the expired TJTC, albeit with several significant changes designed to address problems of the prior law.[18] Retroactive certifications are no longer permitted, with employers now required to determine in advance which newly hired employees meet the criteria for subsidies. In response to criticism that the tax credits merely created an employer windfall without leading to long-term employment, the WOTC increased the minimum employment period for subsidized employees from 90 to 180 days. Finally, compared to the prior law, eligible categories of employees were narrowed and the amount of the credit was reduced slightly. Criticism of these incentives continues, both from employers who want fewer restrictions and from employee advocates who call for narrower targeting.

In the wake of the 1996 federal welfare legislation, the WOTC was extended to eligible employees hired before July 1998 and might be extended further in the future. It is supplemented by two other tax credit incentives for hiring poor people. First, Congress enacted a Welfare-to-Work Tax Credit in 1997 for employers who hire long-term welfare recipients before May 1999.[19] Second, the empowerment zone employment credit[20] has been in effect since 1993. Until its expiration in 2005, the empowerment zone employment credit provides employer incentives for hiring employees who live and work in a federally designated "empowerment zone," which is typically a distressed inner-city locale. HCA in Philadelphia is exploring the creative use of these tax credits to leverage outside investment and to encourage private-sector collaboration with their worker-centered enterprise. This strategy echoes the widespread use of low-income-housing tax credits[21] by nonprofit developers who, over the past decade, have capitalized affordable housing construction by syndicating tax credits through limited partnership structures. With respect to the work credits, HCA would craft relationships with investors and with other health care providers in a way that maximizes the utility of the tax credits, draws needed capital to the worker cooperative venture, and encourages other health care providers to collaborate with HCA.

As a supplement to the work opportunity and empowerment zone tax credits, the 1997 Congressional budget agreement added some $3 billion for a new block grant program to help states build a welfare-to-work transition system for long-term welfare recipients.[22] At the state level, a variety of "grant diversion" programs have channeled funds for individual welfare benefits to employers instead, in order to partially subsidize private sector jobs for welfare recipients. Over a dozen states experimented with such grant diversion programs[23] prior to the 1996 federal welfare legislation, pursuant to federal waivers, and the new TANF block grants will lead to more such efforts in other states in the years to come.

The network experience suggests that employer incentives should be limited to those who provide effective training and the guarantee of a decent job for all successful training participants. Economic studies have shown that more holistic policies, combining wage subsidies with job development and training, have been somewhat successful in improving the employment and earnings of specific targeted groups.[24] Federal and state governments should integrate disparate policies that affect low-wage workers and ensure that the transition from welfare to work is not more punishing financially than remaining on welfare. In general terms, for instance, public assistance recipients should be permitted to keep a larger portion of cash, food stamp, child care, and Medicaid assistance during the early stages of employment, with continuation of modified health coverage and other support for the working poor. Over time, an expanded Earned Income Tax Credit can continue to help make work a rational and feasible choice for the poor.

A clear policy lesson for successful welfare-to-work initiatives is that job opportunities for the poor should "make work pay," offering employment with a livable wage and decent benefits. In addition to the minimum wage laws, federal and state laws have long governed a wide range of employer-employee relations, with baseline standards regarding work hours, health and safety, discrimination, and the right to organize. But more narrowly crafted public policies should address the current crisis of increasingly crowded low-wage labor markets, through employment standards attached to government subsidies or contracts, and through tailored public assistance to the working poor.

In Massachusetts, for example, CHCB has combined its role as an industry employer and an advocate for better work standards by joining in a strategy to secure health insurance coverage for all home health aides. With wages close to the poverty level, many home health aides already are eligible for federal Medicaid coverage for family health insurance. But as the jobs improve, with higher wages and more consistent hours, income limits for Medicaid coverage create a perverse incentive for home care aides and their employers to limit the number of hours worked in order to maintain Medicaid qualification. Even as Massachusetts has increased the family income limit for Medicaid coverage to 133 percent of the poverty level and has expanded coverage further for children, many home health aides continue to fall outside the Medicaid eligibility criteria.

In conjunction with the Massachusetts Council for Home Care Aide Services, an industry association, CHCB has argued that the state government should create a demonstration project that targets Medicaid coverage categorically to all home care workers. Given the large number of home care workers whose wages are directly or indirectly controlled by government reimbursement policies, such as Medicare, public dollars have helped to create and maintain this low-wage labor market. Medicaid coverage, the argument goes, should attach to this reimbursement system—to the benefit of the workers, who would receive medical insurance, and to the benefit of the employers, who would be better able to retain qualified workers without bearing the high cost of private insurance.[25]

On a much larger scale, the federal government can play a pivotal role in ensuring basic wage and benefit standards for home care workers. The federal government is the nation's single largest funder of health care, providing billions of dollars annually to private health care providers through Medicare and Medicaid. This public funding drives much of the home care industry, as these providers rely on government funding to hire paraprofessionals in home care agencies. Arguably, then, the federal government has unintentionally created a low-wage labor market of home health aides, consisting predominantly of women from poor communities.[26]

The federal role in creating and sustaining the home care labor market suggests an opportunity as well for a government role in improving the labor standards for home care workers. The federal government can attach wage and benefit standards to the receipt of public tax dollars, in this case requiring that all employers who receive Medicaid and Medicare funding conform to livable wage and benefit floors for their low-wage paraprofessional employees. Some of the direct cost could be federally supported, as through expanding Medicaid coverage or other individual public benefits to home care workers. Other costs, however, would be borne by employers who themselves profit from federal health care finance subsidies.

Several prevailing wage laws provide precedence for tying wage and benefit floors to contracts funded by the federal government. Although they share a common purpose—providing a wage floor for employees of government contractors—the two main federal prevailing wage laws apply to different sectors: the Davis-Bacon Act applies to the construction industry and the Service Contract Act (also known as the O'Hara-McNamara Services Act) applies to providers of services.[27] Both use the concept of a statutory wage floor based upon the prevailing wage in a given locality, rather than an across-the-board statutory minimum wage. They also apply narrowly to particular government contracts, not more generally to Medicare or Medicaid reimbursements. Nonetheless, the long history of government regulation of labor standards of its contractors by attaching conditions to federal money provides useful precedent for advocates of wage and benefit floors in the government-funded home health care field.

In 1993, President Clinton's failed attempt at health care reform occasioned a number of hearings and reports on the potential economic and employment impact of his proposals.[28] Similarly, in crafting the policy rationale for attaching wage and benefit standards to federal health care finance, an interim step is to document the role that government plays in creating low-wage jobs. In other contexts, such as immigration or international trade, legislative changes have required labor impact assessments by the General Accounting Office or other federal agencies. The Department of Labor and the Department of Commerce are required, for instance, to report to Congress on the jobs impact of the North American Free Trade Agreement. On a larger scale, several failed attempts in Congress during the 1990s would have required an economic and employment impact statement for all significant federal legislation.[29]

Documentation of the government role in maintaining a low-wage labor market in home care would lay bare the marginal economic status of health care paraprofessionals. Assessing the impact of Medicare and Medicaid cuts and of the TANF-driven flood of low-wage workers is likely to show this low-wage labor market squeezed even further. Such documentation would be especially informative if it were sufficiently refined to measure quality—wages, benefits, hours worked, work load, and so on—in addition to overall quantity of jobs.

Illinois took a similar, although modest, step in the context of the child care industry. A 1996 law directed the state Department of Human Services to present an annual survey of average wages and benefits paid to caregivers throughout the state and recommendations for increasing wages to ensure quality care for children. With respect to chore housekeeping and homemaking services under contract with the state, Illinois requires that a set percentage of the rates it pays, and thus of any rate increases, must be allocated to direct-care workers in wages and benefits.[30] In 1996, the Massachusetts legislature appropriated $14 million to fund a wage increase of up to 4 percent for direct-care workers, earning less than $20,000, employed by providers of homemaker or personal care services to the elderly or by human service providers under contract with the state.[31] Modest as these policy initiatives may be, they suggest the potential for targeted work standards on a larger scale.

Conclusion

The experience of the Cooperative Health Care Network foreshadows a changing policy context, particularly the dismantling of the long-standing federal welfare system. Although public assistance to the poor will take shape at the state level, and the federal role will continue in some form, low-wage labor markets will be defined increasingly without reference to the current welfare regime. "Transition from welfare to work" becomes a less meaningful phrase for advocates of the working poor.

The network today identifies its major pool of labor from the welfare rolls, and it has received deserved attention as an exemplary model of a welfare-to-work program. But the network's strategy maintains its integrity apart from the welfare system. It is fundamentally an economic development approach driven by social values—an employer-based sectoral strategy to create quality jobs for workers and to upgrade the status of the home health care work force, to provide quality home health care for clients and to demonstrate the capacity of poor working women for sophisticated enterprise.

The complete story of the Cooperative Health Care Network is yet untold. Its successful track record will be severely tested in the years to come, with dwindling public support for the working poor and consolidation of managed care in the health care industry. A measure of success will be not just survival but, as a collaborative yardstick enterprise, the extent to which its lessons and values influence others in the health care industry and in the public policy arena. The linkage of quality health care with quality of work for the frontline caregivers is a powerful message applicable to many segments of health care delivery and generalizable to employers in other industries. Public policies, beyond today's welfare system, can draw from the network's experience by promoting the creation of decent jobs and by crafting support systems built upon an understanding of the complex and challenging transition from poverty to lasting work.

Notes

Thanks to the Fund for Labor Relations Studies and to the Baldy Center for Law and Social Policy for supporting Peter Pitegoff's research and case study of the Cooperative Health Care Network, and to Anita Costello and Randal Evans for their research assistance. Special thanks to the members of Cooperative Home Care of Boston, Home Care Associates of Philadelphia, Cooperative Home Care Associates in the Bronx, and the Paraprofessional Healthcare Institute for sharing their valuable time and experience.

1. Penny Hollander Feldman, Alice M. Sapienza, and Nancy M. Kane, *Who Cares for Them? Workers in the Home Care Industry* (New York: Greenwood Press, 1990), pp. 17–27. Lynn C. Burbridge, "The Labor Market for Home Care Workers: Demand, Supply, and Institutional Barriers," *The Gerontologist* 33 (1993): 41.

2. A.E. Benjamin, "An Overview of In-Home Health and Supportive Services for Older Persons," in *In-Home Care for Older People: Health and Supportive Services,* ed. Marcia G. Ory and Alfred Duncker (Newbury Park, CA: Sage Publications, 1992), p. 9. William H. Crown, Dennis A. Ahlburg, and Margaret MacAdam, "The Demographic and Employment Characteristics of Home Care Aides, and Other Workers," *The Gerontologist* 35 (1995): 162.

3. Arsen J. Darnay, ed., *Service Industries USA,* 3d edition (Detroit: Gale Research Inc., 1996), p. 355. U.S. Department of Labor, Bureau of Labor Statistics, *The American Work Force: 1993–2005,* (Washington, DC, April 1994), Bulletin 2452. Laura Freeman, "Home-Sweet-Home Health Care," *Monthly Labor Review* 118 (March 1995): 3.

4. National Association for Home Care, *Basic Statistics About Home Care, 1996,* October 1996, p. 4. Cf. Katharine R. Levit, A.L. Sensenig, C.A. Cowan, H.C. Lazenby, P.A. McDonnell, D.K. Won, L. Sivarajan, J.M. Stiller, C.S. Donham, M.S. Stewart, "tional Health Expenditures, 1993," *Health Care Financing Review* (Fall 1994): 247, 256. "Trends in Medicare Home Health Agency Utilization and Payment: CYs 1974–94," *Health Care Financing Review/1996 Statistical Supplement* (1996): 76.

5. *Duggan v. Bowen,* 691 F. Supp 1487, U.S. District, Washington (1988).

6. Penny Hollander Feldman, "Work Life Improvements for Home Care Workers: Impact and Feasibility," *The Gerontologist* 33 (1993): 47. See also Feldman, Sapienza, and Kane, *Who Cares for Them?* supra note 1.

7. The CEO of Cooperative Home Care of Boston captures in the most personal terms the essence of the serious responsibility of home care aides. Before sending a home health aide to provide health care services to a client, he queries: "Would I trust this person to care for my mother?" For an extended discussion of caregiving work and feminism in the context of child care enterprise, see Peter Pitegoff, "Child Care Enterprise, Community Development, and Work," *The Georgetown Law Journal* 81 (1993): 1897, 1920–29. See also Suzanne Gordon, "Feminism and Caregiving," *American Prospect* (Summer 1992): 119, 120. The enormous scale of federal Medicare subsidies, maintained in part by a powerful lobby for senior citizens, enables the network to pursue an enterprise and job development strategy for home health aides that would be more difficult in the context of other caregiving industries—such as child care—that enjoy lesser public subsidies or political support.

8. Among the more successful welfare-to-work programs are the Center for Employment Training (San Jose, CA), America Works (New York, NY), Project Quest (San Antonio, TX), and Project Match (Chicago, IL). With respect to private employer welfare-to-work initiatives, see Hilary Stout, "Clinton Hopes Success of Chicago Bus Operator Will Spur More Firms to Hire Welfare Recipients," *Wall Street Journal,* January 10, 1997, p. A12.

9. Rick Surpin and Peggy Powell, now key managers and leaders at both Cooperative Home Care Associates, Inc., and the Paraprofessional Healthcare Institute, Inc., played central roles in the start-up of CHCA while on staff at the Community Service Society. See Steven L. Dawson, "Start-ups and Replication," Chapter 7 in *Jobs and Economic Development: Strategies and Practices,* ed. Robert Giloth (Newbury Park, CA: Sage Publications, 1998); David Bollier, *Aiming Higher: 25 Stories of How Companies Succeeded by Combining Sound Management and Social Vision* (The Business Enterprise Trust, 1996).

10. Peggy Clark and Steven L. Dawson, *Jobs and the Urban Poor: Privately Initiated Sectoral Strategies* (The Aspen Institute, 1995).

11. For analysis of the legal structure and theory of worker cooperatives, see David Ellerman and Peter Pitegoff, "The Democratic Corporation," *Review of Law and Social Change* XI (1983): 441.

12. Charlotte Snow, "Topsy-Turvy Industry Posts Merger Record," *Modern Healthcare* 26, no. 55 (1996): 54. Kevin Lumsdon, "Home Care Prepares to Catch Wave of Managed Care, Networking," *Hospitals and Health Networks* 68, no. 7 (April 5, 1994): 58. Kevin Lumsdon, "No Place Like Home?" *Hospitals and Health Networks* 68, no. 19, (October 5, 1994): 44.

13. Rick Surpin, Janet Saglio, and Ann Wyatt, *Independence Care System, Inc.: Preliminary Program Plan,* March 1997.

14. Rebecca M. Blank, "Outlook for the U.S. Labor Market and Prospects for Low-Wage Entry Jobs," in *The Work Alternative: Welfare Reform and the Realities of the Job Market,* ed. Demetra Smith Nightingale and Robert H. Haveman (Washington, DC: Urban

Institute Press, 1995), p. 33; Joel Handler, *The Poverty of Welfare Reform* (New Haven, CT: Yale University Press, 1995), pp. 39–44; Sheldon Danziger and Jeffrey Lehman, "How Will Welfare Recipients Fare in the Labor Market?, *Challenge,* (March-April 1996): 31; William Julius Wilson, *When Work Disappears: The World of the New Urban Poor* (New York: Knopf, 1996); Peter Pitegoff and Lauren Breen, "Child Care Policy and the Welfare Reform Act," *Journal of Affordable Housing & Community Development Law* 6, no. 2 (Winter 1997): 113.

15. Steven L. Dawson, "Welfare to Work: An Employers' Dispatch from the Front," Cooperative Health Care Network, 1997.

16. "In Every Hundred, Ten Are Saved," *The Economist,* May 25, 1996, p. 28. Michael Grunwald, "Welfare-to-Work Isn't Cheap: How She Got a Job," *The American Prospect,* no. 33 (July–August 1997): 25.

17. U.S. Department of Labor, Office of Inspector General, Office of Audit, *Targeted Jobs Tax Credit Program: Employment Inducement or Employment Windfall?* Washington, DC, August 18, 1994, Report No. 04-94-021–3-320.

18. 26 U.S.C.S. section 51. The Work Opportunity Tax Credit was enacted as section 1201 of the Small Business Job Protection Act of 1996 (the minimum wage legislation), 104 P.L. 188, 110 Stat. 1755 (1996). The amount of the employer tax credit under the WOTC is generally up to 35 percent of the first $6,000 paid to an eligible employee, or $2,100. Despite a promising introduction of the new law, many employers have expressed frustration and disappointment with its utility in sustaining jobs for former welfare recipients; see, e.g., Rochelle Sharpe, "Great Expectations: A Tax Credit Designed to Spur Hiring Seems Promising—at First," *Wall Street Journal,* August 21, 1997, p. A1.

19. 26 U.S.C.S. section 51A (1997).

20. 26 U.S.C.S. section 1396 (1993).

21. 26 U.S.C.S. section 42 (1986).

22. Departments of Labor, Health and Human Services, and Education, and Related Agencies Appropriations Act, 1998, 143 Cong. Rec. H 6849, 6886 (September 4, 1997). See also Will Marshall and Margy Waller, "Welfare Exit Must Mean Work Entry," *Newsday,* August 21, 1997, p. A53; Testimony of Olivia A. Golden, Administration for Children and Families, U.S. Department of Health and Human Services, before the House Committee on Ways and Means, Subcommittee on Human Resource, February 13, 1997; Testimony of Donna E. Shalala, Secretary, U.S. Department of Health and Human Services, before the Senate Finance Committee, February 13, 1997; Julie Kosterlitz, "Hard Realities," *National Journal,* January 4, 1997, p. 18.

23. E.g., "JOBS Plus," 1993 Oregon Laws 739, title 34, ch. 411; "Work and Gain Economic Self-Sufficiency (WAGES) Act, 1996 Florida Laws, ch. 175, 414; "Family Investment Program," Maryland Annotated Code, Art. 88A, section 44A (1996); "Full Employment Program," Massachusetts Annotated Laws, ch. 118, section 1 (1996); "Work First," Mississippi Code Annotated, section 43-49-11 (1996).

24. Lawrence F. Katz, "Wage Subsidies for the Disadvantaged," Working Paper 5679, National Bureau of Economic Research, Inc., July 1996. Cf. Pascal Courty and Gerald Marschke, "Measuring Government Performance: Lessons from a Federal Job-Training Program," *The American Economic Review* 87, no. 2 (1997): 383; John Harwood, "Welfare Test Suggests Combining Work With Fiscal Incentives for Long-Termers," *Wall Street Journal,* August 28, 1997, p. A16.

25. See, e.g., Section 14, Chapter 203 of the Massachusetts Acts of 1996, "An Act Providing for Improved Access to Health Care."

26. Steven L. Dawson, "The Federal Government and Paraprofessional Health Care Jobs," Home Care Associates Training Institute, May 1996.

27. Davis-Bacon Act, 40, U.S.C. 276a (1931); Service Contract Act, 41 U.S.C. 351(a)

(1965). A third such federal statute, the Walsh-Healey Public Contracts Act, Pub. L. No. 846, 49 Stat. 2036 (1936), applies to the manufacturing and supply industries, but is largely irrelevant today due to duplicative laws and court decisions over the years. State laws known as "Little Davis-Bacon Acts" remain in effect today in 32 states, requiring prevailing wages in state construction contracts.

28. See Jane G. Gravelle, *Employment Effects of Health Care Mandates,* S. Doc. No. 497, 103d Congress, 2d Sess. (1994). *President's Health Care Reform Proposals: Impact on the Economy and Jobs,* Hearings before the subcommittee on Health of the Committee on Ways and Means, House of Representatives, 103d Congress, 1st Sess. (1993).

29. See, e.g., White House Report to Congress on the North American Free Trade Agreement, July 11, 1997, as required by section 512 of the NAFTA Implementation Act (Public Law 103-182; 107 Stat. 2155, 19 U.S.C. 3462). Cf. Paul Blustein, "White House Subdued on NAFTA's Impact," *Washington Post,* July 11, 1997, p. G1; "NAFTA Critics Blast UCLA Study Reporting Job Impact as Modest," *Journal of Commerce,* December 20, 1996. Similarly, the Andean Trade Preference Act of 1991 requires the Secretary of Labor to undertake a continuing review and analysis of the impact of the Act's implementation on U.S. labor, and to submit an annual report to Congress; see, "Trade and Employment Effects of the Andean Trade Preference Act," Economic Discussion Paper 46, U.S. Department of Labor, Bureau of International Labor Affairs, December, 1994, pursuant to Section 207 of the Andean Trade Preference Act, 19 U.S.C. 3201 et. seq. For the generalized bills on labor impact, see, e.g., the Small Business and Private Economic Sector Impact Act, HR 58, 104th Cong., 1st Sess. (1995); the Economic and Employment Impact Act, HR 4006, 103d Cong. 2d Sess. (1994).

30. See Margaret MacAdam, "Home Care Reimbursement and Effects on Personnel," *The Gerontologist* 33 (1993): 55, 60–1 (1993); with respect to child care employment standards, see 1996 Illinois Laws 507.

31. 1996 Mass ALS 151, 1599–6895; 1996 Mass. H.B. 6100.

6

Lucie White

QUALITY CHILD CARE FOR LOW-INCOME FAMILIES

Despair, Impasse, Improvisation

On a Tuesday afternoon in late June of 1997, Lori-Ann Williamston left her two daughters, Kiyah, aged three, and Lacey, eight months, in a stroller in the Robert Bendheim Playground in New York City's Central Park. The stroller was loaded with cereal, a case of baby formula, some clothing, and toys. Before Ms. Williamston left the park, a witness overheard her tell the children that she would be returning with ice cream cones. After the children had been alone for about 45 minutes, a nanny in the park became concerned and notified authorities. The police found Kiyah and Lacey in good condition and placed them in the custody of Children's Services.

According to Valerie Grant, Ms. Williamston's Harlem roommate, Lori-Ann Williamston, an African American woman, was thirty-three years old. She had served in the Navy and earned her high school equivalency diploma but still had trouble finding steady employment. She had taken temporary jobs, including a job collating paper in a warehouse for about $5 an hour. At the time she left her children, she was paying her share of the rent with a $100 a month grant from public assistance and by cleaning the apartment. Ms. Grant had rented the two-bedroom apartment for herself and her teenaged son, Cori, so when Lori-Ann Williamston moved in with her two children, they had to carve out a space for themselves in the living room. "There," according to the *New York Times,* "near the dining-room table and an empty aquarium, the Williamston family would sleep."

After leaving her children in the park, Ms. Williamston apparently returned to the apartment, where she was arrested after Ms. Grant recognized photographs of the two girls on the evening news and called the police. Ms. Williamston explained to investigators that she had been depressed and that she knew that if she left the children in the park, the police would take care of them. The police concluded that Ms. Williamston's actions seem to have been motivated by despair.[1]

Lori-Ann Williamson had good reason to despair about her children. Even with her Navy experience and high school equivalency diploma, the best jobs that Ms. Williamston could find were short-term positions, with irregular schedules, no benefits, and wages that were rarely above the minimum wage. Even with a public assistance stipend supplementing her monthly income, Ms. Williamston could not afford to rent her own apartment, much less pay the tuition for high-quality infant and preschool child care programs for her children for the hours she needed to work. Her only alternatives were to seek child care from unlicensed providers at very low cost, or to barter with relatives or neighbors for whatever care they could offer.

Ironically, the dilemma of women like Ms. Williamston will only get worse as welfare time limits go into effect. After she times out of eligibility for public assistance, Ms. Williamston will lose the $100-a-month cash supplement that has enabled her to rent space for her family in her friend's living room. When this cash income is no longer available, she can try to increase her hours of waged work to make up the difference. Yet the extra hours of work will mean greater child care expenses. Thus, even if she *succeeds* in fully replacing her welfare stipend with wages, her family will be worse off than they were in June of 1997, when she abandoned her children in a playground out of despair.

If Ms. Williamston is not able to replace all of her welfare income through wages, she will probably lose her family's floor space in Ms. Grant's living room. Eventually, after she runs out of friends to help her, her family is likely to end up without shelter. The promoters of the welfare reform "experiment" have dismissed as alarmist the risk that welfare time limits will increase family homelessness. They urge legislators to wait and see whether families without income will actually take such extreme measures as sleeping on the streets. Yet the homelessness of families with children is not an unknown problem in our society. To the contrary, in the late 1980s, a substantial increase in family homelessness in large cities raised great concern among doctors, educators, and urban officials. As a result of this concern, the scope and consequences of homelessness among families with young children were exhaustively documented by social scientists and the federal government.[2] The results of these inquiries were disturbing, but hardly surprising. Family homelessness, even for short periods, has multiple, devastating effects on parental functioning, family stability, and the health and development of children. As a result of this social science research, specific policies for addressing family homelessness were developed and funded. Congress took the lead in mandating and funding an approach to the problem that focused on the integration of intensive services from many agencies and institutions, such as public education, primary health care, mental health services, civil and criminal justice, transitional housing, and social service delivery, with the goal of helping individual children and families become more "resilient" against the massive developmental and psychosocial costs that spates of homelessness could impose. Yet the larger result of this work was a widespread recognition among policy experts that family homelessness was a quintessentially *preventable* condition. A far more rational public policy for addressing family homelessness was to keep it from happening in the first place, in every possible case, by providing families with young children with the income and support that would enable them to maintain stable housing, especially through temporary crises. The availability and, indeed, the expansion of welfare were critical parts of such an approach.

Yet, in the immediate aftermath of this intense national policy focus on family homelessness, PRWORA was enacted. The law's mandatory time limits will require families who are subject to welfare cutoffs to replace their public assistance benefits with waged work, if they are lucky, and therefore to require more child care without more income to pay for it. The time limits are also likely to push many of these families, like the Williamstons, who are stably but marginally housed, into literal homelessness.

The first section of this chapter reviews some of the social science research that has finally shown clearly what women like Lori-Ann Williamston already knew: that quality child care is expensive, and the kinds of child care that they can patch together "on the cheap," without adequate resources, are likely to present grave risks to their children's safety and development. The second section places the child care crisis of low-income working families in the wider context of large-scale shifts in gender roles, family patterns, and the global economy. The third section looks at the prevailing policy approach to the child care crisis of low-income families. This approach calls for demand-side subsidies, either through direct grants or the tax system, to enable lower-income families to purchase high-quality, professionalized day care on an open, but heavily regulated, public-private market. At the same time, supply-side subsidies, channeled through the tax system, government-backed lending, or direct social spending, would bring down the costs of day care for all consumers.

The section will use a popular statutory model for state funding of day care to illustrate and examine this approach. Working from this example, the section identifies the risks that this approach presents for very low-income single-parent households, like the Williamstons. I suggest that these risks require us to rethink the current direction of day care policy advocacy. In order to ensure that policy reforms reach families like the Williamstons, we should let go of rigid notions of professionalism and regulation in favor of more creative, more flexible, and more uncertain approaches for ensuring good enough care for all children. Only such a shift in thinking will help us avoid catastrophic outcomes for the less affluent and powerful among us. Making such a shift will not be easy. It will not be easy for us to give up on bold social democratic visions about universal child care, or to make hard judgments about when loosening up on licensing requirements or professional standards, for instance, contributes to poor-quality care options for poor children. Yet a reluctance to make such judgments will ensure a huge gap between officially endorsed quality standards and day-to-day practices in our least powerful communities, a gap that may become increasingly hard to close.

The concluding section points briefly toward strategies for moving toward good enough day care for all families in this country. These strategies are premised on the idea that two big obstacles must be overcome to achieve such a goal. The first obstacle is a lack of pragmatic knowledge about what *reliably decent* care is and how to supply it. The second obstacle is a lack of political will to make reliably decent day care affordable for the lowest-income families. The dominant current strategy for addressing these closely linked obstacles is first to define a national-level vision of universal, state-subsidized day care, and then to organize diverse support for that goal at the local level.

The new strategy would tackle the problem from the opposite direction. Instead of starting with a big-picture policy vision, the new strategy would start at the local level, but with a keen awareness of the wider history and politics of social welfare policy. Informed by that knowledge, the first step would be to innovate multiple, complementary strategies for decent quality, community-sensitive, and affordable child care within real communities in the current legal and political climate. This approach would not seek a single program or policy for achieving the complex goal of affordable, decent quality day care. Examples of such innovations include encouraging peer networks of low-income, home-based child care providers; supporting well-designed parent education and involvement programs in low-income neighborhoods and day care centers; partnerships between day care centers and providers in different socioeconomic, ethnic, or geographic areas within a city or region; eclectic, well-supervised volunteer programs that supplement a day care center's core teaching staff with a variety of differently skilled helpers; local bond issues or linkage programs for raising capital for facility improvement loans, and the like.

Within each community, the goal of these innovations would be to make decent child care more available, especially for low-income families, given present levels of political will, government funding, and wider local- and state-level support. As those innovations emerge within communities, the systems, practices, state roles, and political will to stabilize, resource, and replicate them can be accomplished through three kinds of work, all of which must move forward at the same time.

In the first phase, the best of these innovations should be implemented at the community level through locally based coalitions of nonprofits, churches, foundations, businesses, local and state governments, the health and education sectors, and social service providers. An important goal of this phase would be to work toward enhancing the power of low-income families' voices and interests in these coalitions. In a second phase, legal and administrative reforms that will bring the state's power and resources solidly behind these local innovations should be worked out. Rather than obligating the state to solve the problem, these law-reform proposals should be locally and regionally specific, leveraging the normative authority, institutions, and fiscal resources of government behind these proposals in multiple ways. The overall goals of these law-reform proposals would be to enable these new innovations to succeed, to guard against inequities in their implementation and design, and to facilitate their adaptation to and implementation in new communities through coalitions in which low-income families' voices and interests take leading roles. In a final phase, coalitions of citizens, across geographic, social, and especially economic boundaries, should be engaged in these initiatives directly, educated about their benefits, encouraged to bring similar innovations into the day care that they use for their own children, and mobilized to support the new legislation that is required to fund and replicate them.

The care-delivery innovations at the center of this new strategy seek alternatives to the bureaucratized, monetized, professionalized, and exorbitantly expensive day care delivery model that current day care policy advocates sometimes uncritically promote. These innovations are likely to command wider political support than the old delivery model for two reasons. First, they will cost less than the older model in hard dollars. And, more importantly, these new innovations will produce more reliably decent child care for all families, regardless of income, because they draw upon interpersonal connection and social commitment, as well as monetary compensation, professional ideology, and regulatory oversight, to ensure good enough care. The older delivery model promotes an abstract notion of universal state-subsidized professional-level care, which sounds wonderful on paper. Yet, ironically, by aiming too high, this model may lead to bad outcomes. For the high- and middle-income working families, promoting this model may lead to care options that are costly to consumers, exploitative of child care workers, and tragically uneven for children, no matter how much money a family is willing to spend for care. And for low-income families, like the Williamstons, promoting this model of day care delivery may lead to no decent options at all.

The Child Care Needs of Low-Wage Families: Good Reason to Despair

Welfare Reform and Child Care

The repeatedly stated goal of welfare reform is to provide strong incentives for recipient families to become self-sufficient, producing all of their income through waged work alone. To accomplish this goal, the federal welfare reform law requires states to impose strict work requirements on most families to whom it grants federally financed public assistance. These workfare requirements typically require most adult members of families receiving welfare to work for as much as 20 hours a week within a few months of going on welfare. Although states may not sanction a recipient who is unable to find state-licensed child care from refusing to cooperate with these work requirements, the law no longer entitles recipients to financial assistance for child care, even while they are doing legally mandated work assignments. Much more problematic than these work requirements on welfare recipients, however, is the five-year lifetime limit that the new federal law places on most families' receipt of federally financed welfare payments.

After this time limit has expired, most families will not be eligible for any federally funded welfare benefits at all, regardless of either the availability for work for adult household members or their level of financial need. After a family's eligibility for welfare has expired, the state is not required to provide most families with any financial assistance to help them pay for day care while working at low-wage jobs.

The federal welfare reform law includes a section that consolidated and expands federal block grants for child care assistance for welfare-related and low-income families. This block grant will extend and expand federal funding, incentives, and technical assistance to the states to enable them to develop systems and subsidies for child care for low-income working parents, as well as the wider population.[3] Other federal child care assistance programs are likely to be expanded and improved in the next decade to provide further support for child care assistance for working parents. The question that must be asked about such initiatives is whether, as these programs are currently envisioned, they are likely to ensure safe and developmentally adequate care for the lowest-income single-parent families for all of the hours that those women will eventually be required to work for wages to make ends meet.[4]

The history of welfare reform initiatives suggests a negative answer. In earlier versions of welfare reform, liberal spending provisions typically have been included in the initial reform package to make work requirements acceptable to liberal legislators. After the reform fails to work, however, the political will to maintain these work-related services ebbs and expensive support programs are cut or eliminated.[5] Let us assume that the current reform follows this pattern, and Congress does not provide deep enough ongoing subsidies for low-income women to enable them to buy decent care for their children while they work. What kinds of care are out there for them, in the market, at prices that they can afford? What choices will they make for child care, when their income must be stretched to meet so many competing basic needs? What consequences are their child care choices likely to have on their children?

Three Boston Families

Before looking at the social science data, consider how these choices are juggled in the lives of three Boston-area families. The following profiles are based on case studies of working families in Massachusetts that were conducted as part of a recent study of those families' child care needs.[6]

The Breens

First, let us consider the situation of Jean Breen. Breen lives in Hyde Park, a lower-middle-income Boston residential area, with her husband and their two children, ages two and four. The family's annual income is $40,000 a year, which makes them ineligible for state-funded, income-scaled child care vouchers. Since having her children, Mrs. Breen has not been working because, as a preschool teacher, she would be earning less than she would have to pay for reliable child care. As a preschool teacher, she could earn $8 an hour, well above the minimum wage. The cheapest child care she could find would cost her and her husband $5 an hour per child. Thus, for every hour that she worked as a teacher, her family would have been *losing* $2 in overall income.

In order to enroll their two children in market-level family day care in the Boston area, the Breens would be required to spend in the range of $378.52 a week, or $18,926 a year, which works out to be about 47 percent of their annual income of $40,000 a year. To enroll their two children in market-level, center-based care in Boston, they would have to pay about $21,464 a year, or about 51 percent of their annual income. Those costs would drop to between 30 and 40 percent of their annual income if they lived in the less expensive central and western areas of the state.

When Mrs. Breen and her husband planned to have children, they did not take into account the high costs of child care. Rather, they assumed that Mrs. Breen would be able to continue contributing to her family's income as a teacher after she had children. As someone who has been trained in child development, Mrs. Breen is concerned that her children are not getting optimal socialization skills by staying at home with her until they enter kindergarten. Therefore, as soon as her son enters kindergarten, she plans to return to work as a preschool teacher, even though more than half of her income will go to pay for her younger child's care. Meanwhile, she works as a bartender three nights a week, leaving her husband to care for the children.

The Grants

Next, let us consider the circumstances of Kaidi Grant. She and her husband, who also live in Boston, have four children, ages seven weeks, four, six, and nine. Like the Breen family, the Grants also earn about $40,000 a year. Prior to the birth of her new baby, Mrs. Grant worked as a reading teacher at her children's school, coming home at three with the two school-aged children. Her four-year-old went to preschool three times a week, at a cost of $100 to $125 a week. On the days their son was not in preschool, her husband worked an evening shift at his job so that he could stay home during the day to care for his son. The next morning, he would resume the early shift, getting only three or four hours of sleep. After the baby was born, Mrs. Grant quit her job to care for the two youngest children at home. Before making this decision, she and her husband calculated that to find reliable, full-time child care for the infant would cost at least $200 a week in the Boston area.

The Wests

Both the Grants and the Breens earn incomes that place them solidly within the broad middle class. A third typical parent in the Boston area, Thrasher West, has less earning power. West is a single mother who lives with her two children, ages nine and three, in metropolitan Boston. Two years ago, her younger daughter was placed in foster care and thus received child care through the Department of Social Services. At this time, she began working in a sales position, for approximately $10,000 a year. When her daughter was returned to her, she was told that she was making too much income to quality for child care subsidies for very low-income parents. When she sought market-level child care, she discovered that it would cost her about $150 to $175 a week, leaving her with only about $25 a week to pay for all remaining expenses. Faced with this picture, she saw two options. She could return her daughter to foster care or she could quit her job and go back on AFDC. She was upset about returning to AFDC, particularly in view of the AFDC time limits that would take effect the following year, but she saw no other option. While on AFDC, she tried to go back to school part-time to improve her skills but was unable to get her daughter into a day care center because she was not yet potty-trained. Now that Ms. West is on welfare, however, she can qualify for short-term day care subsidies to enable her to make the transition from welfare to work. She has no idea how she will continue to pay for day care, while she is working, after those subsidies end.

The Social Science Data

The Trade-off between Quality and Cost

The stories of these three families are not unusual. Indeed, a large body of social science research suggests that many low- to middle-income families in this country face similar no-win choices when they seek high-quality and affordable care for their children while they are at work. Overall, this research provides solid survey data to confirm the picture that the case studies suggest. The two most important headlines from this data are simple. First, high-quality child care, particularly for infants and toddlers, is both very expensive and in short supply.[7] Even for families that have the cash to afford it, high-quality child care services are not widely available on the private market, particularly for the youngest children. And, second, it should be no surprise that the most critical failure of the child care market occurs among the lowest-income consumers, who have the least money to pay for care.

Even in child care centers with state-of-the-art facilities, about 70 percent of the costs of child care inputs go to pay for labor. Thus, the single most important reason that high-quality care for infants and young children is so expensive for families is because of the high costs of paying the human beings that it takes to deliver that care. The single most important strategy for keeping the costs of child care within the budgets of working families is by skimping on those labor costs. The case studies we have examined illustrate some of the ways that those labor costs are kept down. Thrasher West's situation provides an example.

After Ms. West returned to welfare, she became eligible for vouchers to help her pay for child care while she engaged in work or other activities that will supposedly help her eventually to become self-sufficient. Her eligibility for those vouchers will extend for a period of time after she has "transitioned" into full-time waged work. If she arranges child care in a licensed facility, a center or a family day care home, for example, the reimbursement rate for those vouchers will be set by the state legislature or child care funding agency at a percentage of the average rate that such providers charge to unsubsidized parents. The voucher rate reflects the cost-control strategy that those small-scale providers typically use in serving their unsubsidized clients, which is to pay the lowest possible wages to their teachers and other staff that are consistent with floors required by state labor laws and child care regulations. Unless they use this strategy, their unsubsidized clients will be unable to afford the service. In setting voucher rates, the legislatures use a rate structure that is capped by the tuition levels that unsubsidized providers charge. Legislatures are unwilling to raise voucher rates, both because of the absolute cost and for fear that this strategy would inflate the costs of care for non-subsidized consumers.

If, on the other hand, Ms. West arranges care with a relative or baby-sitter within her own home, the state's welfare department (in Massachusetts, the Department of Transitional Assistance or DTA) will provide her a different voucher, with a much lower reimbursement rate. In 1996, this rate was only $2 an hour. Women on welfare, like Ms. West, report that their caseworkers urge them to arrange such informal child care. Indeed, it is only if a large number of welfare recipients "choose" such care arrangements, in which the caretakers are paid significantly below the minimum wage, that state welfare reform budgets can include an entitlement for transitional child care benefits that is not exorbitantly expensive for the state to fund.

The social science data show that in any care setting, low wages to child care workers produce a risk of poor quality care. In group-care facilities, like child care centers or family day care homes, the pressure on providers to cut labor costs in order to balance their budgets produces the same array of labor problems that one finds in any low-wage service job: high turnover, poorly trained and qualified job applicants, poor worker motivation, and low worker morale. In informal care settings, a wider set of issues often compromise the quality of care. If an informal caregiver is a close relative or friend of the family or has a prior emotional bond to the child, then that person may feel motivated to provide high-quality attention and interaction to the child for little compensation. But if the caregiver is not closely attached to the child, there is a strong risk that she or he will deliver poor quality care, for a number of predictable reasons. First, many of the individuals who will be drawn to such employment are likely to be very young, or disabled, or otherwise limited in their capacity to compete in higher-wage labor markets. These caregivers are likely to face the same kind of poverty-related stresses that confront the low-income families and children that they serve. The stresses of living in poverty, whether as a day care provider or a parent, have been correlated with high levels of health problems such as anxiety, depression, and substance abuse. In addition, the low rent housing units where low-income babysitters or relatives are likely to care for children will often be overcrowded or out of compliance with basic housing codes. Furthermore, unlike caregivers in group settings, low-income babysitters and other informal caregivers do not have regular access, through the child care workplace, to training, resources, and support. Thus, it should come as no surprise that the low-cost informal child care that low-wage workers are able to arrange with household members, relatives, or neighbors often scores low on standardized measures of child care quality.[8]

The consensus of research suggests that the best way to respond to these quality problems is through an array of measures aimed to improve the wages of caregivers, or, stated differently, to drive up labor costs. As these costs go up, so too does the tuition that unsubsidized working families must pay, and the voucher reimbursement rates that state government must pay to make the service affordable to the lowest-income families.

These cost-inflating labor enhancement measures are familiar among students of child care policy. One idea is to enact incentives or requirements for decreasing the child-to-caregiver ratio even further. This proposal is particularly important in care sites, like family day care homes or unaccredited centers, that may be state-licensed, but where the ratios that are permitted for infants and toddlers remain suboptimally high. Another idea for improving quality by enhancing the performance of labor is to give more education and training to caregivers on topics related to early education and development. This additional education would improve the quality of care for children, to be sure, but is also costly, and would give caregivers a good basis for demanding higher wages. A third idea for improving quality by enhancing labor's performance is the most fundamental: it is simply to raise the wages and status of day care workers directly, to pay them adequately for the complex and essential work that they perform. The goal would be to upgrade the compensation and status of caregiver jobs from menial labor toward the professional range.

Extensive, comparative social science research on child care shows that from the perspective of the quality of the service that is provided for children, not to mention fairness to waged careworkers, these proposals make good sense. Indeed, the single proven policy for ensuring good enough care for children is to upgrade the caregiver jobs toward a professional level, just as the child care advocacy groups have urged for years.[9] If this is done, the combined force of professional-level status, professional-level educational requirements, and professionalized peer review, through caregiver certification and facility accreditation processes, would make a demonstrable cut into the cluster of problems that create the greatest risks for children. In particular, such measures would cut into the critical problem of staff turnover, a problem that creates a special risk for children in the early years when attachment to specific caregivers seems to be crucial for cognitive, social, and emotional development.

Numerous studies have found that regardless of whether low-income working parents use relative care, babysitters, family day care, or centers, the low cost child care that these families can afford to purchase without subsidies is consistently of poorer quality than child care available for higher-income groups.[10] From the perspective of the Grant and Breen households, however, the strategy of professionalizing the jobs of day care workers in order to improve overall quality runs the risk of tightening their knot of hard choices even further. For if day care workers' wages were upgraded in the way that social science research and advocacy efforts urge, the child care costs that now hover between 30 and 50 percent of these working families' annual budgets will rise to levels that approach or exceed their entire incomes.[11]

The Multiple Costs of Poor Quality Care

A cynic might respond to this data with a quip like, "So what's news: you get what you pay for in this society, and poor people get the worst deal." Yet recent advances in our understanding of child development demonstrate that it is not just the child's parents who lose when a young child spends many hours a day in an unsafe and unstimulating environment. New research suggests that the child's brain undergoes crucial development in the first three years of life. Without adequate attention and stimulation in those early years, the child's neurological and psychological capacities for subsequent development may be irreversibly impaired. Although later interventions can make up for some of this damage, such programs are costly for the public and uncertain in their effects. Thus, long hours of poor quality day care may deprive children of a fair chance to develop into well-adjusted, productive, and responsible adult citizens, no matter how hard they try.[12]

The injury of poor quality child care for low-income families is compounded by the fact that lower-income parents are generally aware of the problem. Studies have shown that low-income working parents generally know quite well that the child care they are using may be harming their children. But this knowledge is of no use to them, because they have no alternatives to inferior care.[13] It has been widely recognized that for any working parent, regardless of income level, concern that her child care arrangements are unsafe or of poor quality will interfere with her performance, motivation, and overall well-being on the job. For low-wage workers, the shortage of high-quality, affordable child care options makes it very likely that child care related job stress will compound the stresses of low-wage work environments that have been documented in the other chapters of this book. Policies, like welfare reform, that seek to *increase* the participation of low-income single parents in low-wage labor markets, are likely to increase this source of stress among poor working parents.

Early results from the National Institute of Child Health and Human Development (NICHD) Study of Early Child Care,[14] a massive, ongoing longitudinal study of child care in this country, confirms several key trends that emerged in earlier research. This study shows that in all family types and ethnic groups, the trend is toward children entering day care at earlier ages and for longer hours. Among poor families, the mothers with the lowest levels of education are particularly likely to place infants in care for very long periods of time. Among the providers of child care to low-income families, nonrelative babysitters are particularly likely to give poor quality care. Although family day care homes consistently score low on measures of the facility's safety and developmental appropriateness, the quality of the child–caregiver interaction tends to vary. Thus, policies that seek to train, support, and license family day care providers can improve the quality of care that they give to poor children.

The quality of center-based care, for infants as well as older children, is clearly correlated to the level of subsidy flows. As the population that is served by a center moves above the income range that is eligible for the deep subsidies that go to child care programs serving the most at-risk children, the quality of care declines. Thus, low-income *working* families are particularly at risk for receiving very low quality center-based care.[15] These families typically use centers that receive no government subsidies except vouchers for individual families. Increasingly, these centers are operated by large, for-profit corporations, which must stretch families' tuition payments to return a profit to investors, meet basic health and safety regulations, and pay their staff the minimum wage. But even if they are operated as nonprofits, the centers that serve low-income working families have little margin for providing high-quality care.

Thus, the NICHD study confirms that ample flows of money improve the quality of service that any type of child care provider offers. Deep flows of public dollars put directly into programs can produce high-quality child care, even for the highest-risk groups of low-income children. Money is most likely to translate into quality, however, if subsidies are combined with other policies that directly ensure the safety and design of the care facility, as well as the skill and training of the caregiver. Small demand subsidies to enable low-income families to arrange their own babysitting are unlikely to ensure any measure of quality. Demand subsidies combined with direct support, training, and monitoring of caregivers can improve the interaction of these caregivers with children but will do little to ensure a safe facility. It is difficult to improve facility quality among small-scale, low-income providers, however, because most of these providers work in their own homes, which are often in substandard rental units.

A Three-Part Policy Vision

Thus, the social science research points directly toward the ambitious three-part consensus child care policy blueprint for low-income working families that many progressive child care policy advocates in the United States have, I argue, understandably but perhaps unwisely endorsed. The first part of the strategy is to expand the supply of licensed, center-based care. The second part is to bring down its cost to affordable levels, even for very low income families. And the third part is to persuade or require families to choose this form of care. This policy blueprint envisions a world in which low-income families will have access to safe day care centers in which professionally trained providers give loving, continuous care to children in child-designed and developmentally appropriate settings. This consensus blueprint suggests specific policies that address the training, salaries, job quality, and professional credentialing of caregivers. It also suggests that policies address the design, construction, and monitoring of child care facilities so that they provide safe, educationally optimal settings for children's education and development. Finally, it suggests policies that address the social environment and educational curriculum in those centers, ensuring that such things as the grouping and supervision of children, the set-up of the classrooms, the spaces and materials, and the children's daily routine are designed in educationally optimal ways.

In addition to policies that directly increase the supply of educationally optimal day care services, the concensus suggests public policies that ensure that all families, even the lowest-income families, can afford licensed, professionalized, center-based care. This might include a range of direct and indirect subsidies to providers for facilities, staff training, and direct operating expenses. Such subsidies might cover the entire cost of the service for all children, regardless of family income, on the model of the public schools. Alternatively, such subsidies might cover only a part of the cost, with tuition payments by families covering the remainder. On this model, additional income-scaled subsidies would have to be made available to the lowest-income consumers to help them meet extremely high tuition costs.

Finally, the consensus blue print suggests policies for educating low-income families to use center-based care. Although the social science data is mixed, some evidence suggests that many low-income families may prefer homelike child care settings to center-based care. Although they recognize the reliability of child care centers, many low-income parents, if given the choice, might still opt for the proximity, trust-levels, and informality that they expect to find in home- or family-based care. In a series of focus groups, interviews, and interactive workshops conducted with low-income Boston-area parents about their child care preferences,[16] for instance, the participants expressed a strong ambivalence about placing their children in day care centers. Many of these women linked day care centers with other institutions, like schools, subsidized housing, health services, and welfare offices, in which they felt disrespected and powerless. They resented the routinized, impersonal, or rude treatment that they often received in these settings. In contrast, they regarded their status and role as mothers as one of their few sources of societal respect and personal efficacy. They described their role as mothers as their central moral anchor in very precarious lives. It gave them a sense of identity and a sense of status in their communities. Therefore, they wanted a say in the care of their children when they were at work. They wanted their caretaker's language and values to mirror their own. And they also wanted a personal relationship with the caregiver, as well as the power and opportunity to supervise what the caregiver did with their child.

Some child care policy advocates would suggest that low-income women express these views because of misconceptions about day care centers or bad experiences with poorly funded or regulated programs in their own neighborhoods. They may not be aware of programs with multicultural curricula, or strong parental involvement in the program's operations, or good two-way communication between the parent and caregiver. In short, they may not have any experience with child care centers in which the parents feel respected and have some real power to infuse the program with their own values. Even if they have heard about such programs, so the argument goes, low-income parents may doubt that this kind of care would ever be made affordable and available for them.

Recapping the Dilemma

Let us summarize the ground that has been covered so far. First, the social science research about child care suggests that the best quality of care for low-income children is likely to be delivered by highly educated child care professionals, in care settings that are physically safe and child-oriented in their design. On the whole, then, center-based care settings may be more likely than in-home babysitters to provide safe, developmentally appropriate care for the lowest-income children. The most obvious way that public policy can move toward this vision would be first to increase the supply of such high-quality care settings, through policies that focus on improving the quality of staff, facilities, curricula, and the like, and second, to make such forms of child care more affordable to lower-income families. The two big roadblocks to this strategy are: (1) it would be prohibitively expensive, especially for toddler and infant care; and (2) many low-income parents express a strong distrust of the kinds of care arrangements that this vision would promote, because of positive experiences with informal caregivers, or distrust of formal programs or the unavailability of such programs, or their exorbitantly high cost.

At this point, one can make one of two decisions. One can either view the obstacles as impediments that must be overcome and push forward with this consensus vision in spite of them. Or one can take the obstacles more seriously, as a signal that the consensus policy vision is itself unworkable and in need of fundamental rethinking. Perhaps a policy vision that would replace the unpaid care work of mothers with a universal scheme of professionalized, commodified care services is itself flawed. If we are either unable or unprepared, as a society, to bear the full cost of monetizing and professionalizing child care for every child, at a level of quality that would ensure real communication and power-sharing between parents and caregivers, then perhaps it is best to rethink the problem from the outset. Otherwise, there is a great risk that the consensus model will never be funded and implemented in ways that reach the poorest families, and a conspiracy of wishful thinking and silence will preclude us from designing second best, but feasible, strategies to fill the vacuum that results.

Stepping Back: A World in Transition

An Overview

If we step back from the day-to-day lives of low-income families, and widen the frame of our inquiry, we can see that a major transformation is under way, throughout the developed world, in the domain of work and care.[17] Over the last several decades, large-scale changes in cultural values, family structures, and the economy have come together to create a crisis in the industrial era's regime of care, and a new care regime has not yet emerged to replace it. The industrial era's normative arrangement for the provision of care for children and other dependent persons was through the unpaid household labor of wives and mothers. That work was indirectly funded through generous wage- and social insurance–benefit levels for the "heads of households," that is, married men.

Increasingly, demographic, cultural, and economic changes have converged into an emerging normative order, in which all adults, women as well as men, are both permitted, and expected, to do public work outside of the home. The gap in caring that has resulted as wives and mothers have entered waged work has been filled by a rapidly expanded, fitfully regulated, and far from perfect market for the private exchange of cash for care. The families that need the greatest quantity of these new monetized care services are those households in which all adult members work extended hours, such as very high-income professional couples, at the one extreme, and very low-income households at the other.

Viewed from one perspective, the recent urgency, in political rhetoric and public opinion, for a drastic reform of the welfare system can be seen as an expression of the crisis in societal arrangements of care. As Joel Handler and Yeheskel Hasenfeld suggest, the recent reforms can be understood as the enactment of a public moral ritual, through which the broad societal care crisis is symbolically represented and magically controlled.[18] Viewed as such a ritual, welfare reform instantiates the societal crisis as the moral failing of a small group of outcast individuals, welfare mothers. These figures are then subjected to punitive sanctions through which they are given the opportunity to correct their own failing. In response to these sanctions, they can choose to become self-sufficient by producing enough income to get off the dole, while caring for their own children without complaint. Alternatively, they can rebel against the sanctions, and refuse to become self-sufficient. If they choose this path, they are free to disappear.

When viewed as such a ritual, welfare reform can be seen as denying, and seeking symbolically to manage, the wider societal crisis of work and care. It can be seen to impose impossible demands on the lowest-income families to ensure the psycho-cultural stability of the wider public. It can be seen to purchase these symbolic benefits for the wider public culture by placing the lowest-income children at a substantial risk of harm from inadequate care and placing their parents at a substantial risk of despair as they are called on to witness that harm to their children without having any power to alleviate it.

At the same time that welfare reform can be viewed as such a ritual, however, it can also be seen very differently. Welfare reform can also be viewed as a bold move for clearing some ground for a postindustrial care regime. From this perspective, welfare reform can be seen as the abrupt, but necessary, ending of a welfare regime that was modeled upon the family wage norm, a regime that wedded single mothers to a patriarchal state in exchange for a highly restrictive subsidy to stay at home, like virgin wives, to care for their children. In this view, welfare reform, for all of its problems, might spark the kinds of local innovation that lead beyond a real impasse in our society's regime of care.

A Closer Look

Looking more closely, we see that the care arrangement of the industrial era, the family wage, was more norm than fact for many households. For roughly the first half of this century, many upper-stratum households did benefit from this arrangement. Wages for some middle- and upper-income male workers were high enough to subsidize a full-time wife, who could devote her time to a wide range of care functions. In addition to caring for the children, the sick, and the elders within the household, she could also care for community institutions like churches, recreational and cultural institutions, libraries, and schools. And finally, she could devote some time to charity, to poor individuals and families, thereby spreading some of her own family-wage subsidy down into lower-end families and communities that did not benefit from the family wage within their own households.

At the high to middle end of the income spectrum, households complied with the norm that wives not work for wages. These households provided cash income, as well as wives' charity services, into lower-end households, however, by hiring servants—waged care workers—to help out the wives: nannies, tutors, and governesses for young children, maids to do the housework, and nurses for sick and elderly adults. At the lower end of the income spectrum, the Mothers' Pensions buttressed the family wage's cultural legitimacy, and the nation's racial and ethnic hierarchy, by rewarding a handful of model single mothers with a stay-at-home care subsidy that was paid to them directly by the state. To qualify for this subsidy, as many feminists have noted, the recipient had to renounce both sexual relationships and waged labor, taking on the restrictions of wifely status, in what amounted to a kind of "marriage" to a patriarchal state. Most very low income mothers, particularly in households of color, were never selected for Mothers' Pensions, however. These mothers had to manage care as best they could, through extended families, church, neighborhood exchanges, ethnic- or race-based care networks, and organized charity.

It was on this foundation that the first extensive state subsidies for day care for children were enacted, during World War II, to enable mothers to take full-time waged work in war industries. After the war these day care programs lapsed in most states. In the half century since then, a maze of fragmented and class-stratified federal programs has been created to provide child care assistance. At the lower end, these day care programs first emerged in the 1960s, when the racial integration and expansion of the Aid to Families with Dependent Children Program (AFDC) (the successor to the Mother's Pensions) led conservative lawmakers to impose gradually escalating work requirements on welfare recipients. For middle- and upper-income families, on the other hand, modest tax benefits provided small subsidies for the costs of child care. Each of these programs was structured to reinforce, rather than move beyond, the family wage arrangement, however, wherever that arrangement was a realistic option for the provision of care.

For Middle- and Upper-Income Families:
Tax Breaks that Buttress the Family Wage

The largest portion of child care subsidy dollars is distributed through several provisions of federal tax laws. First, the tax code offers a deduction for each dependent child in the household, regardless of how the family arranges that child's care. Second, the code declines to tax the imputed income that households receive when wives or other family members provide unpaid care for their own children. By declining to tax the wife's unpaid care work, the tax laws put a heavy thumb on the scale in favor of the wife's decision to care for her own children, rather than working full-time outside of the home. To produce this incentive, the tax system must forego huge potential tax revenues.

And third, the tax code provides a nonrefundable tax credit that reimburses tax-paying families for a portion of the child care costs that they incur to enable adult family members to work outside of the home. Several features of the deduction are worth noting. First, because it is not a refundable credit, it does not flow to families without income tax liability or families who file for taxes but do not seek the credit. Second, unless a family's employer has opted into a flexible-spending program, the family does not get any benefit from the credit until their taxes are filed. Thus, it does not help cash-poor families pay their weekly or monthly day care bills. Third, the credit only covers a small portion of the actual costs to families of full-time day care. Fourth, the credit is not scaled to the number of children in the family. Fifth, the credit places very few strings on the kind or quality of care that qualifies for the subsidy, except that the taxpayer must provide a social security number for the caretaker. Thus, the credit is unlikely to be paid out for care workers who are undocumented, or are evading the payment of income taxes, or for taxpayer families who are not paying employer taxes for the care workers that they employ. In-home babysitters for low-income immigrant households, for instance, may fall into this group. And sixth, at an annual federal price tag of over $2 billion, this tax credit, which flows overwhelmingly to middle- and upper-income families, has been the largest single subsidy for child care that the federal government provides.

If we step back from the details of the federal tax law's care-related provisions, we can make several observations. First, these laws place middle- and upper-class families at the center of the law's attention when it comes to child care needs. This should not be surprising, in view of the greater likelihood of these families to vote, and the greater likelihood that their frustrations will be registered by the pollsters of elected officials. Second, although these laws address the child care needs of middle-income people, they do so in a way that clearly tilts those families toward supporting the family wage arrangement where this is still possible, looking to their own members to provide the majority of the family's care work on an unpaid and untaxed basis and providing only a small credit for a two-earner family's out-of-pocket day care expenses. And third, these huge federal child care subsidies do not help to build the *supply* of good quality day care, particularly in low-income areas where few families are likely to take advantage of them.

Thus, the tax credit will lighten some of the financial burden on families in which all of the adults work outside the home. But it will relieve the pressure in a way that ultimately reinforces, rather than points beyond, the social values and institutional arrangements of the family wage care regime. In sharp contrast to the subsidies that are earmarked to poor people, which set out to change the values and behaviors of the families and individuals to whom they flow, the child care–related tax subsidies leave to individual taxpayers the freedom to make their own choices with respect to child care, in a world that does not offer many good choices, even for middle-income families, except the nuclear family.

For the Poor: Subsidies that Seek to Shape the Soul

As we have seen, the child care–related tax subsidies have comprised the largest share of child care subsidies funded by the federal government, in dollar terms. Yet the array of subsidies that are most commonly equated with the federal government's child care policy are those that are earmarked for the poor. Since the 1960s, those subsidies have fallen into two broad categories. First, there are the specialized subsidies, through programs such as Project Head Start, that provide for model preschool education and family support services for low-income children, with a goal of making up for the cognitive and social deficits that poverty is believed to impose. These subsidies have typically reached only about 10 percent of income-eligible poor children, and have provided a three- or four-hour, part-year program, as opposed to the round-the-clock services that low-income working parents require.

A second set of subsidies has been tied to work requirements in federal welfare legislation. With a few notable exceptions, these subsidies have provided capped sums of money to state and county welfare agencies, permitting them to provide day care for poor children in conjunction with AFDC workfare requirements, or their transition into full-time waged work. These subsidies have reached only a small portion of the AFDC population and have subsidized care of mixed quality.

The Personal Responsibility and Work Opportunity Reconciliation Act of 1996 (PRWORA) requires most recipients of federally funded welfare to move into workfare after a short time and to leave welfare entirely after a fixed number of months. Unlike the prior law, however, the new law does not provide a federally funded child care entitlement for recipients engaging in workfare activities or transitioning off of welfare to full-time work. Rather, PRWORA ends this child care entitlement, while increasing the temporary supply of child care block grant funds to the states. These funds can be used to fund state-level demand-subsidy programs, so long as a fixed portion is set aside for increasing the supply of child care services, monitoring the quality of services, improving state-level regulations, and similar activities.

Thus, when we step back from Ms. Williamston's despair and assess the wider landscape of care in the United States and other industrial countries at the close of this century, we see good reasons for her to feel despair. The primary caring arrangement of the industrial era is rapidly unraveling. An uneven market for monetized care services has sprung up to replace that arrangement. The government's role in supporting that market is fragmented and incoherent, reinforcing industrial-era care arrangements and imposing outdated moral sanctions on the poor. The only policy strategy that has emerged for improving the situation is to professionalize the paid care workers and seek increased state funding to enable consumers to pay the bill.

No industrial nation has moved far beyond the family wage care template to a care regime that is squarely centered in the expectation that all able-bodied adults will do full-time waged work, purchasing care for their children from the wages that they earn. No industrial nation has developed an adequate system for ensuring that the market will deliver reliable, developmentally appropriate care for children in exchange for the amounts of money that wage-earning parents can afford to spend for care. Nor has any industrial nation developed an adequate system for supplementing the earnings of low-wage workers, in order to ensure that they, as well as more affluent families, are able to purchase appropriate care.

No industrial nation has demonstrated that upgrading the caregiver role to a professional or quasi-professional level, with its enormous attendant costs, is the best way, on balance, to ensure that high-quality care is made available to all working families at rates that they can afford or that the government is willing to subsidize.

Yet in spite of the fact that we have not yet devised workable systems for replacing unpaid mother care with something else, PRWORA, the federal welfare reform law, was enacted on the faulty premise that a feasible means of replacing this unpaid care had indeed been found. PRWORA was enacted on the faulty premise that very poor, unskilled single parents of young children, by working full-time in low-wage jobs, could afford to purchase adequate full-time replacement care for their children. What specific policies have been advanced to make this possible, and how likely are they to work?

Affordable Child Care for Everyone? The Massachusetts Example

In Massachusetts, one can observe three different policy responses to the dilemma of providing child care to low-income single parents required to work full-time as a consequence of welfare reform. The first response is to encourage women transitioning off of welfare to arrange informal care with unskilled and inexperienced relatives or neighbors at a very low cost rather than opting for more expensive licensed care. Although the state law does not require women to opt for this kind of care, anecdotal reports from welfare recipients suggest that caseworkers often encourage women to choose it. The fears that low-income women often voice about center-based care, as well as a lack of knowledge about their rights under the law or about high-quality licensed alternatives, will often lead women to accept the informal option. If a subsidy-eligible client agrees to such care, the state, after a pro-forma certification of the caregiver and no monitoring at all of the caregiving arrangement, will reimburse the caregiver at a rate of just $2 an hour. After a transition period, the former recipient's eligibility for this paltry stipend expires, and she is left to fund the caregiver on her own. Such programs, through which states encourage welfare-linked families to use unregulated, informal care, are probably the most common response of states to the conundrum of providing replacement care for low-income parents who are required to work full-time. While such programs control the levels of state expenditures for welfare-linked child care, they do so in blatant disregard of the well-being of children, as we have seen.

The strategy of encouraging women to opt for cheaply reimbursed informal care is limited, however, because both federal and state laws prohibit states from using federal welfare block grant dollars to require women who are receiving welfare to comply with workfare requirements if they are unable to secure adequate care for their children while they are working. In some circumstances care that complies with the rudimentary certification required to receive a state's informal care reimbursement would not be construed as adequate under this standard. A single parent who was aware of her rights could therefore refuse to place her child in such an arrangement. If she was unable to locate a fully licensed arrangement that she could afford with the aid of available subsidies, then she could not be required to comply with workfare obligations.

To get around this legal limitation on the state's freedom to force welfare recipients to choose informal care arrangements, Massachusetts and other states have attempted to use a second strategy. They have attempted to lower their licensing requirements in ways that will reduce providers' operating costs. Thus, soon after the state's welfare reform law was enacted, former Governor William Weld, acting through an emergency executive prerogative, attempted to lower the state's minimum age and educational requirements for directors and teachers in licensed child care centers. This effort was stymied when the state legislature overrode the governor's veto, restoring the original requirements. In other states as well, such as Wisconsin, governors and legislators have sought to lower state child care standards in ways that would bring down the public cost of welfare-linked child care subsidies. Some research suggests that state licensing standards are not always rationally related to the features of "quality" that can be measured by independent means. Yet these attempts to lower state regulations did not arise from careful deliberation about the optimal levels of regulation from a quality perspective. Rather, they appeared to be reactive efforts, by welfare reform proponents, to cut child care costs irrespective of the consequences for children.

A third strategy in Massachusetts for responding to the dilemma of providing child care for low-income working parents has been an effort by progressive child care advocates to promote what I have called the consensus policy vision through legislation that would establish a state-level entitlement to child care assistance for low-income working families. The basic outline of this strategy, which has also been advanced in other states, such as Illinois, as well as Massachusetts, is as follows. The legislation would endorse the principle that no working family should pay more than 10 percent of their income for child care. Subsidy eligible families would receive a monthly child care voucher in the amount of the difference between 10 percent of their income and a "fair market" child care tuition rate that would be set periodically, by region, on the basis of prevailing market rates for different forms of care. The family could then use their voucher at any state-licensed facility that agreed to charge no more than this established fair market rate. The ultimate goal of this strategy is to secure full appropriation for the program, so that every working family is guaranteed state-licensed child care without having to pay more than 10 percent of its income out of pocket.

The basic idea of the legislation derives from federal housing subsidy programs, notably the Section 8 Existing Housing Program. The Section 8 program, which was enacted in 1974, has never been fully funded, in spite of repeated efforts by low-income housing advocates. Congress has viewed full funding of the program as both prohibitively expensive and a dangerous intrusion of government into the private market for rental housing. The costs of full funding of the Section 8 program reflect the high housing-quality regulations with which all Section 8 landlords are required by federal law to comply. These standards set forth uniform norms for minimal safety and amenities in rental housing. Yet some of the standards have been criticized as inflexible, gender-biased, or culturally insensitive. Furthermore, absent sufficient political will to fund the program as an entitlement, these standards have operated to distribute the subsidy funding in arbitrary and uneven ways. Under the program, a few low-income people get housing that provides a high level of amenities. Many other low-income families get no housing assistance, and thus, in too many cases, no shelter at all.

The uneven workings of the Section 8 program came under close scrutiny in the 1980s, when new levels of homelessness among the urban poor made tragically clear how inadequately designed and funded the nation's housing subsidy programs were. The Section 8 program was of limited use to homeless people because some of the quality standards were both too rigid and unrealistically high and therefore could not be used to renovate single room occupancy housing stock, for example. Even outside of the context of homelessness, landlords in some regions have refused to participate in the Section 8 program because they do not consider it cost-effective to bring units up to the level of the federal housing quality standards for the rent levels that the program guarantees or because they do not want to take on what they perceive to be high hidden costs of renting to low-income families, particularly those with young children. In other regions, Section 8 subsidies entering an area may have had the effect of driving up the costs of the lowest-rent housing for nonsubsidized renters.

These lessons from the Section 8 program may be instructive in the child care context. If universal child care bills are enacted at the state level, will the same kinds of problems arise? Will this legislation increase the stratification of the child care market, giving a few lower-income families access to normative, highly regulated care, while locking the rest into an invisible world of risky but, for many families, less intimidating informal care? Will this universal legislation push us farther toward a vision that equates quality with professionalization, even though it may be a suboptimal may to organize care-work, and too costly for all families to access, given present levels of political will? Will this universal legislation produce more upward pressure on state licensing requirements, particularly with respect to facilities, training levels, and compensation, rendering licensed care even less accessible for many of the lowest-income families? While we have no answers to these questions, the history of the Section 8 program gives us little reason to feel sanguine that such problems will not arise.

Loosening the Impasse of High-Cost Professionalized Care

There are no clear answers to the problems that have been raised in this chapter. The social science research points clearly toward both professionalization of the caregiver role and heavy state oversight of provider quality as the most reliable guarantors of adequate day care quality, particularly for the lowest-income children. Professionalized labor, by definition, costs a great deal of money, much more than the states are likely to provide through subsidy payments for the lowest-income children. And the combination of professionalization and heavy state oversight is likely to produce care arrangements that the lowest-income families distrust, and often for good reasons. What paths of public policy might help us work loose of the impasse into which the trilemma of professionalization, bureaucratization, and monetization threatens to lock us? Several paths may be possible.

First of all, public policy might seek to enable parents to care for their own children, particularly infants, in arrangements that do not reinforce the isolation and gender-inequity of the family wage arrangement. Two social movements have challenged the equity and wisdom of the family wage arrangement in recent decades, from the perspective of the women who deliver the care in this regime. The first has been the challenge by the women's movement to the gendered division and isolation of care work in the nuclear family. The second has been the concern that low-income single parents become even more stigmatized, demoralized, and cut off from mainstream society by receiving cash subsidies to stay at home to care for their children. As the Scandinavian experience with paid parental leave has demonstrated, a gender neutral parenting subsidy will not guarantee that fathers and mothers will choose to use the subsidy in equal numbers. And paid parental leave will not counter the isolation of caring for young children at home. Although it is not fashionable for liberals and progressives to endorse conservative diagnoses of "welfare pathology," many studies have shown that low-income single parents who are isolated from social networks often experience negative psychic and social effects. How could public policy encourage and enable parents of both genders, at all income levels to play a major role in caring for their own children, without reinforcing either the gendered distribution of care work or the marginalization of caretakers from waged work and public life?

To promote gender equity, care subsidies—whether they come through the tax system, through firms in the form of family leave provisions or other family-friendly policies, or through direct cash allowances to individuals or households to care for their own young children—might provide specific incentives for fathers' involvement in the caretaking of infants and young children. To counter isolation, particularly of low-income women, neighborhood or workplace parent-child centers might be established, in which parents as well as paid caregivers participate jointly in providing care. Caretaking subsidies might then include incentives or requirements that parents receiving the subsidies participate in such programs, at least part-time.

These centers could be designed similarly to the caretakers' circles and drop-in centers that are springing up in urban and suburban spaces such as museums, shopping malls, public schools, libraries, community centers, primary health centers, courthouses, and churches. They could provide structured programs, parenting support and training, respite, enrichment activities, and community for parents and other at-home caretakers, at the same time that they provide socialization, educational enrichment, and health screening for children and caretakers across class and race lines. The service centers that are described in Chapter 8 of this volume might be good sites for such programs in low-income communities. The subsidies that would enable parents to care for their own children, both at home and at such centers, might be provided through a number of arrangements, such as infant-care insurance programs, the provision of unemployment benefits for parenting leave, or the funding of family-leave policies by firms or government. In order for such arrangements to work, the short-term welfare programs that are authorized by PRWORA would have to be harmonized with these policies. As a start, structured programs in which parents care for their *own* children, such as volunteering at a Head Start or other early childhood program, would have to count as a person's workfare obligation. And sufficient income to enable even the lowest-income parents to spend part of their time caring for their own children would have to be assured. This might come from a combination of welfare, child support, child support assurance, refundable child care tax credits for parental as well as substitute care, and the like.

A second direction for public policy would be to move beyond rigid, professionally oriented approaches to ensuring quality in child care to more flexible, network-oriented approaches. This idea would challenge the spiraling of child care costs that is inevitable if quality is equated with professional training and credentialing. The alternative approach would seek to support the morale and commitment of careworkers through structured peer support, mentoring, and networking among front-line caregivers, between caregivers and communities, and between caregivers and parents. One interesting model for accomplishing this draws from the networks of cooperative enterprises that were established in the Mondragon region of Spain. A network of small child-care facilities within a single neighborhood could be established, supported, and linked together by a community-based development corporation. The development corporation could train, place, and supervise a range of different sources of labor for the entire network, including volunteer labor from youth, elders, and student apprentices within the community; community service volunteers from other, more affluent communities; community members working for "time-dollars"; and paraprofessionals. A small group of highly trained professionals would coordinate these varied forms of labor and ensure that they participated in the delivery of integrated, high-quality, developmentally appropriate services for children. Such arrangements would substitute innovative forms of social organization for the traditional trappings of professionalism—high status, high salaries, and self-regulation—to ensure a high level of commitment and quality among caregivers. The success of some Head Start programs with parent volunteers and semiskilled paraprofessional staff suggests that this alternative model might work in some settings, with appropriate supervision and support. For such policies to work, the fabric of communities must be strengthened in a variety of ways.

Another direction for public policy innovation is reflected in the many efforts that are going on at local and state levels, such as the Smart Start program in North Carolina, to pull all of the groups that have an interest in quality child care, especially nongovernmental groups such as employers and churches, into brainstorming, planning, and problem-solving teams. In some communities such efforts have significantly raised the level of awareness, commitment, and resources for meeting the community's child care needs.

Conclusion

None of these strategies will provide a quick fix for the despair of women like Lori-Ann Williamston. Yet child care policies that lean too heavily on salaried professional labor, no matter how plausible they sound on paper, are not likely to work any better for very low income women. Unless we find new paths for public policy in the domain of caretaking, many children will be left without minimally adequate care. The decision to challenge the taken-for-granted wisdom in the area of child care policy is premised on a determination to do what it takes to ensure that all children get good enough care today and tomorrow, rather than in some imagined future. For it is far more feasible for society to draw parents, extended families, and communities into new community-based practices and institutions of care than it is to expect isolated households to provide all of the care work on their own or to expect them to purchase all of their care needs for cash, as though it were a marketable commodity. If we wait for Congress to provide the money for Ms. Williamston to enroll her two children in full-time, licensed, center-based care, we are likely to be waiting for a very long time. If, on the other hand, we push public policy to allow Ms. Williamston and others in her community to take part in caring for their own and others' children in innovative and supportive settings, we might be able to muster the political will to provide adequate funds and expand such efforts and thus to counter her all-too-astute sense of despair.

Notes

1. D. Barry, "Mother Left Children in Park Out of Despair, Police Say," *New York Times,* June 26, 1997, p. B3.

2. See L. White, "Representing the Real Deal," *University of Miami Law Review* 45 (1990–91): 271–313.

3. See Personal Responsibility and Work Opportunity Reconciliation Act.

4. K. Edin and L. Lein, *Making Ends Meet: How Single Mothers Survive Welfare and Low-Wage Work* (New York: Russell Sage Foundation, 1997).

5. See J. Handler, *The Poverty of Welfare Reform* (New Haven, CT: Yale University Press, 1996).

6. S. Snyder, *The Need for Affordable Child Care for Low and Middle Income Families in Massachusetts.* A Report prepared for Parents United for Child Care, May 5, 1997.

7. M. Culkin, J.R. Morris, and S.W. Helburn, "Quality and the True Cost of Child Care," *Journal of Social Issues* 47 (1991): 71–86, cited in *Consequences of Growing Up Poor,* ed. G. Duncan and J. Brooks-Gunn (New York: Russell Sage Foundation, 1997).

8. L.J. Waite, A. Leibowitz, and C. Witsberger, "What Parents Pay for: Child Care Characteristics, Quality, and Costs," *Journal of Social Issues* 47 (1991): 33–48, cited in *Consequences of Growing Up Poor,* ed. G. Duncan and J. Brooks-Gunn (New York: Russell Sage Foundation, 1997).

9. William T. Gormley, Jr. and B. Guy Peters, "National Styles of Regulation: Child Care in Three Countries," *Policy Sciences* 25 (1992): 381–99.

10. Numerous studies come to this general conclusion. See, for example, E. Galinsky, C. Howes, S. Kontos, and M. Shinn, *The Study of Children in Family Child Care and Relative Care* (New York: Families and Work Institute, 1994); D.L. Vandell and M.A. Corasaniti, "Variations in Early Child Care, Do They Predict Subsequent Social, Emotional, and Cognitive Differences?" *Early Childhood Research Quarterly* 5 (1990): 555–72; C. Howes, "Can the Age of Entry into Child Care and the Quality of Care Predict Adjustment in Kindergarten?" *Developmental Psychology* 26 (1990): 293–303; C. Howes and P. Stewart, "Child's Play with Adults, Toys, and Peers: An Examination of Family and Child Care Influences," *Developmental Psychology* 23 (1987): 423–30; D. Phillips, K. McCartney, and S. Scarr, "Child Care Quality and Children's Social Development," *Developmental Psychology* 23 (1987): 537–43, all cited in *Consequences of Growing Up Poor,* ed. G. Duncan and J. Brooks-Gunn (New York: Russell Sage Foundation, 1997).

11. D. Phillips and A. Bridgman, eds., *New Findings on Children, Families, and Economic Self-Sufficiency* (Washington, DC: National Academy Press, 1995).

12. For two popular press overviews of this new research, see S. Begley, "How to Build a Baby's Brain," *Newsweek,* Special Edition, Spring/Summer 1997, pp. 28–32; J.M. Nash, "Special Report; Fertile Minds," *Time,* February 3, 1997, pp. 48–56.

13. See, for example, F.L. Sonenstein and D.A. Wolf, "Satisfaction with Child Care: Perspectives of Welfare Mothers," *Journal of Social Issues* 47 (1991): 15–32.

14. For a summary of the study's methodology and results, see The NICHD Early Child Care Research Network, "Poverty and Patterns of Child Care," in *Consequences of Growing Up Poor,* ed. G. J. Duncan and J. Brooks-Gunn (New York: Russell Sage Foundation, 1997), pp. 100–31.

15. See D. Phillips, M. Voran, E. Kisker, C. Howes, and M. Whitebook, "Child Care for Children in Poverty: Opportunity or Inequality?" *Child Development* 65 (1994): 472–92. See also D. Phillips, ed., *Child Care for Low-Income Families: Summary of Two Workshops* (Washington, DC: National Academy Press, 1995); D. Phillips and A. Bridgman, eds., *New Findings on Children, Families, and Economic Self-Sufficiency* (Washington, DC: National Academy Press, 1995).

16. These activities included focus groups, individual interviews of low-income parents and providers, and educational workshops for low-income parent groups on child care rights and resources related to child care. They were conducted by students enrolled in a child care clinical program and field-based course on gender, work, and welfare at the Harvard Law School in the spring term of 1996. Papers and reports on these activities are

filed with the author. The activities were conducted in cooperation with the following Boston-area nonprofit child care organizations: Parents United for Child Care; the Cambridge Child Care Resource and Referral Agency; the Boston Child Care Alliance; and the Child Care Careers Institute.

17. See Jane Lewis, "Gender and Welfare Regimes, Further Thoughts," *Social Politics* 4, no. 2 (Summer 1997): 160–77; D. Sainsbury, "Women's and Men's Social Rights: Gendering Dimensions of Welfare States," in *Gendering Welfare States,* ed. D. Sainsbury (London: Sage, 1994), pp. 150–69; T. Knijn, "Care and Gendered Citizenship: Towards a Comparative Conceptual Framework," paper presented at the Women and Public Policy Conference, Rotterdam, 1995; G. Esping-Anderson, *The Three Worlds of Welfare Capitalism* (Cambridge, England: Polity Press, 1990).

18. J. Handler and Y. Hasenfeld, *The Moral Construction of Poverty: Welfare Reform in America* (Newbury Park, CA: Sage Publications, 1991); J. Handler, *The Poverty of Welfare Reform.*

7

Louise G. Trubek

THE HEALTH CARE PUZZLE

CREATING COVERAGE FOR LOW-WAGE WORKERS AND THEIR FAMILIES

The effort to expand health care coverage to low-wage workers and their families is under way. The interaction of a revised Medicaid program and recent welfare reform initiatives has created additional health care options. During the 1980s, Medicaid for low-income women and children evolved into a program with broad support.[1] In the 1990s, however, attempts to reform the welfare system through work incentives were hindered by the lack of health care coverage in low-wage jobs. Congress responded by revising Medicaid, increasing health care coverage for children, and giving states the flexibility to design their own health care coverage programs.[2] With this major legislative initiative, quality health care for low-income working families became a realistic goal. However, certain tensions must still be confronted and resolved in order to ensure that low-wage workers can keep their jobs while obtaining reliable health care coverage for their families: coverage for families versus entitlement for children, Medicaid-based coverage versus private insurance, and access to health care versus workplace success.

Creating health care coverage that merges Medicaid requirements, workplace realities, provider desires, and patient needs is a challenge for advocates, providers, policymakers, and business leaders. This chapter uses Wisconsin's experience to explore the successes and difficulties in resolving this challenge. Wisconsin has built a well-regarded, statewide Medicaid managed-care system that includes consumer protection, patient participation, and an adequate payment rate for managed-care plans. The state has also embarked on an initiative to substantially revise the welfare system to mandate waged work. The welfare reformers who advocated the work initiative understood that health care through the job was essential for a work-based antipoverty program to succeed. When the Medicaid program was expanded in 1997, these reformers used that opportunity to propose "BadgerCare," a plan that extends health care coverage to low-income families by combining Medicaid expansion with private workplace health plans.[3]

Even when BadgerCare is implemented, Wisconsin must continue to refine and adapt policies and procedures to provide working families quality health care in a cost-effective system. Creating health care coverage for these families requires assuring coverage for children, maintaining and improving the private workplace system, and increasing access to health care for working families. This chapter suggests a number of strategies to create quality health care in a cost-effective system, including expanding oversight and patient assistance in both public and private health plans, and developing incentives for workplaces, schools, and community agencies to maintain and expand health care access and coverage for working families. The chapter also explains the complex roles that providers, community and consumer groups, welfare reformers, and state-agency administrators play in the provision of health care through their participation in the development and implementation of health care programs, policies, and procedures.

Evolution of the Medicaid Program

As a result of its link to the Aid to Families with Dependent Children (AFDC) program, Medicaid has been the primary source of health care coverage for poor women and children. Under the old AFDC system, when an individual qualified for AFDC she also became eligible for Medicaid. If that individual met the income and asset tests for Medicaid, she received a substantial package of benefits for her family requiring virtually no patient contribution. Conversely, poor women and children who lost their eligibility for AFDC, usually due to increased income through work or marriage, also lost Medicaid coverage and often became uninsured. According to one expert, "37 million uninsured Americans fall through the cracks in the employment-based health insurance system and do not meet the income and categorical requirements for Medicaid's welfare based assistance."[4]

Enacted as a 1960s safety net health care program for the poor, Medicaid originally was unpopular with providers, was difficult to access, and was inconsistent with waged work. It was the stepsister to the well-loved, comprehensive, and universal Medicare program for the elderly. Since its enactment, three modifications have dramatically increased Medicaid's popularity: the development of managed-care organizations (MCOs),[5] endorsement by health care providers, and expanded eligibility for working families.

Medicaid Managed Care: Oversight and Patient Assistance

As a result of a federal waiver system that allows state Medicaid recipients to enroll in MCOs, a large percentage of women and children now receive health care coverage through Medicaid MCOs.[6] Wisconsin's Medicaid managed-care program is highly regarded because the system promotes collaboration between the Wisconsin Bureau of Health Care Financing (the state Medicaid administrator); MCOs; and community, public health, and consumer groups.[7] This positive view of the Wisconsin program shared by HMOs, advocates, and state officials is the product of a decade of hard work and energy.

The Wisconsin MCO system utilizes agency oversight and patient assistance to ensure quality service at a reasonable cost. The system is built on contracts between the Medicaid agency and MCOs that enforce agency oversight and mandate participation.[8] Through contract requirements, the Medicaid agency encourages MCOs to utilize community groups, public health units, and schools to provide prenatal care, immunizations, and transportation to health care services. These contract terms also require MCOs to collect usage data to demonstrate their progress in providing underutilized services, such as preventive dentistry. Before MCO contracts are renewed, the Medicaid administrator assesses compliance with these specific contract terms.

Patient assistance complements agency oversight. Wisconsin has developed an innovative approach to incorporating advocacy into its Medicaid managed-care system; "HMO advocates" are one of these innovations. In Wisconsin, Medicaid contracts stipulate that patient advocates must be employed by HMOs to assist clients, promote programs such as HealthCheck within their HMOs, and cooperate with community coalitions.[9] Carola Gaines, a licensed practical nurse, is one example of an HMO advocate. In addition to providing internal advocacy for patients, Ms. Gaines develops programs to promote positive health outcomes in prenatal care and children's preventive care. She also participates in the Madison Regional Health Coalition, a group of health care providers, state administrators, public health workers, and activists that advocates for quality health care, and she has organized the HMO advocates in her region into a group that meets regularly to share experiences and coordinate activities.[10]

MCOs are obligated to provide quality health care while maintaining their own financial solvency. Because of their dual roles as patient advocates and MCO employees, HMO advocates experience the tension between patient needs and the business interests of their HMO employers. To maintain balance and support, advocates like Ms. Gaines form alliances with health care providers and community groups. These alliances are able to place the needs of clients within a broader perspective and propose policy solutions using media outreach and legislative lobbying.

Provider Endorsement: Political Power

Provider support for the Medicaid program is increasing. Traditionally providers were hesitant to participate in the Medicaid system. They complained about low reimbursement rates, burdensome paper work, and uncooperative clients. However, this hesitancy has evolved into modified enthusiasm due to increases in Medicaid payment structures, decreases in revenue from private health insurance plans, concern about the burden of uninsured patients, and external pressure for quality care.

With provider support, federal legislation requiring states to use a market standard for determining reimbursement rates has resulted in increased Medicaid funding.[11] While the Medicaid reimbursement rate is increasing, private health insurance companies are placing substantial cost containment pressure on health care providers by lowering reimbursement rates and encouraging fierce competition. Increased competition, in turn, has made it more difficult for providers to service the uninsured since those that provide uncompensated care will be at a competitive disadvantage when their rates reflect these expenditures. Providers view Medicaid expansion as a solution to the problem of a costly uninsured population.[12]

Providers are also subject to increased external quality reviews by businesses, government, and the public. Protocols are being developed and other quality of care indicators are being enforced through quality assurance systems and accrediting agencies.[13] As a result, providers are now accountable for preventive care, such as immunizations, mammographies, and prenatal services. In response, they have adopted oversight and review systems, similar to those provided by Medicaid, which allow them to meet outcome requirements.

Quality assurance requirements encourage providers to employ individuals who serve as liaisons with clients and community groups. For example, Lisa Monagle, a registered nurse, directs a prenatal clinic at a large Milwaukee hospital. She is also an active member of Health Watch, an advocacy group on issues relating to Medicaid in Milwaukee. Monagle uses her extensive knowledge of clinical issues in health care for low-income pregnant women to advocate within the hospital, join with community groups in speaking out for quality prenatal and postnatal care, and lobby in the legislature on behalf of additional funding for these services.[14]

Thus, health care providers can simultaneously serve both their own financial interest and the public interest by advocating for an ample Medicaid program. The existence of this powerful health care constituency to advocate for quality care for low-income families has proved crucial. Resources and contacts of provider-lobbyists, combined with the client stories of advocates like Lisa Monagle, are effective tools in guarding the Medicaid program. Providers can quickly unite to advocate at a turning point in legislative debate and can offer extensive resources to facilitate timely participation.

Expanding Medicaid to the Workplace: Linking Work with Health Care

Over the past decade, the expansion of Medicaid to cover non-AFDC families has broken the exclusive eligibility link to AFDC. Medicaid legislation has added health care programs—such as Healthy Start, "continuation coverage," and the medically needy program—that have allowed more working-poor families to enroll and retain their eligibility. Healthy Start allows women and children otherwise not eligible for AFDC to qualify for Medicaid. States provide coverage up to 200 percent of the poverty level with no asset limits for pregnant women up to six months after birth and children up to 18 years.[15] Additionally, Medicaid allows families to continue their coverage for eighteen months after exceeding program income limits, which enables families to work and maintain coverage.[16] The medically needy program creates a "spend down" option where families who must spend down their assets and income for medical expenses are eligible for medical assistance. This permits working families not eligible for AFDC to obtain Medicaid coverage.[17]

In addition to these universal Medicaid expansion programs, the federal Medicaid agency has granted waivers to states to develop experimental programs covering higher-income working families.[18] As a result of the waiver option, state bureaucrats and legislative leaders have developed an understanding of how to use Medicaid to improve health care for uninsured and vulnerable populations. States have taken the lead in designing programs that combine Medicaid, charity care, and client contributions to create health care coverage for working families who cannot meet the Medicaid eligibility requirements.

The Intersection of Medicaid with Welfare Reform

Job stability for poor women is linked to the availability of health care coverage. The low-wage job market, where most women find jobs, often does not offer health care plans for employees.[19] Even when insurance is available, a worker may have to contribute to premiums, family coverage may not be offered, and the benefit package may be limited. Government efforts to provide private insurance coverage in the low-wage workplace have been ineffective. The creation of small-business health plans during the 1980s, the Health Insurance Portability and Accountability Act (HIPAA),[20] and tax credits have not substantially increased employer-based coverage. Evidence indicates that the number of uninsured people at the workplace is not decreasing.[21]

In Wisconsin, as welfare reformers sought to promote waged work, they saw that the lack of health care coverage in the low-wage workplace acted as a barrier to those wishing to leave AFDC. A Republican leader in welfare reform indicated:

> Health care is the 600-pound gorilla blocking successful welfare reform. Small business employers insist that tax credits and other private insurance incentives are not sufficient to get them to provide coverage for their employees. . . . I now believe that welfare reform won't be successful if people can't access coverage for their children. Expansion of Medicaid to the working poor is the only realistic route to make welfare reform work. People will stay in community service jobs rather than take private sector jobs so they can keep their Medicaid. They would rather accept lower wages.[22]

This leader recognized that efforts to increase health care coverage in the workplace through private insurance have failed. He also believed that the Medicaid program in Wisconsin, with its focus on managed care and community and provider support, could provide a framework for covering working families.

Personal Responsibility and Work Opportunity Reconciliation Act of 1996 and Wisconsin's W-2: Laying the Groundwork

At the federal level, the push toward a revised welfare system culminated in the passage of the Personal Responsibility and Work Opportunity Reconciliation Act of 1996 (PRWORA). Wisconsin embarked on a welfare reform initiative of its own, which was dubbed W-2. Introduced in the summer of 1995, Wisconsin's W-2 plan was billed as a comprehensive welfare reform program intended as a national model. W-2 proposed an early effort to create a health component to accompany welfare reform. The health plan attempted to create a new system for the working poor to have health care coverage. This was to be achieved by expanding income eligibility for Medicaid, requiring co-pays for every recipient no matter what the level of income, and eliminating Medicaid eligibility if the employer offered any type of health care coverage and paid at least 50 percent of the premium.[23]

Proponents of welfare reform recognized that providing health care coverage was essential if women were to be integrated into the labor market. They also realized that Medicaid dollars were necessary in order to craft a system that enabled workers to maintain health care coverage in jobs that did not offer health benefits, but they were interested in encouraging employers to provide coverage.

As the proposal worked its way through the legislature, the Policy Group on Welfare Reform in Wisconsin was created to advocate for an effective antipoverty strategy. This coalition of religious groups (the Catholic Conference, the Lutheran Group on Public Policy), direct service providers (affordable housing and teenage counseling services), and nonprofit organizations (public interest law firms and children and domestic violence advocacy groups) analyzed the W-2 health plan proposal.[24] The analysis highlighted the drawbacks of the plan: an unrealistic co-pay requirement, an unregulated private insurance option, and elimination of the Medicaid entitlement. In addition, it emphasized the positive aspects of the proposal: integration of the working poor into Medicaid and the linking of Medicaid to the private workplace health care coverage system.

Health care providers were also concerned about the limitations of the W-2 health plan. To address this concern they initiated a collaborative effort with individual hospitals, physician clinics, MCOs, health care provider trade associations, and a public interest law firm. They lobbied and testified for specific changes in the health plan. Specifically, they worked to preserve the medically needy and Healthy Start programs and to maintain Medicaid eligibility unless the workplace offered comprehensive, affordable insurance. When the W-2 legislation was enacted some positive changes had been made; however, private insurance requirements remained weak and Healthy Start eligibility was reduced.

At the federal level, when PRWORA was enacted it did not include any changes in the Medicaid system; the Medicaid entitlement was frozen at the July 1996 level. Therefore, Wisconsin's W-2 health plan, if implemented, would have been substantially out of compliance with the federal Medicaid program. To rectify this problem, the state applied for a waiver to allow its W-2 health plan to be enacted, despite the fact that it required substantial deviation from the existing Medicaid requirements. The waiver was denied.

Balanced Budget Act of 1997 and Wisconsin's BadgerCare: A Second Try

One year later, in the summer of 1997, Congress enacted the State Children's Health Insurance Program (SCHIP). SCHIP initiated a massive expansion of health care coverage for uninsured children with substantial latitude provided to states to design their own health care system.[25] Welfare reformers realized that changes in health insurance for low-income families were essential in order to have a work-based strategy succeed. Medicaid's evolution emboldened states to believe that they could create programs to cover uninsured children and families. Governors led the effort in Washington to gain additional federal funds; their participation was an essential ingredient in the push toward transforming Medicaid to a health care plan for low-income families. At the federal level, children's advocates created public support for uninsured children.[26] They expressed concern that welfare reform would produce health care cutbacks and a diminution of quality care, adding to the impetus for the enactment of SCHIP. Thus, the job-based welfare strategy and a positive view of Medicaid, combined with public support for children's health care programs, created the environment for the passage of SCHIP. However, children's advocates opposed SCHIP's flexibility, fearing expansion to families would reduce benefits and coverage for children.[27]

Wisconsin immediately responded with BadgerCare, a revised state health plan providing health care coverage to all uninsured families below 185 percent of the federal poverty level. The state took its original W-2 health plan and altered it to meet the requirements of the new federal guidelines and to answer the earlier criticisms of state-based advocates. For example, BadgerCare maintains a health care entitlement for all currently eligible Medicaid participants and creates several new categories of eligibility. Additionally, the plan substantially reduces the patient co-pay requirements contained in the W-2 proposal and enrollment is free to all families with incomes up to 150 percent of the federal poverty level. Families with incomes between 150 percent and 185 percent of the federal poverty level may participate in Badgercare by paying premiums equal to 3 percent of their income. Individuals retain their eligibility for BadgerCare unless an employee's workplace insurance option includes an employer contribution of 80 percent and a comprehensive set of benefits. BadgerCare was submitted for required federal waivers, but federal administrators have raised objections.[28] This conflict between Wisconsin and federal Medicaid administrators over BadgerCare demonstrates the difficulty of creating and implementing health care coverage for low-wage workers. Any comprehensive plan must confront serious objections. Will the plan maintain quality of care for participants? Can workplace health plans be integrated with expanded Medicaid eligibility? Will the plan address the need for increased access to health services?

Low-Wage Workers and Health Care: Tensions and Strategies

SCHIP appears to provide an opportunity for states to fully transform Medicaid into a program that provides quality health care coverage for low-wage workers. It transfers significant authority and revenue to states to modify current Medicaid programs.[29] However, innovative policies and proposals will be required to change Medicaid into an effective program for working families. Creating these policies and proposals will require providers, advocates, and agency administrators to confront and resolve three tensions: coverage for working families versus entitlement for children, Medicaid-based coverage versus private insurance, and access to health care versus workplace security.

Coverage for Families versus Entitlement for Children

Federal SCHIP funds were targeted for uninsured children, but the legislation gave states some flexibility to design state-based health care programs for working families. Some states plan to use these additional federal funds to expand health care coverage for working families rather than exclusively to cover uninsured children.

Those that support expansion of health care coverage for working families assert that the well-being of families requires health care for all members and that children can be protected within a comprehensive family plan. They maintain that high-quality health care for children will emerge from health care coverage for the working family. They assert that strong families come from secure parents, and, if families fear losing health insurance and their jobs, children will be adversely affected.

However, proponents of expanded coverage for children argue that a shift to family coverage will jeopardize SCHIP's protections and funding, specifically for children. They have two levels of concern: that the special attention needed to provide children with comprehensive care will be undermined and that expanded family coverage will create unexpected revenue requirements. These proponents advocate using Medicaid to ensure that all children receive needed medical care. Children without health insurance are six times more likely to go without needed care, five times more likely to use the hospital emergency room as a regular source of care, and four times more likely to have necessary care delayed.[30] In addition to basic care, expanded social and psychological services to at-risk children are proving efficacious.[31] The crucial importance of basic and expanded health care services for the health, social, and educational development of children is a powerful argument for keeping the focus on children's health.

A second concern is based on anticipated federal and state government resistance to providing the additional revenue required to adequately fund health care expansion. The argument is that if Medicaid undertakes to cover uninsured families, the eventual revenue shortfall will result in sacrificing children's coverage. There is some evidence to suggest that as attention focuses on workplace coverage, other programs to assist health care access may be curtailed to contain expenditures; a program to provide extra funding for hospitals that disproportionately serve low-income people was slashed in the recent Medicaid expansion legislation. Thus, the concern that both the quality and the long-range visibility of coverage for children could be jeopardized by underfunded expansion to families has some validity.

In Wisconsin, the debate has been resolved in favor of working families. The philosophy behind BadgerCare is that "[b]y extending health coverage to low-income families, [the state is] making sure that work does pay for [working] families and that their children receive quality care."[32] However, the tension between expanding Medicaid exclusively to cover uninsured children and the desire of welfare reformers to include working families continues to be an issue. This tension emerges due to the perceived limited pool of health care funds and philosophical differences on how best to cover children.

One strategy to resolve the tension between health care coverage for working families and coverage for uninsured children is to strengthen the protections for children within an expanded health care system. In Wisconsin, BadgerCare is integrated into the Medicaid managed-care system. Federal agencies, local providers, and community organizations have confidence that Wisconsin's Medicaid managed-care infrastructure, which provides for agency oversight and patient assistance, can protect quality health care for children. However, careful attention is required to ensure that these systems actually benefit children. Children's advocates should continue to press for additional protections for children. For example, advocates of family coverage may resist paying for increased health outreach and intensive services for children; however, both preventive care, such as immunizations and regular dental check-ups, and outreach programs for children's enrollment must be maintained. Continued oversight through contract requirements for these services is essential. In addition, an HMO advocate's job description should require the advocate to speak out for the inclusion of special programs that assist at-risk children. Agency personnel and HMOs recognize the benefit of incorporating additional safeguards to avoid expensive care and liability. They can be allies in the fight for children's protections. Providers and community groups must be vigilant in strengthening the health care infrastructure to provide coverage for all while ensuring that adequate protection is maintained for children. Ultimately, a universal health care system is the best way to meet this goal.

Medicaid-Based Coverage versus Private Insurance

SCHIP provides an opportunity to develop health care coverage for low-income families that is continuous and seamless. There are tensions, however, in integrating the Medicaid program into private workplace coverage. Creating a publicly funded system that provides accessible and appropriate health care for low-income families can conflict with the need to maintain existing workplace coverage. The availability of government-subsidized programs to cover workers and their families may encourage employers who currently provide health insurance to drop their policies. This so-called "crowd-out effect" might be especially attractive if the Medicaid expansion programs provide outreach and preventive services at a lower cost to the worker.[33] The risk of the crowding-out effect is that the cost of Medicaid expansion will be prohibitive and a political backlash could cause the program to be slashed.

Resolving this tension requires both discouraging employers from dropping existing coverage and strengthening the quality of private workplace coverage—a stick-and-carrot approach. Wisconsin is proposing a law that requires employers who offer insurance to offer it to all employees. The legislation would also prohibit employers from dropping insurance if they currently offer coverage.[34] This "stick" approach only preserves the existing workplace plans. It does not provide the consumer protections that can be found in the Medicaid program. Improving the quality of workplace plans would complement the stick approach. In Wisconsin, initiatives are under way to create consumer protection mechanisms in private health plans that parallel Medicaid's oversight and patient assistance requirements. These consumer protection mechanisms include expanded health care data collection, a Consumer Bill of Rights, private sector advocates, and hotline/ombuds programs.

New state legislation will enable the Wisconsin Office of Health Care Information, the state health care data collection agency, to better monitor health care cost and quality. In addition to increasing the scope of data collection, the legislation transfers this agency to the Bureau of Health Care Financing, the department that oversees the Medicaid program. This location allows expert data collection analysis and outcomes studies crafted for Medicaid to be shared with the workplace oversight agency that monitors health quality and cost in the workplace.[35]

Several health care Consumer Bill of Rights packages have also been proposed as legislative initiatives. These packages contain specific substantive requirements for health care policies, such as continuity of care in MCOs and increased access to specialists. They also contain due process requirements, such as providing appeal rights.[36] The response from the MCOs has been to resist such regulation. However, a health care Consumer Bill of Rights is likely to be enacted at both the federal and state levels.[37]

In addition to expanded agency oversight, health care providers are making efforts to increase patient advocacy. For example, one Wisconsin health care provider employs advocates to assist low-income patients or other patients facing barriers to care. Jeanan Yasiri and Bob Richards work for a large Madison multi-specialty clinic. Both have television and newspaper backgrounds. They describe their role as liaisons between the community, clients, and the clinic. Ms. Yasiri runs the Community Care program, which assists uninsured patients in receiving care. As a patient advocate, Mr. Richards resolves patient complaints and communicates client and community concerns to the clinic staff. Both are active in community coalitions working to increase coverage for the uninsured and to improve patient protections.[38] In addition to patient advocates, the state association of MCOs has proposed a statewide hotline/ombuds program to be operated and funded by providers, MCOs, and consumers. This program would serve all MCO patients by offering them health care rights information and assisting them in utilizing appeal processes.[39] Both the patient advocate and the health care ombudsperson work under the same tensions as the HMO advocates, confronting the conflict between patient needs and the financial solvency of an employer. The emergence of these mechanisms in the private sector may presage a convergence of private and public advocacy systems. Overall, these private-sector initiatives represent a positive reaction to the pressure to expand patient protections within a private health coverage environment.

Access to Health Care versus Workplace Security

Maintaining a job and meeting family health care needs create a tension for women as they move from welfare to work. Welfare reformers who advocate "work not welfare" confront the revolving door problem of keeping people in their jobs. The absenteeism of former welfare recipients is a major concern of employers. Employers realize that health care needs can be a reason for job failure. For example, one employer, discussing the employer's role in assisting welfare reform, noted, "Employers worry about absenteeism related to sick children. . . ."[40]

The concern is real. Women with small children who are placed in jobs that require early and late shifts will have difficulty locating health care for sick children. Workers who have 9-to-5 jobs may have to leave work if a child becomes ill. In addition to parental concerns, health care providers worry about their ability to deliver quality health care if patient-workers cannot come to them because they risk losing their job. The upsurge in preventive care requirements and attention to quality assurance oversight contributes to this provider concern. For example, Medicaid managed-care contracts require MCOs to reach immunization and mammogram targets. Quality assurance initiatives required by Medicaid and private insurers force providers to ensure that enrolled patients receive treatment.

Resolving these workplace tensions will require changes in the health care system, schools, community agencies, and workplaces. The health care system must ensure that care is accessible to all workers. Health care providers have a stake in assisting workers who have health care coverage to access care and overcome job loss concerns. Because providers are monitored by internal advocates and external quality assurance mechanisms, they must demonstrate their provision of quality care. For example, if women forego prenatal examinations because they are unable to take time off from work, providers may receive sanctions from Medicaid and, ultimately, experience community outrage if infant mortality rates increase. Additionally, public health pressure for immunizations and control of infectious diseases will also create pressures for increased health care access. Thus, providers may find that it is in their best interest to not only provide extended hours[41] but also to lobby for community-based delivery systems and workplace protections.

In addition, Medicaid is now paying for health care services at schools. School-based health care sites can help working mothers by expanding child care services and clinic hours, and by developing more flexible policies toward sick children. Creation of community sites for health care enrollment and delivery is another way of providing support for working mothers. This approach locates health care facilities in specialized social service agencies. Importantly, community organization-based health care offers much-needed convenience and an expanded support system to working mothers. For example, health care services could be combined with domestic violence shelters or day care centers. These agencies could expand their holistic care to include health care services, such as enrollment, claims advocacy, preventative care, and education. Using multiple sites as entry points can be an important innovation.

A funding mechanism has been created by PRWORA to encourage enrollment in health care plans. This system establishes a $500 million fund to assist states in coping with the unlinking of Medicaid from PRWORA. This additional funding provides an opportunity to initiate innovative systems to enroll individuals in health care programs. The dollars can be used for expenses directly attributable to the increased administrative costs of Medicaid eligibility determination incurred because of the transition from AFDC to PRWORA. Activities that can be included are outstationing, public service announcements, and assistance to beneficiaries. As such, funding can be used to encourage enrollment by outstationing workers at MCOs and other health care provider locations, schools, and community organizations. In Wisconsin, this expanded enrollment system will be integrated into the BadgerCare program. The state Medicaid agency has indicated that it will provide funding incentives to multiple sites to encourage workers to enroll and use health care services.[42]

Family friendly workplaces should also be encouraged. A local Wisconsin official has urged businesses to support welfare reform by creating workplaces that reflect an understanding of basic family needs.[43] Workplaces may also be able to provide sites for enrollment and preventive care, enabling workers to receive health care while on the job.

The Family and Medical Leave Act (FMLA) represents an early attempt to resolve the tension between work and health care.[44] FMLA protects workers by allowing time off for childbirth and health care treatment for workers and their families. The act is enforced, in part, through client grievances. FMLA, however, is virtually unknown to health care providers, job support centers, and community advocates. Informing workers of their rights under the FMLA is one effective strategy for assisting workers. However, the FMLA has several limitations in its ability to assist low-wage workers, namely coverage is limited to unpaid leave and its protections extend only to serious health conditions.[45]

Conclusion

Welfare reform has provided a catalyst for the significant expansion of health care coverage for low-wage workers. However, the challenge remains to create a health care system that effectively serves low-wage workers and their families. Transforming the health care system so that it provides quality health care coverage requires provider, government agency, and community group collaboration to expand Medicaid health care coverage, maintain children's protections, strengthen workplace health coverage, and increase health care access at community agencies and in the workplace.

The Wisconsin story demonstrates that unlikely allies can be united to achieve health care reform. The shared concern among welfare reformers and community groups to "make work work" has contributed to the enactment of the federal SCHIP program. Continued collaboration can ensure that federal health care funding is maintained and, ultimately, increased. Both health care providers and community activists have an interest in improving the level of patient care. Collaboration between these groups may increase patient protections in all health care policies. In addition, state Medicaid administrators and welfare reformers are interested in promoting job security and improving access to quality care. These shared goals can be achieved by initiating enrollment and health care delivery in nontraditional sites, such as community agencies and schools. Creating multiple sites can assist low-wage workers in balancing their work with family commitments.

Because control over health care design has devolved to the states, collaboration among states is also essential. An alliance of state government actors has already emerged. The strength of the National Governors Association (NGA) has been demonstrated by the intervention of the governors on federal Medicaid legislation, which increased the ability of states to design their own health care programs. In redesigning health care, states will consider expanded proposals of varying quality. To combat inadequate, low-quality plans, interstate sharing of information, strategies, and success stories must be encouraged among concerned advocates, government agencies, and providers must be encouraged to share information, strategies, and success stories among states. This networking is essential if high-quality state health care initiatives are to emerge.

Notes

Special thanks to Cristine Nardi for her thoughtful and dedicated research and editorial assistance.

1. This chapter uses the word, "Medicaid," only to refer to the section of the Medical Assistance program that provides health care coverage based on family status and income.

2. The State Children's Health Insurance Program (SCHIP), 143 Cong. Rec. X6029–01 (daily ed. July 29, 1997). This program is included in the Balanced Budget Act of 1997, Pub. L. No. 105–33 (1997).

3. The Federal Health Care Financing Administration as of June 1998 had not yet approved all waivers necessary to implement Wisconsin's proposed BadgerCare. Memorandum from Angie Dombrowicki, Managed Care Section, Bureau of Health Care Financing to Interested Parties, June 8, 1998, hereinafter Dombrowicki memorandum.

4. *Hearing on the Perspectives on the Transformation of the Medicaid Program, Before the Committee on Commerce,* 104th Cong., 1st. Sess. 1995, statement of Diane Rowland, senior vice president, Henry J. Kaiser Foundation.

5. Managed-care organizations (MCOs) encompass a diverse group of arrangements for the financing and delivery of health care services. David A. Hyman, "Consumer Protection(?), Managed Care, and the Emergency Department," *American Bar Association Health Law Sec. Mono.* 5 (1997): 57, 61.

6. See Jane Perkins, Kristi Olson, and Lourdes Rivera, *Making the Consumers Voice Heard in Medicaid Managed Care: Increasing Participation, Protection and Satisfaction,* Los Angeles, CA: National Health Law Program, 1996, p. 5.

7. See Louise G. Trubek, "Making Managed Competition a Social Arena: Strategies for Action," *Brooklyn Law Review* 60 (1994): 275.

8. See 1998–99 Department of Health and Family Services, *Contract for Services between HMO and Wisconsin Department of Health and Family Services,* 1997, hereinafter *HMO Contract.*

9. Ibid. Health Check is the name for required preventive screening for Medicaid-enrolled children. See also Perkins, Olson, and Rivera, *Making the Consumers' Voice Heard,* p. 66 (noting uniformly positive assessment of member advocates in Wisconsin).

10. Interview with Carola Gaines, HMO Advocate, Unity Health Plans, in Madison, WI, April 10, 1997.

11. See U.S.C. s.13960(a)(13)(A)(1982); see also *Wilder v. Virginia Hospital Assoc.,* 496 U.S. 498 (1990).

12. Tamar Lewin, "Hospitals Serving the Poor Struggle to Retain Patients," *New York Times,* September 3, 1997, p. A1.

13. See John D. Blum, "Introduction," *American Bar Association Health Law Sec. Mono.* 5 (1997): 3.

14. Telephone interview with Lisa Monagle, manager of Ob-Gyn Clinic, Sinai-Samaritan Hospital, April 11, 1997.

15. See 42 U.S.C. s. 1396(a)(1) (1991).

16. See Tit. 42, Ch. 7, sec. 1396r-6 (extension of eligibility for medical assistance).

17. See 42 U.S.C. s. 1396(a)(10)(C) (1991 and Supp. 1996).

18. See *Medicaid Waivers,* Health Care Finance Administration's Web site http:\\\www.hcfa.gov\medicaid\obs7.htm (visited May 20, 1997).

19. See Peter Kilborn, "Illness is Turning Into Financial Catastrophe for More of the Uninsured," *New York Times,* August 1, 1997, p. A10 (There are "23 million uninsured working adults, 17 million of whom work full time. . . . Nearly half of the working poor do not have health insurance").

20. Health Insurance Portability and Accountability Act, Pub. L. No. 104–191 ss. 341–342, 2723 and 2744–2747 (1996); see also Robert Pear, "Health Insurers Skirting New Law, Officials Report," *New York Times,* October 5, 1997, p. A1 (discussing HIPAA noncompliance).

21. See Kilborn, "Illness is Turning Into Financial Catastrophe," p. A10.

22. Telephone interview with John Gard, Wisconsin Assembly representative (R-Dist. 89) (April 8, 1997).

23. Act 06 April 25, 1996, 1995 Wis. Laws 289 (The "Wisconsin Works" or "W-2" welfare reform legislation was enacted but the required federal waiver was denied so the program was never implemented).

24. Louise Trubek and Ann Batio, "Welfare, Health Reform Must Go Hand in Hand," *Wisconsin State Journal,* October 20, 1995.

25. See the State Children's Health Insurance Program (SCHIP), 143 Cong. Rec. H6029–01 (daily ed. July 29, 1997). This program is included in the Balanced Budget Act of 1997, Pub. L. No. 105–33 (1997).

26. See Marian Wright Edelman, *10 Million Uninsured U.S. Children in Working Families,* Children's Defense Fund website http:\\www.childrensdefense.org\ insurememo.html (visited May 20, 1997).

27. "A Choice on Children's Health," *Washington Post,* July 17, 1997, p. A18.

28. The debate over the granting of the waiver rests in part on the cost-effectiveness of providing health insurance to children by also insuring the whole family and the extent of states' flexibility to design programs. See Dombrowicki memorandum.

29. Barbara Wolfe, professor of economics, University of Wisconsin. Remarks at the First Annual Health Care Forum in Madison, WI, September 16, 1997.

30. See note 29.

31. Wisconsin Legislative Council, Special Committee on Prevention of Child Abuse, Proposed Legislation on Medical Assistance for Case Management Services, Committee Print, 1997.

32. Statement on Family Health Insurance Program, Office of the Governor of Wisconsin, August 4, 1997,"BadgerCare."

33. Lisa Dubay and Genevieve Kennedy, "Scare Talk About 'Crowd-Outs'," *Washington Post,* August 28 1997, p. A21.

34. Joe Leean, secretary of the Wisconsin Department of Health and Family Services, Remarks at the First Annual Health Care Forum in Madison, WI, September 16, 1997.

35. See staff of Wisconsin Legislative Council, Special Committee on HealthCare Information, Revision of Wis. Stat. ch. 153, 1997).

36. See Patient Protection Act (State Med. Soc'y of Wis. ed., 1997); see also Proposed Provisions: Health Care Consumer Protection Act, Center for Public Representation, Inc., edition, 1997.

37. See Blum, "Introduction," p. 5.

38. Telephone interview with Jeanan Yasiri, manager, Community Care Program, Dean Medical Center, April 7, 1997; telephone interview with Bob Richards, director of Patient Advocacy, Dean Medical Center, April 7, 1997.

39. Policy statement from the Association of Wisconsin HMOs. Adopted September 12, 1997.

40. Marvin Balousek, "Local Committee Focuses on Problems of W-2 Plan," *Wisconsin State Journal,* July 22, 1997, p. 4B.

41. Memorandum from Peggy L. Bartels, Director, Bureau of Health Care Financing to Interested Parties, October 7, 1997.

42. Ibid.

43. Kathleen Falk, Dane County Executive, Address to the W-2 Steering Committee, July 31, 1997.

44. 29 U.S.C. s. 2601–2654 (1994).

45. Ibid.

Lucy A. Williams

UNEMPLOYMENT INSURANCE AND LOW-WAGE WORK

Introduction

Empirical studies have increasingly documented that the majority of women who received Aid to Families with Dependent Children (AFDC), now Temporary Assistance for Needy Families (TANF), exit welfare for work within two to four years or combine welfare with labor market income. Ignoring these experiences of many single mothers, much of the rhetoric regarding welfare policy over the past few years has singularly highlighted the image of the welfare mother as not being a participant in paid labor; it has often focused on the alleged economic incentives of AFDC to discourage wage work. Current welfare policy is designed to push women who are *assumed* not to be paid laborers into paid labor.

This book, and much of the recent discourse and research, is dedicated to identifying and overcoming barriers that keep women from getting into, maintaining, and thriving in paid labor. But no matter how many barriers to entering and maintaining wage work are overcome, for some people there will always be periods of unemployment. The very enactment of an unemployment insurance system legitimates the existence of unemployment in paid labor markets and embraces an economic growth model that assumes unemployment is a functional necessity to a growing economy. Because of the panoply of reasons relating to both job structure and personal circumstances discussed earlier, low-wage workers, in general, and low-wage mothers, in particular, often experience more frequent and cyclic/recurrent periods of unemployment than the general population.[1] Once we have embraced the complex and fluid experiences of women receiving welfare *and* participating in wage work, we must determine which cash assistance programs are available to tide them over in times of inevitable unemployment.

Although the unemployment insurance program is thought of as the program that provides benefits for virtually all wage workers who lose their jobs, the design and implementation of the program is such that many in paid labor are ineligible. In 1996, only 36 percent of those technically covered by the unemployment insurance categories actually received benefits when unemployed.[2] This percentage has been falling slowly, but consistently, since the 1940s; it sharply declined between 1980 and 1984 and has remained at a low rate since that time.[3] A study by the National Commission for Employment Policy (NCEP) highlighted the gender discrepancy, finding that 80 percent of unemployed women did not meet the eligibility criteria (as opposed to 74 percent of men).[4]

In particular, unemployment insurance has *not* been the program that has assisted many low-wage single mothers when they become unemployed. In one study of women-maintained families in which the mother was employed at least three months, almost three times as many families turned to welfare as to unemployment insurance.[5] In another study of 1,200 single mothers who received AFDC for at least two months in a 24-month period, 43 percent also worked, averaging just about half-time. However, only 11 percent of those who worked received *any* unemployment insurance. Those who did not receive unemployment insurance had slightly higher education than those who did receive unemployment benefits, but they had lower wages, fewer jobs, slightly fewer hours per year (an average of 894 hours per year as opposed to 1,050 hours per year for those who did receive unemployment benefits), and fewer weeks of full-time work. In other words, those who received little or no unemployment benefits represented a longer-term, but less intensive, work effort (more weeks/months of work but with fewer hours per week and at lower hourly wages). Also, those who did not receive unemployment benefits were substantially more likely to be African American.[6]

While there are, of course, many reasons for the decline in recipiency, a substantial portion of the discrepancy between those unemployed and those receiving benefits appears to be the result of expanded state disqualifications based on (1) findings of individual worker-fault in job terminations and (2) insufficient wages.[7] By time-limiting the TANF program (i.e., restricting welfare as a cash support in times of unemployment for single mothers), policymakers must rethink unemployment insurance as key to assisting women in maintaining their connection to paid labor.

This chapter explores the ways in which unemployment insurance policies are infinitely malleable and value-laden. Moving beyond the false dichotomy of wage work and welfare receipt, I then set forth a new model of unemployment insurance, which integrates some of the costs of unpaid labor into the costs of production.

The Current Program and Low-Wage Single Mothers

The United States federal unemployment insurance statute was enacted as part of the broader Social Security Act in 1935 in response to the high level of unemployment following the stock market crash of 1929. The program was designed as a joint federal-state system;[8] states are authorized to implement the program pursuant to the federal requirements set forth in Title III of the Social Security Act. State noncompliance may result in higher tax rates for businesses[9] and the loss of federal administrative funds.[10] But each state is left to determine most eligibility standards, the amount of most taxes to be collected, and the level of benefits to be paid.[11] As a result, there was and continues to be great variation from state to state.

Despite this local flexibility, there are several overarching themes. The unemployment insurance program was and continues to be uniformly designed as a fault-based (only for those who are involuntarily unemployed), non-needs-based (all covered employees are eligible for benefits regardless of destitution, but coverage is restricted by amount of earnings and/or number of hours worked), and short-term (generally 26 weeks) program.

However, the application of these themes has varied considerably and evolved since 1935 as the composition of the United States labor force has changed dramatically. The massive entry of women into the paid labor force and the rapid expansion of part-time, temporary, or contract work (filled largely by women, workers of color, and low-wage workers) has been well documented and much discussed.[12] This latter group, the so-called contingent labor force,[13] is disproportionately affected and therefore marginalized by unemployment insurance qualifications.[14] It is here where the impact of unemployment insurance policy and implementation on TANF recipients is most pronounced.

Involuntary Unemployment

In order to be eligible, claimants must be unemployed through "no fault of their own."[15] While the federal structure leaves to state discretion both the definitions of the disqualifications and the penalties for losing a job for fault, most states incorporate versions of disqualifications if claimants have voluntarily quit their jobs without good cause, have been fired for work-related misconduct, are involved in a labor dispute, are not available for and actively seeking work, or have turned down a suitable job.

In the last fifteen years, states have expanded the scope of these nonmonetary disqualifications, increasing the significance of the worker's "fault."[16] For example, an increasing number of state laws restrict "good cause" for voluntarily quitting a job to reasons attributable to the employer or the employing unit, thereby excluding domestic and other compelling individual circumstances; the number grew from sixteen states in 1948 to twenty-six by 1971 to 37 by 1990.[17] The interpretation of "voluntarily" quitting a job has significant gender ramifications; the impact on low-wage single mothers may be reflected in a number of ways. The NCEP study found that the main reason for male unemployment was layoff or plant closing (26.5 percent of men as opposed to 15 percent of women), while the main reasons for women to be unemployed were family/personal (17 percent as opposed to 3.3 percent of men) or the loss of a job due to pregnancy or childbirth (an additional 7.5 percent of women as opposed to 0 percent of men).[18] Yet thirty-two states find an individual ineligible if she leaves her job due to marital or domestic obligations (e.g., illness in the family), and thirty-one states disqualify an individual who leaves her job because of domestic violence.[19] In addition, in the increasing temporary market, if one accepts a temporary job, she may be held to have "voluntarily" quit when the job ends.

Likewise, states have increased the duration of the period of ineligibility. Perhaps in recognition of the dearth of available jobs at the time of the enactment of the Social Security Act, most states disqualified "at fault" workers for only a designated number of weeks.[20] After that period, the state laws incorporated the assumption that unemployed workers who were actively looking for employment might not be able to find jobs on their own, ended their fault disqualification, and found the claimant eligible for benefits.[21] Thus, regardless of initial worker fault, at some point the unemployment became involuntary and attributable to economic circumstances.

Yet, currently all but five states disqualify a worker who voluntarily leaves her job for the entire duration of unemployment rather than for a fixed period,[22] all but 12 do so for workers who are discharged for misconduct,[23] and all but 13 do so for workers who refuse a suitable job.[24]

In addition, the unemployment insurance system has increasingly emphasized the individual's responsibility for obtaining, as well as retaining, a job.[25] As initially drafted, the program scheme required only that the worker be able to work and be available for work.[26] By 1955, however, 26 states had added a requirement that unemployed workers affirmatively demonstrate that they were "actively seeking work," and had registered for job referrals at the local employment office.[27] The number of states that required an explicit statement of work-search activities grew from 15 in 1948 to 30 in 1971 to 40 in 1990.[28] The underlying assumption is that although a worker may be involuntarily unemployed on the day that she is laid off due solely to the action of her employer, she may immediately thereafter become *voluntarily* unemployed by not searching assiduously for new work.[29]

Part-time workers are frequently penalized under the "able/available/actively seeking" requirements. Over 68 percent of all part-time workers are women, and 56.7 percent of all unemployed seeking part-time work are women.[30] Yet in at least 39 states, individuals are considered not to be available for and actively seeking work if they are only seeking part-time work even when they are doing so because of compelling personal circumstances or domestic circumstances, such as caregiving.[31] Likewise, most states find individuals ineligible if they restrict their available hours to certain shifts, hours, or days (unless they are available for the hours that are normally worked for their occupation in their locality), even when the restriction is due to domestic or compelling personal circumstances, transportation limitations, or medical or physical conditions.[32] Similar disqualifications apply as a "refusal of suitable work" if an individual turns down a full-time job because she needs to work part-time in order to care for her children.[33]

Thus the unemployment insurance system has historically stigmatized some workers, regardless of the length of their previous labor attachment, who allegedly created or perpetuated their own unemployment or destitution. But, as we will see, terms such as "involuntary," "attributable to the employer," and "actively seeking work" are indeterminate and incorporate and construct societal values and ideologies in their interpretations in each case. Those disqualified under these terms can include low-wage single mothers who are fired for absences due to lack of child care, are fired when they refuse a night shift for which they have no child care, quit their job because they are running from domestic abuse, or seek part-time work consistent with their domestic obligations. Many of these women previously relied on AFDC as their temporary income support until they could move back into wage work. However, under time-limited TANF, this option is greatly restricted. The very existence of the fault-based disqualifications, by emphasizing the innocence of some unemployed workers, creates an "other" category of those who are not innocent,[34] and for whom little governmental assistance is available.

Attachment to Labor Markets

The unemployment program, in sharp contrast to welfare or "relief" programs for the needy, bases eligibility for unemployment benefits on attachment to labor markets, not need. Unemployed workers are not required to exhaust their assets to be eligible for unemployment benefits.[35] In fact, an important premise of unemployment insurance is the maintenance of economic stability in the unemployed worker's life until she is able to find another job, and much of the debate at the time of the federal enactment centered on the need to maintain the worker's self-respect.[36] In establishing unemployment insurance as a non-needs-based program tied to labor market attachment and funded through employer contributions rather than general tax revenues, Congress and the states developed a two-tiered system of social welfare, again differentiating those who are "worthy" (i.e., "sufficiently attached to the labor market,") from those who are unworthy.

But simply having worked will not qualify a worker for unemployment insurance coverage; rather, unemployment insurance requires that the worker must have worked *enough*. The failure of the unemployment insurance program to provide support for many low-wage mothers who become unemployed, forcing them to resort to welfare in times of unemployment, and the inability of policymakers and the public to critically assess the impact of expanded state disqualifications on low-wage women workers, defines them as "not attached to the labor force." This in turn reinforces the perceived dichotomy between welfare recipients and wage workers that continues to resonate so deeply with much of the American public.

Each state requires workers to meet a standard of labor force attachment[37] in order to be eligible for unemployment insurance, setting a "base period," or specific period of time, during which the worker must have earned wages in a specified dollar amount and/or worked a specific number of hours.[38] As with the nonmonetary eligibility standards, over time states have increased the required degree of labor attachment,[39] although there is wide variation in the amounts. Various studies have found that higher minimum earnings requirements are responsible for 5.1 percent of the decline in recipiency,[40] increases in qualifying weeks account for 3.4 percent of the decline,[41] and that each increase in the minimum earnings requirement of $1,000 results in a 2.4 percent drop in recipiency.[42]

This labor market attachment requirement disadvantages those who work, but retains those who are low-wage and contingent workers. For example, to meet monetary eligibility minimums, low-wage workers must work more hours than higher paid workers.[43] In nine states, a half-time, full-year (1,040 hours of work) worker who earns minimum wage is completely ineligible for benefits, while the worker who earns $8 an hour for the same hours of work is eligible.[44]

In addition, requirements in some states that wages be earned during certain quarters[45] negatively impact part-time low-wage workers. For example, nine states would disqualify a half-time full-year minimum wage worker (who worked 1,040 hours), but only one state would disqualify the same worker if she worked the same number of hours full-time for 26 weeks and did not work at all the rest of the base period.[46] The NCEP study found that 9 percent of all unemployed part-time workers received unemployment insurance as opposed to 36 percent of full-time workers.

The result for women is pronounced. The NCEP study found that 20 percent of women were excluded based on minimum weeks of prior employment as opposed to 8 percent of men. Ten percent of women were disqualified based on the required amount of earnings in the highest earning quarter versus 4 percent of men. Minimum earnings requirements disqualified almost twice as many women as men (4 percent versus 2 percent). Taken together, prior earnings requirements excluded 34 percent of women versus 15 percent of men, after accounting for nonstudent status and covered employment issues.[47]

Furthermore, all but seven states define the "base period" in a manner that does not incorporate an individual's most recent earnings, that is, does not count the earnings in the two most recent calendar quarters. As a result, single mothers in low-wage jobs that have higher turnover, and create a more sporadic work history, are disproportionately found monetarily ineligible. One California study found that, if the state counted the most recent earnings for purposes of unemployment insurance eligibility, it would save almost $41 million in *welfare* benefits currently paid to 28,200 workers.[48]

Finally, the classification of "covered employment" in the unemployment insurance system has historically been racially biased. Although the 1935 exclusion of agricultural and domestic workers[49] was revised in 1976 to include domestic workers earning more than $1,000 per quarter and farm workers employed on large farms, the current exclusion in many states of seasonal workers and certain farm workers has a disproportionate impact on low-wage workers of color.[50] In addition, many domestic workers remain outside the system both because of the dollar minimum in the definition of employment and because of employer failure to pay payroll taxes.

Thus choices about what constitutes a "sufficient attachment to the labor market" and "covered employment" for purposes of unemployment insurance eligibility are political choices laden with value judgments. The stratification embedded in unemployment insurance systems excludes from coverage a very large number of workers, people who actually do wage work. This exclusion is even more problematic in its failure to acknowledge the rapidly changing composition of paid labor markets. Existing societal biases, including race, gender, and class distinctions, are incorporated in the selection of these groups, with significant impact on TANF recipients.

Duration and Amount of Benefits

The unemployment insurance system generally provides for 26 weeks of regular unemployment insurance benefits, except for periodic federal enactments of an extension in times and geographical areas of high long-term unemployment.[51] The implicit economic model is one in which labor markets have little friction and great fluidity, and fails to appreciate, let alone account for, the increased structural unemployment in recent years. Unemployed workers are far less likely to return to their previous jobs after spells of unemployment.[52] The percentage of unemployment insurance claimants who exhaust their 26 weeks of benefits without finding another job has been steadily increasing during recessions since 1970.[53] Similarly, the average duration of unemployment and the percentage of individuals experiencing long-term unemployment has increased.[54] When one adds to this general economic trend the experiences of many single mothers who have to leave a previous job due to domestic crises, such as fleeing an abusive spouse, the short length of benefits becomes even more acute.

Finally, since benefit levels are calculated according to a formula based on a fraction of prior earnings, low-wage workers often receive insufficient benefits. According to a study done by the Advisory Council on Unemployment Compensation (ACUC), workers who earn between $10,000 and $15,000 spend a minimum of 65 percent of their pretax income on necessary expenditures, as opposed to those earning between $20,000 and $30,000 who spend a minimum of 42 percent on essentials. Yet 38 states pay sufficient unemployment insurance to cover the essentials for the higher-paid worker, while only three states pay sufficient benefits for the low-wage worker.[55]

Likewise part-time workers are penalized in terms of benefit amounts. Weekly and total potential benefit amounts vary considerably among workers who have worked at the same wage for the same number of total hours in their base period. For workers at most wage rates, benefits are significantly higher if their hours of work are concentrated in two quarters of the base period. For example, a worker who earned $10 per hour and worked for 1,040 hours in the base period would be eligible for an average weekly benefit amount of $191 if the work was distributed 40 hours per week in 26 weeks that fall within two calendar quarters. The same worker, however, would receive an average weekly benefit amount of $110 (only 58 percent of $191) if the work was distributed 20 hours per week for 52 weeks.

These interpretations of non-neutral concepts have resulted in policies that exclude many low-wage, part-time, or temporary workers from the receipt of unemployment insurance benefits in various states:

- disqualification as a "voluntary quit" of workers who leave their jobs due to family or medical emergencies, or due to sexual harassment;
- longer disqualification periods, so that now most states disqualify a worker for the entire period of unemployment;
- disqualification as "unavailable" of workers who are able or willing to only take part-time work, even when they meet the monetary eligibility requirements;
- disqualification of many part-year or seasonal workers, who are disproportionately women, by excluding more recent earnings from the base period used to calculate monetary eligibility;
- disqualification because the amount of earnings required to qualify as sufficiently attached to the labor force is too high for low-wage workers, or is required in an intensive, full-time attachment;
- discontinuity between an unemployment insurance system designed to respond to short-term unemployment and the increasing presence of long-term unemployment;
- inadequate benefit amounts for low-wage or part-time workers.

As a result, many single mothers, who have substantial ties to paid labor, but whose ties are through part-time, temporary, recent, and low-wage jobs, or who are required to leave their jobs due to conflicts between their paid labor and their unpaid labor, are ineligible for unemployment insurance.

Reenvisioning the Program: Valuing Paid/Unpaid Work

Traditional Unemployment Insurance Advocacy

Policymakers and advocates often see the unemployment insurance system as a classic democratic reform system that does not call into question, but rather supports, the dominant institutions of labor markets. Unemployment insurance, while having some potential to redistribute wealth, is not an actor in redistributing power or transforming core institutions. Even though the unemployment insurance program was the "worthy" program contrasted to AFDC, the program from its inception still treated income insecurity as individual misfortune. The development of unemployment insurance was partly a response to more radical proposals for universal jobs and a social wage—for example, the contemporaneous Lundeen, or Worker's, Bill, which "forced recognition of the social nature of the costs of the production system and of the reproduction of the labor force."[56] Thus the establishment and development of unemployment insurance was an alternative to policies that might have realized full employment and a guaranteed income. The unemployment insurance system provides a humanitarian check on, as well as a legitimation of, an economic policy that views unemployment as necessary for economic growth. It provides an income cushion for core employees, but it also has co-optative dimensions and does not serve the needs of peripheral employees, who are disproportionately low-wage women and workers of color. As a result of these conflicting views, we largely do not have a history and practice of thinking of unemployment insurance in transformative terms.

That is not to say that the idea of degendering or interstitially reshaping unemployment insurance is new. The Ford administration in 1975 pledged to "support and strengthen [unemployment insurance] laws prohibiting discrimination based on sex."

> Although many States have repealed discriminatory provisions, a number of State laws still include special disqualifications for pregnancy or automatically consider unavailable for work any pregnant claimant, without regard for the facts concerning her actual physical ability to work or availability for work. Some impose special disqualifications against those who leave work because of marital or domestic obligations, regardless of the actual period of their unavailability for work; this type of provision applies almost exclusively to women.[57]

The Congressionally established Advisory Council on Unemployment Compensation (ACUC), in existence from 1994 to 1996, recommended some incremental steps in this direction. In terms of nonmonetary eligibility, it recommended that workers not be disqualified merely because they are seeking part-time employment and that seasonal exclusions be eliminated.[58] It also recommended that the U.S. Department of Labor work with the states to develop measures of access to the unemployment insurance system, and that some of the factors to consider are whether individuals are excluded because they quit their job for legitimate family-related reasons, they are unable to accommodate an employers' change in job conditions, or they are unable to accept shift work.[59]

In terms of monetary eligibility, the ACUC recommended that states use a "movable base period" which would allow an unemployed worker to financially qualify for unemployment insurance based on earnings in the most recently completed four quarters, if they were not eligible based on the first four of the past five quarters. It recommended that states set base-period earnings at no more than 800 times the state's minimum hourly wage (i.e., measure labor market attachment by number of hours worked) and that earnings requirements in a single high quarter be no more than one-quarter of that amount. If the earnings were set at that level, the number of individuals eligible for unemployment insurance would increase by 5.3 percent.[60] In terms of duration of benefits, it recommended that long-term unemployed workers should be eligible for extended unemployment insurance benefits provided that they are searching for work or in education or training activities to enhance reemployment.[61]

While certainly each of the recommendations should be implemented by states in order to cover many currently ineligible wage workers, they do not go far enough in structuring an unemployment insurance program that integrates wage work and family.

The Unemployment Insurance System Is Value Laden and in Turn Creates Identities and Employer–Employee Relationships

Each choice in unemployment insurance policy and implementation implicates and legitimates social values, and creates broader cultural and societal values about people's worth. In the context of its connection to poor single mothers, unemployment insurance, as currently constituted, reinforces a lack of recognition or devaluing of paid work that is low wage, done part-time or done while juggling home/child care obligations. Both monetary and nonmonetary unemployment insurance criteria are often contradictory to the goal of single mothers staying connected to wage work. Thus the choices made in the development of the unemployment insurance program marginalize certain "workers" and reinforce and create societal stratification.

"To be attached to the labor force," "to be available for and actively seeking work," or "to have voluntarily quit a job" are not terms of art with concrete meanings; they are indeterminate concepts that are infinitely malleable. By making decisions about these terms, judges, administrators, and legislators formulate the law to reflect their cultural values. For example, a woman who is underemployed leaves her job to accept employment that pays a better wage. Much to her surprise, she is laid off from the new job shortly thereafter and is disqualified from receiving benefits because she has not held the new job long enough for it to count as "employment." Did she "voluntarily quit" her job? Or, a woman who is concurrently employed at full-time and part-time jobs resigns from the part-time job because working both jobs is too demanding. She is then laid-off from the full-time job. Should she be denied benefits based on the voluntary separation from her part-time job? Likewise, of course, whether something meets the definition of "attributable to the employer" is frequently a mixture of demands at home and at wage work, for example, demands by the employer that are inconsistent with domestic responsibilities. Why should any of these situations be disqualifying if the worker is currently "available for and actively seeking work" and has "sufficient" earnings to show an "adequate" attachment to the labor force?

In addition, in defining these terms and deciding who gets unemployment insurance, the law constructs cultural values through people's identities and relationships. The failure to incorporate low-wage women into the "worthy" unemployment insurance system portrays and creates the single mother's identity not as a valued member of paid labor, but primarily as a mother. This has ramifications both for how the woman views her attachment to paid labor and in how society generalizes about her "laziness."

The interpretations of these terms also create new relationships within labor markets. In the context of low-wage single mothers, the exclusion from unemployment insurance might create relationships of increased dependency—a job structure that disempowers women as paid workers who can negotiate for higher wages or better working conditions. If single mothers know they can no longer receive TANF beyond the time limit, and if they are also ineligible for unemployment insurance, they may be less willing to openly challenge job conditions.

Of course, while policymakers try to use unemployment insurance systems and the corresponding constructed relationships to create incentives they believe will increase the productivity of labor, the effect on workers' discipline and motivation are complex and produce indeterminate results. For example, exclusion of workers from unemployment insurance might make them feel insecure, leading them to hoard specific skills, and to resist retraining and technological advancement. On the other hand, this insecurity might also enhance worker motivation because the worker fears losing her job.

Thus unemployment insurance statutes and regulations reflect and contribute to the development of broader, contested visions of both economic growth and societal value.

Unemployment Insurance as a Transformative Program

Understanding this dynamic requires us to expand our thinking and begin to reconceive unemployment insurance programs with an awareness of the interplay between wage work and family obligations. Policymakers have allowed unemployment insurance to ignore many wage workers, particularly low-wage workers and women of color who have historically been required to be in wage work. The development of unemployment insurance and welfare laws has obscured the fact that AFDC has served as the fall-back program for many single mothers in low-wage work, thereby defining welfare recipients as nonworkers. But under the Personal Responsibility and Work Opportunity Reconciliation Act, in an era of time-limited welfare, low-wage single mothers can no longer rely on TANF as their "unemployment insurance" program. Therefore we must conceptualize a new unemployment insurance structure that recognizes single mothers' ties to paid labor, but also recognizes the centrality and value of unpaid labor in labor markets.

Economic theories of "productivity" largely do not include the value of unpaid labor as a factor, or as a cost of production, within labor markets. Workplace productivity assessments are based on factors that isolate one's role in wage work, and ignore other parts of one's life as influencing, contributing, or detracting from wage work productivity.

The unemployment insurance system is an excellent example of this in its exclusion of many caregivers who are in wage work. Thus economists can discuss or speculate about increased efficiency or productivity by ignoring the costs of resource reallocation that are currently absorbed by the household, such as provision of health care and child care to allow others to be in paid labor. But what is "productivity," what is an "efficient outcome," is not a fixed or "natural" concept, but is developed by those who draft the definitions and define the factors included in "productivity." Thus an alternative economic formulation can be devised that challenges the coherence of "productivity" or "efficiency," altering the basic underlying premises in a gender-remedial direction by incorporating into the costs of production a portion of the unpaid labor costs.

As a first step toward this type of reconstruction, one can envision the incorporation of the unemployment insurance system with the Family and Medical Leave Act (FMLA). The FMLA was enacted in 1993, guaranteeing employment upon return from a medical- or family-related absence. Of course, the FMLA is quite limited, both in duration of leave (12 weeks) and in coverage (the employee must have worked for the employer for at least 12 months and for 1,250 hours during the year preceding the leave).[62] As a result, it covers only about one-half of the United States workforce.

Yet according to the Congressionally established Commission on Family and Medical Leave, "the major reason employees in FMLA-covered businesses do not take FMLA leave is that they cannot afford to do so." In order to make it possible for workers to take needed leave, the commission recommended that serious consideration be given to the development of a uniform system of wage replacement. Specifically, the commission suggested that states extend unemployment compensation qualifications to employees on family and medical leave. The Carnegie Corporation has made similar suggestions.[63] Congress has articulated a societal value in leave for family and medical emergencies, and by building that into our market structure, has incorporated the costs of these emergencies into the cost of production. Yet if we allow individuals to have release time from paid work because of family or medical necessities, we cannot then set up a monetary system that only allows those with sufficient income to take advantage of the leave benefits. In other words, if we want low-wage women to retain their connection to paid labor, we must provide a system that supports them when they must leave their jobs. We must provide a comprehensive income support system for individuals in paid labor who become unemployed.

Integrating the FMLA with the unemployment insurance system would need to be accomplished in a number of ways. For example, when an individual leaves her job or gets release time from her job due to reasons allowed under the FMLA, unemployment insurance should be available for the time leave is allowed with no disqualification for "voluntary quit" or requirements for being "available for and actively seeking work." If that leave time is exhausted, the individual should continue to be available for unemployment insurance if she is actively seeking work; there should be no penalty for having voluntarily left her job. Absences caused by personal or family sickness that qualify for leave under the FMLA should not count against a worker's attendance record for purposes of a misconduct disqualification. A worker should have "good cause attributable to the employer" to terminate employment if the employer refuses to grant a worker leave she is entitled to under the FMLA. The unemployment insurance base period should be suspended during the time that family and medical leave is used so that an individual is not penalized, in terms of the required labor force attachment, for taking FMLA leave.

A proposed Vermont bill moved in this direction, by providing that workers on leave under Vermont's family and medical leave act are deemed to be able and available for work, and the disqualification as a "voluntary quit" is limited.[64] The Regional Unemployment Insurance Director of the U.S. Department of Labor sent a letter to the Vermont unemployment insurance agency commissioner stating that the bill was not consistent with the federal interpretation of "able and available."[65] However, this opinion itself is merely the incorporation and interpretation of a societal value. In fact, a number of states have provided for unemployment insurance in analogous situations; for example, eleven states exempt workers who are ill or disabled from "able and available" work search requirements. To exempt workers on leave under the FMLA merely provides a gender-remedial application of this principle.

Under a model that incorporates some of the costs of unpaid labor into the costs of production, the unemployment insurance program responds to family needs that require the caregiver to take a leave from paid labor on occasion. It recognizes that this individual is still part of the labor force, and that she can become available for paid labor again. It incorporates a family schedule into the types of jobs she may need, thereby not disqualifying her when she seeks part-time jobs or has shift restrictions. It recognizes that there is high turnover in low-wage/part-time jobs, and that if TANF is structured to encourage/expect single mothers to be in these jobs, then the unemployment insurance programs must be reenvisioned in ways that incorporate the experiences of low-wage single mothers into the income support system. By better integrating the values of caretaking into the costs of production, the unemployment insurance system can contribute to the self-construction of low-wage single mothers as valued paid laborers, enhance human capital, and contribute to reconstructing the marketplace as a viable arena for low-wage single mothers.

Notes

1. See Chapter 1.
2. U.S. Department of Labor, "All Weeks Claimed as a Percent of Total Unemployment," January 1996.

3. Advisory Council on Unemployment Compensation, *Report and Recommendations* (Washington, DC: U.S. Government Printing Office, 1994), pp. 17, 31–37, (hereinafter ACUC, 1994 Report).

4. Young-Hee Yoon, Roberta Spalter-Roth, and Marc Baldwin, *Unemployment Insurance: Barriers to Access for Women and Part-Time Workers,* National Commission for Employment Policy, 1995, p. 30.

5. Diana M. Pearce, Statement of the Women and Poverty Project, Wider Opportunities for Women, to the National Advisory Council on Unemployment Compensation, May 11, 1993; Roberta Spalter-Roth, Heidi Hartmann, and Beverly Burr, *Income Security: The Failure of Unemployment Insurance to Reach Working Mothers* (Washington, DC: Institute for Women's Policy Research, 1994).

6. Roberta Spalter-Roth, Heidi Hartmann, and Beverly Burr, "Income Insecurity: The Failure of Unemployment Insurance to Reach Working AFDC Mothers." Presented at the Second Annual Employment Task Force Conference, 1994), p. 2. (Available from Institute for Women's Policy Research).

7. ACUC, 1994 Report; pp. 39–41, 117 citing to Walter Corson and Walter Nicholson, "Causes of Declining Claims During the 1980s"; The Secretary's Seminars on Unemployment Insurance, "Unemployment Insurance Occasional Paper" 89–1 (1989): 13–60 (finding that 21–54 percent of the decline between 1980 and 1986 was due to state policy changes); Marc Baldwin and Richard McHugh, "Unprepared for Recession: The Erosion of State Unemployment Insurance Coverage Fostered by Public Policy in the 1980s," briefing paper, Economic Policy Institute, 1992 (on file with author) (finding that 54 percent of the recipiency decline between 1979 and 1990 was due to state policy changes).

8. See Joseph E. Hight, "Unemployment Insurance: Changes in the Federal-State Balance," *University of Detroit Journal of Urban Law* 59 (1982): 615 (discussing the historical debates and shifts in the balance of federal-state power).

9. 26 U.S.C. §3302(a),(b).

10. 42 U.S.C. § 503(b) (West 1991); William Haber and Merrill G. Murray, *Unemployment Insurance in the American Economy: An Historical Review and Analysis* (Homewood, IL: R.D. Irwin, 1966), p. 446.

11. Margaret Weir, Ann Shola Orloff, and Theda Skocpol, "Understanding American Social Politics," in *The Politics of Social Policy in the United States,* ed. Margaret Weir, Ann Shola Orloff, and Theda Skocpol (Princeton, NJ: Princeton University Press, 1988), p. 6.

12. See generally Karl E. Klare, "Toward New Strategies for Low-Wage Workers," *Boston University Public Interest Law Journal* 4 (1995): 245; Eileen Appelbaum, "Introduction, Structural Change and the Growth of Part-Time and Temporary Employment," in *New Policies for the Part-Time and Contingent Workforce,* ed. Virginia L. duRivage (Armonk, NY: M.E. Sharpe, 1992); Deborah Maranville, "Changing Economy, Changing Lives: Unemployment Insurance and the Contingent Workforce," *Boston University Public Interest Law Journal* 4 (1995): 291; Mary E. O'Connell, "On the Fringe: Rethinking the Link Between Wages and Benefits," *Tulane Law Review* 67 (May 1993): 1421, 1476–8.

13. Contingent work slots are those that fall outside of the traditional full-year, full-time job for a single employer, such as temporary or contract work. Involuntary part-time employment accounted for 40 percent of new part-time jobs between 1979 and 1989, and the entire increase in part-time employment between July 1990 and January 1992, so that by January 1992, 21 million, or almost one-fifth of all U.S. workers, were working part-time. Appelbaum, "Introduction, Structural Change and the Growth of Part-Time and Temporary Employment," ibid., p. 1. Of these, the number desiring full-time employment rose by 1.5 million, ibid. Employment in the temporary help supply industry grew from

340,000 in 1978 to 695,000 in 1985. Francoise J. Carre, "Temporary Employment in the Eighties," in duRivage, ed., *New Policies,* p. 47; these workers are disproportionately female, young, and African-American (ibid., p. 50).

14. O'Connell, "On the Fringe," pp. 1468–70; Spalter-Roth, Hartmann, and Burr, *Income Security;* Diana Pearce, "Toil and Trouble: Women Workers and Unemployment Compensation," *Signs: Journal of Women in Culture and Society* 3 (1985): 439; Richard McHugh and Ingrid Kock, "Unemployment Insurance: Responding to the Expanding Role of Women in the Work Force," *Clearinghouse Review* 27 (1994): 1422; Maranville, "Changing Economy, Changing Lives," p. 304–30.

15. Shortly after the act's passage, the Social Security Board described the program as compensating "only employable persons who are able and willing to work and who are unemployed through no fault of their own. . . ." Social Security Board, *Unemployment Compensation: What and Why?* Publication No. 14, 1937, p. 7.

16. Advisory Council on Unemployment Compensation, *Report and Recommendations* (Washington, DC: U.S. Government Printing Office, 1995), p. 102, (hereinafter ACUC, 1995 Report); Saul J. Blaustein, Wilbur J. Cohen, and William Haber, *Unemployment Insurance in the United States: The First Half Century* (Kalamazoo, MI: W.E. Upjohn Institute for Employment, 1993), pp. 282–9. For documentation of an earlier but much less pervasive expansion of disqualification periods, see Arthur Larson and Merrill G. Murray, "The Development of Unemployment Insurance in the United States," *Vanderbilt Law Review* 8 (1955): 181, 203–4 (documenting that by 1955, 16 states had an indefinite disqualification for voluntary quit, 9 states for misconduct, and 15 for refusal of suitable work).

17. Blaustein, Cohen, and Haber, *Unemployment Insurance in the United States,* p. 283. See also ACUC, 1995 Report, p. 110 (finding that states have become more restrictive in defining "voluntarily leaving without good cause," focusing more on reasons attributable to the employing unit and less on the worker's personal circumstances).

18. Yoon, Spalter-Roth, and Baldwin, *Unemployment Insurance,* p. 28.

19. ACUC, 1995 Report, p. 114.

20. All but one state imposed a limited period or no disqualification for voluntary quit, all but two states did so for misconduct discharge, and all but six states for refusal of suitable work. Larson and Murray, "The Development of Unemployment Insurance," pp.198–9.

21. Blaustein, Cohen, and Haber, *Unemployment Insurance in the United States,* p. 166.

22. ACUC, 1995 Report, p. 110; Blaustein, Cohen, and Haber, *Unemployment Insurance in the United States,* p. 284 (documenting that only 11 states did so in 1948 and 28 did so in 1971).

23. ACUC, 1995 Report, p. 107–9; Blaustein, Cohen, and Haber, *Unemployment Insurance in the United,* p. 284 (documenting that only six did so in 1948 and twenty did so in 1971).

24. ACUC, 1995 Report, p. 107–9; Blaustein, Cohen, and Haber, *Unemployment Insurance in the United States,* p. 284 (documenting that only 12 did so in 1948, 23 did so in 1971, and 41 in 1990).

25. One of the reasons suggested for this eligibility tightening and resulting lowering of expenditures is federal policy encouraging the states to increase the solvency of their unemployment insurance trust funds, e.g., by charging interest on loans to states that do not repay the loan during the same fiscal year. ACUC, 1994 Report, pp. 100–111, 114–5.

26. Larson and Murray, "The Development of Unemployment Insurance," p. 198 (discussing draft Social Security bills, and resulting state legislation).

27. Ibid., p. 203.

28. Blaustein, Cohen, and Haber, *Unemployment Insurance in the United States*, p. 287.

29. Haber and Murray, *Unemployment Insurance in the American Economy*, p. 136.

30. Yoon, Spalter-Roth, and Baldwin, *Unemployment Insurance: Barriers to Access*, p. 8.

31. ACUC, 1995 Report, p. 104–5. ·

32. Ibid.

33. Ibid., p. 117.

34. Kenneth M. Casebeer, "Unemployment Insurance: American Social Wage, Labor Organization and Legal Ideology," *Boston College Law Review* 35 (1994): 259, 317.

35. Haber and Murray, *Unemployment Insurance in the American Economy*, pp. 28–29, 42. Contrast the prior Aid to Families With Dependent Children program, which had an asset limit of $1,500 (42 U.S.C. §602 (a)(7)(B)) and Food Stamps, with an asset limit for families that do not contain a member over age 60 of $2,000 (7 U.S.C. §2014(g)). Applicants for these and other programs are ineligible if they retain assets in excess of the specified amount, and often if they seek to expend assets in order to be eligible for the program. 7 U.S.C. §2015(h) (Food Stamps); 42 U.S.C. §1396p(c) (Medicaid).

36. Haber and Murray, *Unemployment Insurance in the American Economy*, pp. 34, 42–43.

37. ACUC, 1995 Report, p. 91.

38. Ibid., p. 92.

39. While many states originally applied an annual earnings test, states have moved to more restrictive weeks-of-work or multiple of high-quarter wages tests. Blaustein, Cohen, and Haber, *Unemployment Insurance in the United States*, pp. 278–80. Seventeen states used the flat annual earnings test in 1948, as opposed to seven in 1990; one required more than twenty weeks of employment in the base period in 1948, as opposed to six in 1990; two used the multiple of high-quarter wages test in 1948, as opposed to twenty-four in 1990. Ibid., p. 279.

40. Marc Baldwin, "Benefit Recipiency Rates Under the Federal/State Unemployment Insurance Program: Explaining and Reversing Decline," (diss., Massachusetts Institute of Technology, 1993), p. 168, Table 3.6.

41. Walter Corson and Walter Nicholson, "An Examination of Declining UI Claims During the 1980's," Unemployment Insurance Occasional Paper 88–3, p. 119, Table VI.1.

42. Marc Baldwin and Richard McHugh, "Unprepared for Recession: the Erosion of State Unemployment Insurance Coverage Fostered by Public Policy in the 1980s," Economic Policy Institute Briefing Paper, February 1992, pp. 2, 17.

43. ACUC, 1995 Report, p. 17.

44. Likewise, a two-day-a-week, full-year worker earning minimum wage would be ineligible in 29 states, but the same worker earning $8 an hour would be eligible in all but two states. ACUC, 1995 Report, p. 17.

45. Thirty-three states require that a minimum amount of earnings be received in an individual's high-wage quarter. Thus workers who concentrate their work hours in a shorter period are more likely to meet the eligibility requirements. ACUC, 1995 Report, pp. 94, 98.

46. Ibid., p. 98.

47. Yoon, Spalter-Roth, Baldwin, *Unemployment Insurance: Barriers to Access*, p. 24.

48. Al Lee, Chief Deputy Director, California Health and Welfare Agency, letter to the Hon. Patrick Johnston, California State Senate, November 22, 1996.

49. Historically, the principal exception to state discretion in this area was the initial Congressional exemption of certain categories of workers, most notably agricultural and domestic workers, from coverage. Social Security Act of 1935, Pub.L. 74–271, ch. 531, 811(b)(1), (2) (codified as amended at 26 U.S.C. §3306 [West 1989]). This exception meant that large numbers of African Americans were not covered, particularly in the

South. Jill Quadagno, *The Color of Welfare: How Racism Undermined the War on Poverty* (New York: Oxford University Press, 1994), p. 20.

50. Larry Norton and Marc Linder, "An End to Race-Based Discrimination Against Farm Workers Under Federal Unemployment Insurance, Special Issue, Unemployment Compensation: Continuity and Change," *University of Michigan Journal of Law Reform* (1995): 21. ACUC, 1995 Report, pp. 118, 165–7 (describing current exemptions for these workers).

51. Extended Benefits was established in 1970 as a permanent program to provide additional weeks of unemployment insurance benefits in periods of high unemployment in a state. The Federal-State Extended Unemployment Compensation Act of 1970, Pub. L. No. 91–373, Title II, 84 Stat. 708 (1970). Emergency supplemental benefits programs have been enacted by Congress during every recession since 1958. ACUC, 1994 Report, p. 58; Extension of Emergency Unemployment Compensation Act of 1993, Pub. L. No. 103–6, 107 Stat. 34 (1993), as amended; Pub. L. No. 102–164, 105 Stat. 1049 (1991), amending Emergency Unemployment Compensation Act of 1991; Emergency Unemployment Compensation Act of 1977, Pub. L. No. 95–19, 91 Stat. 39 (1977); Emergency Compensation and Special Unemployment Assistance Extension Act of 1975, Pub. L. No. 94–45, 89 Stat. 239 (1975); Emergency Unemployment Compensation Act of 1974, Pub. L. No. 93–572, 88 Stat. 1869 (1974), as amended; Emergency Unemployment Compensation Act of 1971, Pub. L. No. 92–224, 85 Stat. 811 (1971), as amended; The Federal-State Extended Unemployment Compensation Act of 1970, Pub. L. No. 91–373, 84 Stat. 708 (1970); Temporary Extension of Unemployment Benefits Act of 1961, Pub. L. No. 87–6, 75 Stat. 8 (1961); Temporary Unemployment Compensation Act of 1958, Pub. L. No. 85–441, 72 Stat. 171 (1958).

52. ACUC, 1994 Report, p. 7.

53. Ibid., pp. 20–21.

54. Ibid., pp. 20, 22.

55. ACUC, 1995 Report, pp. 132–3.

56. Casebeer, "Unemployment Insurance: American Social Wage," pp. 262–3, 266, 268–9, 295, 300.

57. U.S. Department of Labor, Unemployment Insurance Program Letter No. 33–75 1–2(1975).

58. ACUC, 1995 Report, p. 18.

59. Advisory Council on Unemployment Compensation, *Report and Recommendations* (Washington, DC: U.S. Government Printing Office, 1996), pp. 12–3.

60. ACUC, 1995 Report, pp. 16–8.

61. ACUC, 1994 Report, p. 8.

62. 29 U.S.C. §2611 (2) (A) (i), (ii) (West Supp. 1997).

63. U.S. Department of Labor, Commission on Family and Medical Leave, *A Workable Balance: Report to Congress on Family and Medical Leave Policies* (Washington, DC: Women's Bureau, 1996), p. 198–9; Task Force on Meeting the Needs of Young Children, *Starting Points: Meeting the Needs of Our Youngest Children,* The report of the Carnegie Task Force on Meeting the Needs of Young Children (New York: Carnegie Corporation, 1994), p. 47.

64. Vermont S. 143 (1997).

65. Gail H. Backus, Regional Director for Unemployment Insurance, U.S. Department of Labor, letter to Ms. Susan D. Auld, Commissioner, Vermont Department of Employment and Training, March 12, 1997.

9

Joel F. Handler and Yeheskel Hasenfeld

COMMUNITY-BASED, EMPLOYMENT-RELATED SERVICES FOR LOW-WAGE WORKERS

As described in earlier chapters, low-wage women workers face considerable barriers in the labor market. In this chapter, we propose a social service agency that can help these women. The agency will be community-based, focusing primarily on employment and related services. Most employment service models—at least those that have been evaluated and discussed in the literature—are welfare-to-work demonstration projects. While we will use these models for purposes of analysis, the model that we are proposing will have no formal connections with welfare. Rather, the services will be available to all who need them, free to low-income applicants, with a sliding fee scale for others. For example, as discussed in Chapter 5, the Cooperative Health Care Federation could use this service to help screen and train job applicants. Welfare recipients, indeed welfare agencies, may want to use the services, but they will be strictly voluntary.

The agency will provide information, outreach, and advocacy. It will be a one-stop agency offering a range of basic social services, staffed by interdisciplinary service workers, many from the local community. Clients will be active participants in decision making. The services will reflect the particular employment needs of the community. Ideally, the funding for the range of disparate employment training should be consolidated, allowing each local community to establish the mix of services most suitable to its particular circumstances.

Needed Services

What kinds of services are needed? One way of approaching this question is to look at the stories of those women who are successfully employed.

Getting a Job

Most low-skilled workers find their jobs through informal networks. They hear about jobs through friends or relatives, usually already employed at the particular establishment. Employers of low-skilled labor rely on the personal recommendations from their existing labor force. An essential ingredient of a work group is that the workers get along with each other—that they cooperate. Hiring—even of low-skilled labor—is a costly decision.[1]

Network recruitment has a number of advantages for employers. Using the existing social structure to recruit new workers saves costs by screening out potentially undesirable employees. Employees know who will make a good recruit and whom they want as coworkers. The social network both socializes and disciplines the worker. Employers of low-skilled jobs emphasize attitudes and demeanor more than job skills. Because these traits are not readily observable, using current employees as recruiters ensures that persons with the right "attitude" will be hired.[2] The key factors that employers looked for in sales and customer services jobs are appearance, communication skills, and personality, and not education.[3] Employers preferred the demeanor associated with white middle-class behavior. While basic language and math skills were tested for clerical jobs, high premium was placed on interpersonal skills and appearance. For low-skilled blue-collar and service jobs, key factors were dependability and a willingness to work hard and to cooperate with others. Race, locality, and class were used as markers for such traits.[4] Thus, employers are more likely to use race, ethnicity, class, and residence as proxies for desirable work traits. One of the consequences of group-based markers is that they reproduce the characteristics of the existing work force.

Child Care

As Chapter 6 on child care points out, this is a critical condition of work. Mothers have to have a stable, reliable child care arrangement. Many low-wage workers use paid family members. While these arrangements are often satisfactory, they can become unstable, and many mothers would prefer more formal arrangements. A critical issue concerns information about the availability and quality of child care. As stated in Chapter 6, most mothers—for understandable reasons—tend to rate their child care arrangements higher than independent experts. There is a need for independent, professional monitoring and evaluation. Then, there is the issue of cost. Public and private subsidies may be available. Here, there is a need not only for information but also to help the mother process the application and provide advocacy services, if necessary. Then, there has to be temporary back-up support in case of a breakdown in the child care, a school emergency, and so forth.

Health Care

As discussed in Chapter 7, many jobs do not provide any health insurance at all. Or, if health care is provided, it is either not available for the employee's family, or if available, it is costly. Successfully employed low-wage mothers either rely on another family member's insurance—most likely the husband—or more likely, the local emergency room. Health care remains an important problem for both the employed and those trying to work. The most preferred alternative would be free or low-cost primary care clinics in the community. More likely, the need is to provide information as to the terms and conditions of policies, where health care consumers can find services, and advocacy services. There are examples of health care hotlines, which are heavily used.

Transportation

A significant constraint on finding and keeping a job is transportation. Not surprisingly, car owners have a much better employment experience than those without cars; they have a wider choice of jobs, work more regularly, and earn more money.[5] Conversely, workers who have to rely on public transportation have more limited choices, spend a great amount of time commuting not only to and from the job but also for day care, health care, and shopping, and have an especially difficult time with shift-work. Almost all have stories about arriving late for work because of public transportation delays. Successfully working mothers not only tend to have transportation, but they also have a backup in case of a breakdown. In most cases, it is family, but often, employers help in cases of emergency. Back-up transportation services are needed.

Benefits; Programs

There are a wide range of programs—federal, state, local, and nonprofit—that are employment-related, for example, the Earned Income Tax Credit, child care subsidies, various income tax provisions with regard to expenses, and others. There are programs that apply when work ends (and we have seen that an increasing proportion of jobs are temporary), such as unemployment insurance, and welfare. Then, there are programs that are alternatives to work, such as disability. There are programs that apply to children—school lunches, health care, special education services—and to pregnant women. With the increasing trend of devolution from the federal government to the states, more state and local programs will be funded. As pointed out in Chapter 2, there are many provisions in the TANF block grants of which the states can take advantage. Again, there will be a great need for information, outreach, and advocacy services at the community level. The myriad programs are not well publicized and they are often complex and difficult to negotiate. For example, the New Hope pilot demonstration project (see Chapter 1), offered significant employment benefits, including a guaranteed job if one could not be found. Despite aggressive outreach efforts, only about 20 percent of the eligible adults heard about the project and fewer than 12 percent knew any of the details.[6]

Providing Services

First, we consider the needs of woman who are relatively qualified—for example, they have a high school diploma or some work experience—then, we consider the needs of those who need more assistance. Many examples of service agencies are welfare-based. While the services that we proposed are not connected to welfare but available to all, the welfare examples are relevant because, contrary to the stereotype, most welfare recipients are in fact very similar to the working-poor single mother not on welfare—that is, they are adults, they usually have a fairly extensive work history, they are in and out of the labor market generally using welfare because they do not qualify for unemployment insurance, and they exit welfare usually fairly quickly via employment. However, while welfare-to-work programs that help in the process of exiting welfare through employment are relevant, the difference, of course, is that most welfare-to-work programs are mandatory, at least in theory, if not in practice, whereas the services proposed here are strictly voluntary. But this distinction should not be overemphasized since the more successful welfare-to-work programs rely more on cooperation and trust than on sanctions.

The first need, then, for these low-income workers is finding a job. The task of the social services agency would be to supply the network-referral function for those women who lack these connections. The services would not be limited to merely supplying lists of openings. What is needed is *job development.* This does not mean that social service workers create jobs. Job development consists of three components: (1) the workers go out and canvass prospective employers as to their needs; (2) the workers recruit job applicants, assess their capabilities, and provide necessary information and training; (3) prospective employees are then referred to the employers with the assurance that the applicants will not only fit the employers' needs, but that the agency will stand behind the applicant and provide back-up, if necessary. In other words, the agency becomes a reliable source of labor, much as the employed friend or relative. Welfare agencies that have engaged in job development have succeeded in becoming reliable sources of labor.[7] Job development is to be distinguished from the current job club and job search emphasis of most welfare-to-work programs. These are services that teach welfare recipients basic job search skills over a short period of time. However, the burden of finding a job is on the recipients themselves. While job clubs and job search are useful, the emphasis is on the client rather than the labor market.

Successful job development reduces the costs of hiring and retaining workers. To accomplish this, the agency has to work closely with the employers to gain an understanding of their particular needs. As community-based agencies, they are in a position to develop knowledge of the particular hiring needs and practices of local employers. Second, they have to recruit and orient the job seekers with the employer's particular expectations in mind. As discussed, quite often employer requirements have less to do with specific job skills than with appearance, attitudes, and communication skills. Quite often job clubs are effective in presenting and working with these expectations. Third, the service agencies have to be in a position that when employers have job vacancies, the agencies will have available appropriate applicants who will most likely meet their needs. Fourth, the services have to provide postemployment support that will minimize the risk of absenteeism or tardiness. This means keeping in touch with newly placed workers in order to handle emergencies (e.g., transportation, child care) or other kinds of problems that may come up. Postemployment support is particularly crucial for single parents.

As discussed later, the service agencies will also provide additional human capital investments, such as supported work experience, remedial education, and skill training, as needed, to job seekers. Thus, the pool of job seekers referred by the agencies may be more qualified and more productive than ones reached through informal networks. This, in turn, may lead employers to prefer the agency services rather than informal networks or general advertisements. At the same time, job seekers, knowing that the agency services are the preferred referral source and, in addition, that they offer postemployment support, are more likely to use the agencies.

There is indirect evidence to suggest that programs that emphasize job development and supportive services can be effective. The Massachusetts Employment and Training (ET) for Aid to Families with Dependent Children (AFDC) recipients engaged in marketing to potential employers.[8] Letters were sent to potential employers encouraging them to turn to ET for their employment needs. A media campaign advertised the program to the business community. ET provided an Employment Network, which involved job development and job placement. Performance contracts were issued in which job development and placement contractors were paid, in part, on the number of participants who obtained full-time jobs lasting over 30 days and paying at least $5 per hour.

ET offered a range of support services, including extended child care subsidies for 12 months after obtaining a job. Health care benefits were also extended to 12 months after leaving AFDC. Education and training were available to recipients even after leaving the program.

The success of ET in increasing employment and earnings cannot be attributed to these features alone; many participants received education and vocational services, and this was a period of strong economic growth.[9] Nonetheless, job development and placement and postplacement support services were important in moving welfare recipients into the labor market.

Perhaps the strongest case for the job development and placement comes from the Greater Avenues for Independence (GAIN) program in Riverside, California, which has been the most successful program in moving welfare recipients into the low-wage labor market. Riverside case managers were evaluated and rewarded in terms of their success in placing their clients in jobs. There were strong incentives to seek out job opportunities. Often jobs would be lined up while participants were still in job club. Each local office had its own job developer whose task it was to establish contacts with employers and to encourage them to call the program when they had job vacancies.[10] The program engaged in aggressive marketing by making presentations at various business forums and contacting potential employers. Employers were offered not only pools of applicants but also screening and follow-up. Again, while many factors contributed to the success of the Riverside placements, there is little doubt about the importance of job development and job placement.

While less is known about the effectiveness of postemployment support services, it would seem evident that it is important to find ways to assist the newly hired workers, especially single parents, to remain employed by preventing and reducing work-related emergencies and stress. The employers too need to know that they can obtain assistance when they experience difficulties with the workers.

Accordingly, a community-based service agency should engage not only in job development and placement services but also in postemployment case management, at least for a set period of time after the initial employment. In addition to providing material resources, such as back-up child care and transportation, case managers ought to have counseling and mediation skills to handle interpersonal issues that may arise in the workplace. In many respects, the case managers need to supply some of the services often provided by employee assistance programs that are common in many workplaces.

Individualized Employment Services

More specialized, individual services are needed for more disadvantaged job seekers—those who lack a high school diploma or have other kinds of educational needs, lack specific work skills, or have intermittent work experience, deficiencies that may limit the person's ability to find and hold a steady job. The service agency would provide remedial education, work experience, on-the-job training, or vocational training. The approach here is to provide individualized services that are geared to the specific needs of the client. Clients who completed the individual services programs would then be referred to the job development and placement services.

While many of the needed services, such as remedial education, might seem to be available in the community, these services must be specific to the needs of the particular clients, which may differ from the needs of the usual consumer. For example, welfare recipients often do not gain much from adult education. The reason is that adult education, in general, is not suitable for a population that has already experienced educational failure. When adult education programs are specially geared for such students, they are more successful.[11]

If these more intensive programs are to succeed, the clients have to become active participants in all aspects of the program. The clients, in consultation with service counselors, have to have the responsibility for making their own decisions to participate. A trusting relationship has to develop between the employment counselors and the clients. Counselors gain trust by maintaining close contact with their clients, engaging the clients in the decisions, mobilizing the necessary services, advocating on their behalf with service providers, and handling emergencies and crises that might disrupt the learning process.[12]

An example of this kind of service is the Options Program in Baltimore initiated in 1982.[13] Options emphasized long-term employability through education and training.[14] It offered, among other services, job search, unpaid work experience, basic skill and GED instruction, vocational training, and on-the-job training. Services were individualized according to the participant's background and needs after a careful assessment of educational background, employment history, skills, attitudes, goals, and barriers to employment.[15] The staff emphasized the importance of active involvement of the participants in the program assignment decisions. Legally, the program was mandatory but the staff emphasized cooperation. Sanctions were rarely threatened. Even though the program emphasized human capital investment, most activities were of modest duration— for example, work experience required 40 hours per week up to 13 weeks, on-the-job training was 10 weeks, on average, and education and training activities averaged about 19 weeks.[16]

Options, as well as three other welfare-to-work programs, were evaluated using experimental design and long-term data (five years).[17] The gains were modest (as is true for all of the "successful" programs) but what is unique about Options, in contrast to the other three programs that emphasized job placement, is the persistence of the treatment effect. In contrast to the other programs, in Options, after five years, the experimentals were earning more than the controls.[18] In other words, the human capital investments in the participants seem to have paid off (although, again, the gains were modest). The short-term evaluation of Options indicates that the program had greater impact on those with no recent work experience.[19] Thus, the experience with Options suggests that such a program will be even more effective if it can target those with greater human capital deficits.

Intensive Employment Services

For job seekers who have more serious human capital deficits—for a example, a lack of education, training, and work experience—there has to be a combination of services. Neither remedial education, nor skill training or work experience by themselves will be sufficient. It used to be thought that basic education alone can improve the employability of welfare recipients. However, a two-year follow-up study of the impact of basic education in the GAIN program failed to show that the improvements in education alone had any impact on employment, earning, and welfare.[20] Welfare recipients tend to view Adult Basic Education (ABE) less favorably than other service components, such as training, probably because they cannot see how ABE could result in a better job. In addition, passing the General Education Development (GED) test alone may not improve earning capacity.[21] In contrast, the combination of education and postschool training seems to be more effective in getting higher-wage jobs. Therefore, for persons with more serious human capital deficits, there needs to be an integrated approach that combines education, skill training, and job development.

The Center for Employment Training (CET), located in San Jose, California, provides a relatively effective employment training program for disadvantaged women seeking employment-women who are poor, minority, with very young children, on welfare, and without recent work experience.[22] By integrating skill training, remedial education, job development, child care, and supportive services, CET has achieved impressive results, with the experimentals earning more than the controls.[23]

The success of CET seems to lie in the program's guiding philosophy and the design and delivery of its services, which emphasize confidence in every participant; practical skill training in relevant occupations, even while some participants are improving basic literacy, math, and language skills; adjusting the pace and content of the training to take account of individual needs; and support services that create a supportive "family" environment.[24]

Participants are recruited through active community outreach, which includes presentations to community groups. Prospective participants identify the occupational skills in which they are interested. Assessment is followed by a three-day trial period in the training class itself to ensure that each prospective participant understands the nature and requirements of the training course.

The training classes are tailored to the needs of potential employers. As with other successful job development programs, CET developed a close relationship with local employers who, in turn, rely on the program for trained employees. Programs reflect local market conditions. During the time of the study, CET offered courses in basic office skills, data entry and word processing, bookkeeping, shipping and receiving, electronic assembly, industrial maintenance mechanic, and custodial services.

Education and training were directly related to those specific skills that were needed for particular jobs. Thus, the training course combined instruction in both technical job skills and "feeder" skills—the specific reading and math skills needed for the skill. When the skill required a certain knowledge of math that the participant lacked, she then took the necessary math module, and when she mastered it, she returned to the skill training. In addition, the participant may also spend one or two hours a day in a supplementary class to complete a GED certificate or in an English as a second language (ESL) class to improve fluency. The key to the effectiveness of the training program then was the integration of the skill training with the remedial education. In contrast to the conventional training approach, here, participants can see the value and importance of the educational component as it relates directly to their vocational interest.

Instruction is based on individual coaching rather than on the conventional classroom pattern. CET has an open-entry policy; therefore, each class may include participants at different stages of training, with the advanced trainees helping the less advanced. On average, participants spend 26 weeks in training and education. CET provides a child care center at the training site especially designated for infant and toddler care.

CET engages in significant job development activities. There is an Industrial Advisory Board, consisting of representatives of the major employers in the community. A cadre of job developers is assigned to cultivate relations with employers, identify job openings, prepare the participants to enter the job market, refer the participants to employers, and follow-up after employment placement. The job developers actively scan the labor market, visit potential employers, and promote close relations between them and the program. As a result, CET regularly gets job orders from employers. The job developers are also responsible for job placement, which is greatly facilitated by their knowledge of the employers. Indeed, one of the attractions of the program to potential participants is the recognition that the program has access to jobs.

CET is expensive, but not excessively. The average cost per enrollee is estimated to be $3,573, while the average cost per woman entering education and training was $5,232 (1986 dollars).[25] By comparison, the average costs for the educational and training component of Massachusetts ET ranged from $1,660 to $1,988[26] and was about $3,000 in the Maryland Employment Initiative Program.[27] In the GAIN program, the average cost per experimental ranged from a high of $6,622 in Alameda County, which emphasized education and training, to a low of $2,963 in Riverside, which emphasized job placement (1993 dollars). Thus, the costs of CET are not unusually high, especially if one keeps in mind that the program provided on-site child care services. On average, child care costs represented 28 percent of the total cost of the program.

Despite the high costs, CET was cost-effective. From a social perspective, CET produced a net benefit of $1,200 per treatment group member over five years, or a return of $1.28 to society for every dollar of cost. From the participant perspective, CET generated a modest net benefit of $2,371 per treatment group member over five years.

The experience with CET suggests that such a program, coupled with appropriate support services, might be useful for women seeking work but who lack the requisite education and work experience. It provides them with an opportunity to acquire the necessary skills and work experience to make them employable, but through a gradual and controlled process that is not overwhelming.

Thus far, we have described what we believe should be the substance of employment services. How should these services be organized?

The Organization of Employment-Related Services

Effective employment services are individualized and flexible, responding to the different needs of clients; workers and clients enter into mutually supportive, trusting, cooperative relationships; and services have to be patient for clients that have long-term needs.[28]

What are the organizational prerequisites for such employment services? First, there has to be an articulated mission that can be translated into a set of clear objectives. For example, ET, CET, and Riverside, while very different, each had a coherent and unambiguous mission that was institutionalized throughout the organization and manifested in every service component. ET believed that welfare recipients wanted to work, that these desires would be fulfilled if the recipients acquired the necessary human capital improvements and placement services, and that recipients must make their own choices voluntarily. In Riverside, it was the notion that work, any work, is better than being on welfare and that employment placement is the most critical step in the road toward self-sufficiency; while recipients had the responsibility to take a job, both success and failure was the joint responsibility of both the client and the agency.

The mission statement reflects the agency's *moral conception of the client.* All human service agencies explicitly or implicitly construct a moral conception of the clients. This moral conception defines the program's commitment to its clients, the expectations that it sets for them and for its staff, and the type of relations the staff will develop with their clients. In contrast, when the agency views the client as an object rather than a subject, the program will circumscribe its investment in the clients, lower its expectations about what results can be achieved, and the staff will develop an impersonal, if not, distrusting relationship with their clients. Self-fulfilling prophecies that are set in the recruitment process extend throughout the program, including evaluation during which the staff in their behavior and the clients in their response will confirm the negative moral conception. In a word, clients with problems become problems. Conversely, to be successful, human services agencies must ascribe to their clients a high social worth, assume that they are amenable to change, and grant them the capacity to be active participants in the decisions about their fate. When clients are viewed as subjects, workers become partners. The first step, then, is for the agency to define the client.

Agencies, whether public, not-for-profit, or private, require political support from the external environment for legitimacy. This is especially true for community-based agencies. Program leaders have to establish links with and mobilize supporting constituencies, interest groups, and stakeholders. Especially if agencies are publicly funded, they need the support of important political office holders. They also need support from other important stakeholders. For employment-related agencies, stakeholders would include, first and foremost, the business community and especially local low-wage employers; they would also include other civic organizations, and educational and training programs. At the same time, the program also needs to be buffered from political interferences by interest groups that may wish to use it to obtain side-benefits, such as political patronage, or a supply of cheap labor. Thus, the legitimacy of the program must be based on the professionalism of its staff, which we discuss shortly.

Effective programs must have sufficient external resources. Many public work programs fail because, among other things, they have insufficient resources. In contrast, all of the successful programs were adequately funded.

Resources not only have to be sufficient, they also have to be stable. A program that struggles year in and year out with the uncertainty of resources cannot take a long-term view of its mission and have the patience to work with clients who have more long-term needs.

A comprehensive employment service has to develop a network with other community-based services to complement its core services.[29] Links with employers are, of course, essential, but the network must also include educational and training programs, child care services, health care, mental health and counseling services, and so forth. Clients who are referred must not only obtain the necessary services, but the services have to be structured in the same manner as described for the employment services—that is, the clients must be co-participants in the decision-making process, and the services have to flexible and individually tailored. This asks a lot of cooperating agencies; it can be accomplished only if, among other things, each of the cooperating agencies perceives that a distinct benefit will be derived from the relationship. That is, an educational program will respond favorably to referrals of clients if, for example, it obtains additional resources or its legitimacy is enhanced. As pointed out, standard ABE programs usually are not appropriate for students who have had poor educational experiences. Again, considerable research on interorganizational relations points to the importance of such an exchange network to the effectiveness of the organizations.[30]

Finally, the program must be embedded in the local community. This includes not only the local formal structures but also informal networks. Residents of the community, especially those who might need its services, must become stakeholders in the program. Thus, the program must engage in extensive outreach—to neighborhood organizations and other grass-roots activities. Behn defines such outreach activities as being "close to the customer."[31] He describes, for example, how ET used focus groups consisting of current and former welfare recipients, teen parents, and residents of public housing to try to identify the most effective ways to reach out to these potential clients.[32] Louise Trubek, in Chapter 7, describes the various roles of patient–community group liaisons with health care institutions; there are locally based organizations that provide information and advocacy services to uninsured, as well as insured, patients. Successful organizations use local workers and former clients. Residents are much more likely to use a program when they develop a sense of ownership.

As to internal structure, the mission of the employment services has to be translated into a set of concrete and measurable outcome objectives. Successful employment programs have developed a number of performance criteria—for example, the number of clients with limited work experience that are placed in jobs lasting for a certain period, the number of clients whose reading and computational skills have been raised above a certain level, the proportion of clients needing child care that are, in fact, enrolled in licensed child care facilities, and so forth. Once such accountability is agreed upon, the staff should be given considerable autonomy, relying on their professional knowledge and experience, to accomplish the objectives. It is the combination of clarity and specificity of outcomes and internal flexibility in attaining them that is a key prescription to organizational effectiveness in people-changing organizations.

The success of the staff must be tied to the success of the clients. Staff success has to be both material and ideological, that is, the tangible, material rewards reinforce the agency conception of the client and the worker's professional self-identification as a partner with the client. Tangible, material rewards should be linked to the service outcomes. The more successful the clients are at becoming employable and self sufficient, the greater the rewards their staff obtain. To avoid creaming, the rewards should be weighted by the degree of difficulty the clients present. By granting staff discretion on how best to serve their individual clients, the service technology must encourage individualized attention so that the staff can tailor the services to the specific needs of the clients. The ideological component builds on the moral conception of the client. As stated, the clients must become active participants in the service delivery process. They must be given a real voice in deciding what services they need, and they must be given choices if they are to have a stake in getting successful outcomes. When clients are given choices and an active voice, they also share with their workers the responsibility for the consequences. Having such responsibility means that the clients, as well as the staff, have a stake in the rewards of success and the costs of failure. The relationship becomes interdependent. It is through such interdependence that a trusting relationship, so fundamental to the success of the program, can begin to emerge.[33] In other words, the relationship between staff and client is based on a moral conception of the client as a subject, on the staff recognition that the client must be an active part of the employment project, and on the development of a trusting relationship, and is strengthened by material benefits for both the staff and the client. A service technology so defined requires staff with professional training and expertise. Professionalism involves not only technical skills, but also adherence to a code of conduct that grants clients high moral worth, acknowledges their potential to succeed, and respects and protects their rights.

As stated, the services are to be community-based. Traditionally, local communities (e.g., counties) have been given considerable discretion in how to implement their work programs, often under broad and vague outcome requirements. In many cases, these programs succumb to the local political and economic forces that push the program and serve to benefit various local interest groups rather than the needs of the clients. The model that is proposed here recognizes that for the program to be effective it must be sensitive to the local community. But, by requiring the program to adhere closely to very explicit outcome objectives, and by making the resources available to the program contingent on attaining these objectives, hopefully, the program is prevented from subverting or displacing its service goals.

Replication

A major failing in social policy is the blind replication of seemingly successful programs, which are more often than not, demonstration projects. The present example is the Riverside welfare-to-work program. First California, and now most state programs, want to apply the Riverside model as *the* welfare-to-work program. However, Riverside crucially depended on certain features that are probably unique to that agency. The first, and most obvious feature, was the charismatic head of the agency. Lawrence Townsend had a missionary zeal, which he was able to impart to his staff. Even though there was some evidence of staff dissatisfaction, it surely is unusual for the average welfare bureaucracy to experience this kind of totally committed leadership and staff organization. Second, as discussed, the staff developed a cooperative relationship with the clients rather than a bureaucratic one. And third, the staff engaged in extensive job development. As compared to the average welfare agency, the Riverside changes are profound. It is precisely this reason—the depth and extent of the change required—that makes the Riverside model so problematic when applied throughout the country to the thousands of welfare offices. This is not to say that some, or even several offices, may not be able to change, but surely it is idle to think that such a far-flung, decentralized, field-level bureaucracy as AFDC will change in such a meaningful way that while primarily engaged in income-maintenance, they will at the same time become a professionalized, cooperative, employment service.

To some extent, the same objection also applies to this model of community-based employment services. While the services will be free-standing, that is, totally unrelated to an income-maintenance, welfare bureaucracy, and completely voluntary, nevertheless, they are based on a few exceptional, successful demonstration projects. Furthermore, this model, although voluntary, is designed to target the more difficult cases, which means that the failure rate (however defined) is bound to be high and that the agencies will always feel pressure to show supporters "positive results."

In the end, one has to admit that replication will be problematic. At the present time, good systematic knowledge about the important conditions of replications is lacking. We even lack good outcome measures; for example, so many variables, in addition to effective services, will affect the employment of particular individuals especially as the years go by. Patience and experimentation are needed. Hopefully, these will be easier to come by with services that are divorced from welfare, are community-based, are universal, and are designed to help those who want to help themselves.

Conclusions

The problems facing most low-wage women workers are, first and foremost, access to jobs with decent wages and benefits and, second, support services to handle life crises and workplace stresses in order to keep them employed.

Any employment strategy must be based on the availability of jobs. With rare exceptions, policy and programs assume that jobs are available and that employment difficulties are due to deficits in the unemployed. However, the evidence is clear that lack of jobs, especially steady, decent jobs, is a fundamental cause of unemployment among vulnerable less-skilled working populations. Therefore, the success of the employment services hinges on the existence of a policy that ensures employment to those who can work.

The proposed model of community-based employment services has the following features. First, services are individualized to the needs of the clients such that those with greater human capital deficits receive more intensive educational and training services. The provision of social services is based on a professional model that relies on expert judgment and skills. Service decisions are based on an assessment of the particular attributes and problems presented by each client, and a judgment as to the most effective way to respond to them. Interaction with clients is continuous and extensive; the worker is interested in the range of client attributes that might affect their well-being. The effectiveness of the worker is based on problem-solving skills learned through extensive training and is contingent on developing a sustained trusting relationship with the clients. People-changing programs, as described here, require individualized services, a cooperative relationship based on information and trust that develops into a partnership between the worker and the client. This relationship is founded on a *moral* conception of the client as a subject, rather than an object, as a person who is worthy of trust and support. Both the client and the worker have to believe that the client is there because she wants to be there, that she wants to participate, and even though there may be setbacks, she will succeed. The worker will not or cannot afford to enter into such a relationship unless the worker believes that the client is a reliable source of information, that the reasons given by the client are in fact true. And the same applies to the client; she has to believe that the worker has her best interests at heart. Organizationally such a technology requires a professional structure. In such a structure, staff are given considerable discretion, authority is collegial rather than hierarchical, and supervision is advisory.

Second, job development is a central activity. The onus shifts from the clients to the staff to develop and make the jobs available to their clients. Third, ongoing support services are always available. When the clients experience difficulties either at work or at home that endanger their ability to remain on the job, needed services can be mobilized to alleviate or reduce the problem. These services may include emergency child care, transportation, temporary cash assistance, mediation at the workplace and counseling. The point of these services is to buffer the workers from life circumstances and workplace situations that often lead them to quit or lose their jobs.

The proposed model builds on the best experiences and lessons learned from various employment programs, including welfare-to-work, that have shown to be successful, especially with regard to poor single mothers. Two key features of these employment services are that they are community-based and they are universally accessible. By being community-based, they can be sensitive to the local needs of both employers and job seekers. By being universally accessible, they open the doors to serve men—to the men and boys in the lives of these families, and to the fathers who could contribute to the support of their children if they were gainfully employed.

Notes

This chapter is based on Joel Handler and Yeheskel Hasenfeld, *We the Poor People: Work, Poverty, and Welfare* (New Haven, CT: Yale University Press, 1997), chapter 7. Reprinted with permission from The Century Foundation, formerly the Twentieth Centuryy Fund, New York.

1. The CEO of a meatpacking plant said that it costs between $2,000 and $3,000 to train a beginning worker. Kirstin Grimsley, "U.S. Corporations Look for Incentives to Entice Low-Wage Workers to Stay," *International Herald Tribune,* March 24, 1997. "Fast-Food Restaurants Rely on Cooperation to Cut Down the Serving Time," *New York Times,* June 22, 1997, News of the Week in Review, p. 4. Harry Holzer reports that the single most important characteristic of low-wage workers is "people skills." Harry Holzer, *What Employers Want: Job Prospects for Less-Education Workers* (New York: Russell Sage Foundation, 1996).

2. Roger Waldinger, "Black/Immigrant Competition Reassessed: New Evidence from Los Angeles," *Sociological Perspectives* 40 (1997): 365–86.

3. Joleen Kirschenman and Katherine Neckerman, " 'We'd Love to Hirm Them But': The Meaning of Race for Employers," in *The Urban Underclass,* ed. Christopher Jencks and Paul Peterson (Washington, DC: Brookings Institution, 1991).

4. Ibid.

5. Jane Gross, "Poor Without Cars Find Trek to Work Can Be a Job," *New York Times,* November 18, 1997, A1.

6. Michael Wiseman, *Who Got New Hope?* (New York: Manpower Demonstration Research Corporation, August 1997), pp. viii–ix.

7. The major example is Riverside, CA. See County of Riverside Department of Public Social Services in GAIN Program, *JOBS Program: Transferability Package for High Output Job Replacement Results* (Riverside, CA.: DHSS, March 1994).

8. Demetra Nightingale et al., *Evaluation of the Massachusetts Employment and Training (ET) Program* (Washington, DC: Urban Institute Press, 1991).

9. June O'Neill, *Work and Welfare in Massachusetts: An Evaluation of the ET Program* (Boston: Pioneer Institute for Public Policy Research, 1990).

10. James Riccio, Daniel Friedlander, Stephen Freedmann, and Veronica Fellerath, *GAIN: Program Strategies, Participation Patterns, and First-Year Impacts in Six Counties* (New York: Manpower Demonstration Research Corporation, 1992).

11. Handler and Hasenfeld, *We the Poor People,* p. 69, n. 46.

12. Yeheskel Hasenfeld and Dale Weaver, "Enforcement, Compliance, and Disputes in Welfare-to-Work Programs," *Social Service Review* 70 (1996): 235–56.

13. Janet Quint, *Interim Findings from the Maryland Employment Initiatives Programs* (New York: Manpower Demonstration Research Corporation, 1984).

14. Daniel Friedlander, Gregory Hoerz, David Long, and Janet Quint, *Maryland: Final Report on the Employment Initiatives Evaluation* (New York: Manpower Demonstration Research Corporation, 1985).

17. Daniel Friedlander and Gary Burtless, *Five Years After: The Long-Term Effects of Welfare-to-Work Programs* (New York: Russell Sage Foundation, 1995).

18. Friedlander and Burtless, *Five Years After,* pp. 16–18. In all four programs, AFDC payments impact also converged toward zero by year five, but this is to be expected, given the dynamics of welfare.

19. Friedlander et al., *Maryland: Final Report.*

20. Karen Martinson and Daniel Friedlander, *GAIN: Basic Education in a Welfare-to-Work Program* (New York: Manpower Demonstration Development Corporation, 1994).

21. Lisa Lynch, "Entry-level Jobs: First Rung on the Employment Ladder or Economic Dead End?" *Journal of Labor Research* 14 (1993): 43; Cameron and Heckman show that persons with a GED "are statistically indistinguishable in their labor market outcomes from high school dropouts." Stephen Cameron and James Heckman, "The Nonequivalence of High School Equivalents," *Journal of Labor Economics* 11 (1993): 1–47.

22. Ann Gordon and John Burghardt in *The Minority Female Single Parent Demonstration: Short-Term Economic Impacts* (New York: Rockefeller Foundation, 1990), p. 22.

23. The average monthly earnings of the experimental group in the fourth quarter of the experiment by $133. By way of comparison, the GAIN program in Riverside improved the average monthly earnings in the fourth quarter by $76.

24. Alan Hershey in *The Minority Female Single Parent Demonstration* (New York: Rockefeller Foundation, 1988), p. x–xi.

25. Sharon Handwerger and Craig Thornton in *The Minority Female Single Parent Demonstration: Program Costs* (New York: Rockefeller Foundation, 1988).

26. O'Neill, *Work and Welfare.*

27. Friedlander, et al., *Maryland: Final Report.*

28. See Lisbeth Schorr, *Common Purpose: Strengthening Families and Neighborhoods to Rebuild America* (New York: Anchor Books, Doubleday, 1997), pp. 5–12.

29. Jan L. Hagen and Irene Lurie, *Implementing Jobs: Progress and Promise* (Albany: Nelson A. Rockefeller Institute of Government, State University of New York, 1994).

30. E.g., Catherine Alter and Jerald Hage, *Organizations Working Together* (Newbury Park, CA: Sage, 1991).

31. Robert D. Behn, *Leadership Counts: Lessons for Public Managers from the Massachusetts Welfare, Training, and Employment Program* (Cambridge, MA: Harvard University Press, 1991), pp. 95–103.

32. The program managers discovered through these groups that one effective way to recruit welfare recipients was through the testimonials of the children of the participants in ET about the impact of the program on them and their mothers.

33. Joel Handler, *Down From Bureaucracy: The Ambiguity of Privatization and Empowerment* (Princeton, NJ: Princeton University Press, 1996).

10

Kathleen A. Sullivan

THE PERILS OF ADVOCACY

LISTENING, LABELING, APPROPRIATING

Lawyers for poor mothers often learn the most personal and private details of their client's lives. The legislative debates and media coverage accompanying the end of "welfare as we know it" have been particularly painful for advocates for poor mothers, though no more so than for their clients. Federal and state legislative debates and attendant media coverage have often projected negative images of poor women, images at variance with what those advocates see. This chapter questions the legitimacy of advocates' use of stories based on the lives of poor women to counter such images. Poor mothers face diminishing public benefits and increasing suspicion of child neglect and abuse. This background might properly be understood as the political and social context of poor mothers' lives. Like the personal and private details of their lives, understanding this context is crucial to understanding poor mothers' stories.

Background

Even before federal legislation ending the Aid to Families with Dependent Children (AFDC) program, many states had achieved reductions in their AFDC caseloads.[1] This reduction of welfare rolls has been accompanied by an increase in child protection activity. The numbers of poor women charged with neglecting their children have increased dramatically.[2] The number of poor children removed from their homes and placed in foster care has increased at an alarming rate.[3]

There is reason to suspect that the number of mothers accused of neglecting their children will continue to increase as state-administered welfare programs, faced with declining federal resources, provide fewer financial benefits to poor mothers.[4] When adjusted for inflation, AFDC expenditures have remained largely flat for the last twenty-five years. Even before the new federal legislation, unadjusted AFDC benefit expenditures fell slightly.[5] However, from 1990 to 1994, the average monthly benefit (in 1995 dollars) decreased 15 percent, from $458 to $386.[6]

In this same four-year period, child protection activity, the process of identifying children as neglected or abused, and intervening into their families, has increased dramatically. In 1990, approximately 2.58 million children were the subjects of reports of alleged maltreatment that were referred for investigation. By 1994, 2.94 million cases were reported.[7] In 1990, states found approximately 800,000 children to be victims of maltreatment. In 1994, states substantiated maltreatment reports involving 1,011,628 children, an increase of almost 27 percent from 1990.[8]

In 1995, prior to the passage of federal legislation imposing a five-year bene-fit limit on benefits under Temporary Assistance for Needy Families (TANF),[9] the state of Connecticut implemented its own welfare "reform" program, called Reach for Jobs First. The program included AFDC benefit cuts ranging from 7 to 18 percent, and a 21-month time limit on benefits, one of the shortest in the nation. Between 1995 and 1996, while the number of families receiving AFDC diminished, the caseload of the state child protection agency swelled from 19,800 to 28,100 and the number of children in foster care increased 43 percent, from 3,300 in 1995 to 4,750 in 1996.[10]

The single largest reason for reporting children as maltreated is neglect, rather than abuse.[11] As scholars of child intervention systems have noted, neglect has everything to do with poverty. In fact, neglect is substantially overreported and poverty is often mistaken for neglect.[12] The inadequate financial support pro-vided to children in foster care is regularly cited as an issue in need of reform, yet state AFDC systems provide only a fraction of the financial support provided to children in foster care.[13] It is not surprising then that mothers receiving wel-fare benefits are especially vulnerable to allegations that they have neglected their children.

In addition, charges of neglecting children are visited disproportionately on families of color. Children born into families of color are more likely than their percentages in the population to be in poverty.[14] Nationally, children of color are roughly twice as likely to be found maltreated as white children. African Ameri-can children may be particularly vulnerable. In Connecticut, for example, Afri-can American children are roughly three times more likely to be found maltreated than are white children.[15]

As welfare "reform" proceeds, more children will not have their basic needs met. The Urban Institute projects that federal welfare reform will increase the number of children in poverty by 1.1 million (12%).[16] As changes to welfare result in cuts in cash assistance to families, more state intervention into families, particularly minority families, will result. Children who are identified as mem-bers of minority groups are found to be victims of maltreatment at rates that are higher than their percentage in the population would predict.[17] Furthermore, a child born into a family of color is more likely to be the subject of a confirmed report of maltreatment than a child born into a white family.[18]

Congress and the states have responded to the crisis in foster care by weaken-ing the requirement that states make reasonable efforts to keep families together and by easing restrictions on adoption and termination of parental rights.[19]

Poor families have always been disproportionately subject to state intervention. The elimination of income maintenance benefits for mothers and children has been linked to the removal of poor children from their parents. The number of children placed with agencies and orphanages mushroomed in the United States at the end of the nineteenth century as many communities abolished or restricted "outdoor relief," or the provision of cash assistance to the needy.[20] In the twentieth century, the Mother's Pension programs that were the forerunners of AFDC required as a condition of eligibility that mothers maintain suitable homes and be fit and proper custodians for their children. State and localities routinely found homes of unmarried mothers and mothers of color unsuitable. Officials often used the "suitable home" requirement to discourage parents from applying for AFDC, unless they were willing "voluntarily" to place their children outside their homes.[21] The standard invited moral judgments about a mother's worthiness and intrusion into her personal life that were fed by race-based stereotypes, and those in turn continue to feed today's myths about the worthiness of mothers on welfare. States in the AFDC program continued to use the suitable home requirement until the Supreme Court invalidated it in 1968.[22]

Most parents accused of child neglect are single mothers whose income is below poverty level. Many receive welfare benefits and a disproportionate number are women of color.[23] The debate surrounding the dismantling of the AFDC program has revealed that politicians and the media have successfully capitalized on an image of welfare mothers as inadequate, not only as citizens but as mothers. The current wave of increasing state intervention to separate poor children from their families is a logical extension of the rhetoric of the welfare reform debate that projected AFDC mothers as failed caregivers. This rhetoric projects women, by virtue of their poverty, their status as welfare recipients, and their race and class, as being "bad" mothers; in neglect proceedings, the state undertakes to label them as such. The inevitable consequence of neglect proceedings is the threatened or actual separation of parents from their children.

There are risks in talking about mothers accused of neglecting their children as a surrogate for welfare mothers. Clearly the vast majority of welfare mothers do not neglect their children; nor are most welfare mothers explicitly accused of doing so. In another sense, however, women who have been subject to state intervention in the context of allegations of neglect are simply formally given the label "bad mother," which the current debate about welfare has given all welfare mothers informally.

There is also a huge overlap between mothers on welfare and mothers who are subject to state intervention in the context of allegations of neglect. The statistics suggest that welfare families are disproportionately subject to state intervention.[24] Families involved in child protective proceedings often receive benefits from AFDC (or now TANF), or state general assistance programs or disability benefits under Social Security or SSI.

Further, we have seen explicit acknowledgment in the debates on the dismantling of welfare that the reduction in the availability of AFDC benefits will result in more state intervention in families. In Connecticut, for example, the original proposal for the Reach for Jobs First program included a plan to report any family whose benefits were terminated because of the time limit to the Child Protection Agency.[25] In Congress, during the debates that led to the passage of the Personal Responsibility and Work Opportunity Act (PRA) of 1996, House Speaker Gingrich proposed eliminating minor parents' eligibility for AFDC benefits and using the savings to build orphanages for their children.[26] This suggests that the people who are dismantling AFDC expect there to be increased state intervention into families as a result, though they know it is not popular to say it.

Sadly, therefore, we can project more state intervention in poor families in the coming months. For that reason it makes sense to look more closely at the experience of mothers subject to state intervention. This chapter explores how the experience of being labeled a "bad mother" in this context reflects the silencing of women's lives and survival strategies in ways that parallel the rhetoric during the debates on the elimination of welfare. Similarly, state intervention involves the disclosure and misappropriation of the stories of mother's lives in ways that reflect a lack of respect for their privacy, confidentiality, and autonomy. Finally, this chapter proposes a model of lawyering against this kind of subordination and what that lawyering might look like.

How Stories Fuel Myths about Women on Welfare

The linking of AFDC benefit reductions with stories of women on welfare being bad, inadequate, or even dangerous mothers has been a conscious theme of welfare "reformers."[27] The ways that state power is exerted to intervene in poor families is therefore a particularly important context for a consideration of the implications of federal welfare reform on the ability of poor women to participate successfully in the labor market.

The myths that contribute to the portrayal of women on welfare as bad mothers persist even in the face of contradictory objective evidence. There is a belief, for instance, that women on welfare have large numbers of children out of wedlock even though the size of welfare families is no larger than U.S. families generally. The size of welfare families has been declining steadily; the average welfare family is slightly smaller than the average U.S. family.

There is also a common belief that many young women on welfare are having children just so that they can get welfare benefits or that women on welfare are having more children to get more welfare benefits, even though that hypothesis has never withstood empirical scrutiny. In fact, unmarried teen births have declined steadily over the last several years. Furthermore, the highest rates of unwed teen births are in states like Alabama and Mississippi, which historically had the lowest AFDC benefit levels.

Myths that drive public attitudes and policy initiatives rely on stories for their power. Despite the fact that statistics and other empirical proof refute much of the popular ideology about welfare recipients, the myths persist. A single anecdote about an able-bodied, substance-abusing mother neglecting and mistreating her child while refusing to get a job has more power than a mountain of statistics that prove she is an aberration. Stories resonate; statistics do not.

Many of the myths that have driven the current effort to "end welfare as we know it" were the result of misappropriation of the life stories of the women struggling to survive on AFDC. These myths derive from details of women's lives disclosed without their consent in the service of telling a story about them they would not have told about themselves. The details were often themselves mythologized (embellished or spun), and their seizure often violated the privacy or confidentiality of the woman who was the subject of the story. An individual woman's story, thus misappropriated, became the composite or stereotype of every AFDC mother as a bad, neglectful mother who refuses to accept work as the vehicle to better her family's life.

How Myths Silence Poor Women, Concealing the Structural Issues that Constrain Them, while Disclosing the Stories of Their Lives

Myths permit denial about the painful realities of poverty in the United States and silence conversations about structural issues that need to be reformed: for example, that welfare benefits are inadequate to support a family (and that low-wage work is too), that single mothers, poor mothers, welfare recipients, and women of color are especially vulnerable to being accused of neglecting their children. These myths permit society to deny the realities of poverty and they demonize poor mothers. They silence poor mothers struggling to cope with economic poverty, particularly welfare mothers.

Our denial of the realities of life as a poor mother drives women's coping strategies underground and defines them as deviant. The details of poor women's lives are also driven underground because of the risk that any aspect of their lives might be characterized as deviant in a way that has profoundly negative consequences.

Welfare mothers have always been required to provide for their families while being deprived of the means of doing so. Welfare benefit levels are inadequate to meet the basic subsistence needs of the families who depend on them. In every state, AFDC benefits paid less than the poverty level, even when the value of food stamps were combined with the cash welfare grant.[28] Under AFDC, states were required to articulate, though not to pay, a standard of need, the minimal subsistence amount a family needed to survive. Most states failed to pay even their own standard of need. In their book, *Making Ends Meet,* Kathryn Edin and

Laura Lein report on their research with 214 "welfare-reliant" mothers in four cities. Every mother interviewed was unable to meet her basic subsistence living expenses on the benefits she received.[29]

Survival options for the welfare mother with insufficient resources are limited, and society has defined all of them as deviant or criminal. She can find a way to supplement her welfare grant, but in general, she must do this without the welfare department knowing about it, since if she reports receiving income her grant will be reduced or terminated. This is defined as fraud. She can get the things she needs without paying for them—by not paying the rent or electric bill, for instance. This is also called fraud, or theft, or being a deadbeat. Finally, she can do without the things her family needs by going without heat or electricity, or becoming homeless. We call this neglect.

The delegitimizing of poor women's survival strategies subjects poor women to stigma and shame. It requires silence in the face of the day-to-day stress of needing to provide for their children with insufficient resources. Not only are poor women silenced but their lives and survival strategies need to be kept from outsiders who have defined them as deviant. Poor women's lives are forced underground—they keep secrets.

Yet, by virtue of their poverty, of their dependence on public assistance, society justifies intrusion into poor women's lives such that they come into greater public view. "Outsiders" fairly systematically appropriate poor women's stories, revealing their secrets in ways calculated to harm them: that is, they label them as bad mothers and separate them from their children. That misappropriation is sometimes the way the story is taken, sometimes the way it is told, and sometimes the way it is used by the outsiders who hear it. This view is judgmental, one that characterizes poor women as deviant. Thus, for poor women, the stakes have been raised to maintain control of their lives and their privacy in whatever way they can.

As Lani Guinier has described in criticizing the suppression of conversations about race, welfare recipients function "as the miner's canary—the fragile bird that suffocates first from the poisoned gas in the metaphorical mines."[30] The experience of welfare mothers, if openly acknowledged, could force society to confront the dilemmas of poverty, work, and parenting. By labeling the problems of welfare mothers as their own shameful problems, society avoids responsibility for their solutions.

How Poor Women are Subordinated by Neglect Allegations and Attendant State Child Welfare Intervention in Ways that Parallel the Mythmaking of the Anti-Welfare Rhetoric

Ideology has always linked poverty and neglect, projecting the single mother who relies on public assistance as a bad mother. A similar process happens on the individual level, when the state charges a mother with neglecting her children and begins the process of intrusion into her and her family's life. Building on the myth of the irresponsible welfare mother, state child welfare authorities construct a story about the individual mother, one that presents her as having neglected her children. Like the broader myth, the individual story is constructed by misappropriating the life story of the mother. The story is misappropriated in the sense that it is a story she would not have told about herself, it is composed of details of her life taken without her consent, and frequently the state gains access to the details it uses by violating relationships that would otherwise have been confidential.

State child welfare intervention is often triggered by a report of neglect or abuse filed by a "mandated reporter." More than half of all reports of suspected child neglect are filed by mandated reporters, professionals who are required to report suspicions of child abuse or neglect or face state sanction.[31] In most states, educational, social services, medical, or child care workers are mandated reporters of suspected child neglect or abuse. Almost by definition, a mandated reporter is someone whose relationship with the person they have reported would otherwise be confidential. Most interactions with social workers, health care professionals, psychologists, or teachers, and generally the records they keep, are required by law to be kept confidential.[32] Even with respect to information that is not explicitly entitled to confidentiality by law, professionalism presumes discretion in maintaining confidences and not divulging private details of people's lives. And yet women labeled as "bad mothers" most often come to the attention of the state intervention system by virtue of the very breach of what might otherwise be considered a confidential relationship. State mandatory reporting statutes either conflict with or override the confidentiality that otherwise attaches to professional relationships.

The vast majority of neglect allegations are found to be unsubstantiated. Although the media decries the increased incidence of serious abuse and neglect, leading experts of the child protection system believe that the definition of child abuse and neglect has steadily expanded, that poverty is frequently mistaken for neglect, and that mandatory reporting laws have led to significant overreporting of children as abused or neglected.[33]

After an allegation of abuse or neglect is made, the state or local agency charged with the protection of children investigates the allegation. That investigation can involve not only interviewing the person against whom an allegation of neglect has been made, but their children, members of their family, their intimate associates, and their neighbors, as well as other professionals who may be treating them or who may have interacted with them, such as school officials.

Much of what is reported as abuse or neglect is based on a single incident or observation, such as a school-age child observed out of school, or a child observed unattended, or a child dressed in clothing that to the reporter appears dirty or otherwise inappropriate, or a child observed with a bruise. State law generally provides that every report of suspected abuse or neglect be investigated.

An investigation of child neglect exposes a parent at her most vulnerable, calling for her to explain what may be a pattern of behavior, a momentary lapse in judgment, or an unfounded scurrilous rumor. The investigation often reveals the fact that she has been reported and the substance of the allegations to the people she would least wish to have find out about them. In the course of the investigation and in the record that results from the reporting and the investigation, the complex interactions of mothers' lives are reduced to sound bites in which the agency uses labels like "physical or emotional neglect," "medical neglect," "educational neglect," "sexual abuse," "physical abuse," to describe an extraordinary range of suspected or actual conduct. The power of the reductionist term that is used to describe the conduct is palpable. The labels appear in documents that are generated and maintained by the state in case another referral is ever made.

Sometimes an investigation results in a conclusion that the allegation is unsubstantiated.[34] Often, however, the report itself triggers additional scrutiny by the state agency charged with the protection of children. At every step of the way, a failure to invite the investigator in, to answer all of the investigator's questions, and to behave passively, even cordially, is characterized as an aberrant lack of cooperation, which in turn can justify further intervention.[35]

Sometimes a department's investigation can result in an informal resolution, whereby the mother being investigated is required to sign an agreement as a condition of keeping her children. Sometimes the agreement requires that the parent accept services from providers who will advise the department of her "cooperation." Domestic violence victims can be required to sign a contract to stay away from their abuser, on pain of losing their children. Sometimes agreements are made with members of the mother's family, requiring a relative to take custody or care of the child as a condition of keeping the children out of state custody.

When a mother will not agree to an adhesion contract of this sort, the state agency initiates a formal court action—a neglect proceeding—against the mother. In a neglect proceeding, state law requires the agency to prove its allegations against the mother, and may provide that the mother has a right to remain silent. She can, however, be required to open her home or otherwise cooperate with a state caseworker, who can then testify to the substance of those interactions. The mother can be ordered to submit to mental health or substance abuse evaluations, the results of which can be used against her. She can be required to accept counseling, parenting classes, or other services. And all of the professionals she encounters along the way can be compelled to testify against her. She can be compelled to release records of her own or her children's medical or psychiatric treatment.

Often, the first time she comes to the attention of the judicial system is because the state agency has gone into court without her knowledge to seek temporary custody of her children. She learns of this court proceeding when workers come with police officers to take her child away. Whether or not her child is taken away from her at the commencement of the court proceeding, an attorney will be appointed for her child. This attorney has a right to weigh-in on whether she has committed any acts of neglect and has a right to question her child without her consent and outside her presence.

If her children are removed at the commencement of a neglect proceeding, she has a right to a hearing to contest their removal. The hearing may not be scheduled for two weeks or longer after her children are removed, however. In most states, if she is indigent, the state appoints a lawyer to represent her. Like the professionals who likely reported on her, the lawyer promises her confidentiality. In this context, it would not be surprising if the woman were suspicious of the promise of confidentiality.

An Approach to Advocacy for Low-Income Mothers Accused of Neglect

A mother who has experienced this kind of disruption of her family may not come to a relationship with a court appointed lawyer prepared to trust that lawyer. She may not be willing to confide in that lawyer; she may need to keep secrets. She may wish to avoid her lawyer in the same the way she seeks to avoid the intrusion of the state. Any hope this lawyer-outsider has of gaining a mother's trust requires that the lawyer respect her privacy and confidentiality more than the players she has met in the system so far.

Most mothers resist the label that they are bad mothers or have neglected their children. Mothers accused of neglecting their children, at least those I have encountered, profess the love for their children that I profess for my child. Most mothers accused of neglect face enormous obstacles in caring for their children (and do so nonetheless).

Ideally, a lawyer defending the mother accused of neglect collaborates with her in resisting the bad mother label and its attendant state intrusion into her family. Such a model of lawyering may contribute to the client's telling of her own story in ways that break her silence and challenge labeling of her as a bad mother.

Collaboration with the mother accused of neglect looks very different from the prevailing model of lawyering in this setting. The prevailing model of advocacy for mothers accused of neglect is often less than fully adversarial. It encourages admitting neglect allegations and consenting to the attendant state intervention, even when it means the state retains custody of the children. I will call this a strategy of cooperation. A lawyer might pursue this cooperation strategy unselfconsciously, the theory being that most mothers in this situation need services anyway, so what is the harm? An attorney representing a mother may not have a very good relationship with the client and may not stay in close contact with her, not just because the lawyer does not make an effort to do so, but because the client does not either. Clients, not surprisingly, often find it hard to distinguish their lawyer from the other nosy, intrusive people who want to "help" them. This is particularly the case when a lawyer sees the focus of her representation as encouraging a client to cooperate with the authorities, as opposed to resisting them.

The cooperation strategy, while not designed to forge alliances with clients, allows the lawyer to develop allegiances with other attorneys, judges, and agency workers. (Perhaps not coincidentally, these players, like the lawyers but unlike the clients, are most often white.) The cooperation model is inhibited when the client does not tell the lawyer everything. (For one thing, it inhibits the lawyer's ability to share that information with the state.) Secrets are a problem for the cooperation model. It is relatively easy for the lawyer to detach himself from the mother and her objectives.

The alternative model endeavors toward collaborating with the client in pursuing her strategy of resistance. One obvious feature of this model is that it is more adversarial than the cooperation model. In this model, the lawyer, conscious of the ways she appears complicit with the state, operates in ways that offer the potential to differentiate her from those state players in the process and convince the mother that the lawyer really is "on her side." One way the lawyer can make herself look different is by recognizing and objecting to violations of the client's confidentiality by others. The lawyer moving toward a collaboration with her client in resisting the state's bad mother label and its attendant intervention is not detached, but passionate in her attempts to collaborate with her client, even if her client appears to be resisting her.

A lawyer seeking collaboration with a mother accused of neglect must mean more by confidentiality than what is traditionally meant by other players in the system. She may even need to hold herself to a higher standard of confidentiality than that contemplated by the Lawyer's Code of Professional Responsibility. For example, the Lawyer's Code permits intrafirm disclosures, so that a lawyer is free under the code to share client information with her law partners and other staff members. The lawyer seeking collaboration with her client will make sure that her client understands this exception to the confidential relationship she promises and may not act on it without the client's consent. Even then, she may refrain from sharing information about the client and her case within the firm unless doing so assists the lawyer in handling the client's case more effectively.

The lawyer seeking to collaborate with her client distinguishes herself from other players in the system by showing greater attention to the client's privacy. Appearing at the client's home unannounced, a strategy often employed by caseworkers, child protection investigators, and "service" providers, will be inherently suspect. Even if the client does not have a telephone, or has been difficult to reach, the lawyer seeking collaboration will avoid communicating with her client in ways she is likely to find intrusive.

The Dilemma of Storytelling for the Anti-Subordination Lawyer

This brings me back to the dilemma of using stories to counter negative myths about welfare mothers and mothers accused of neglecting their children. The public conversations that have resulted in the dismantling of the AFDC program have mythologized a pathology of welfare mothers, misappropriating the stories of women on welfare in the process. I am tempted to tell a counter-narrative from my perspective as a lawyer and law professor who represents mothers on welfare. The story I could tell would portray these mothers more sympathetically and, I believe, more accurately.

However, I come into contact with women who live in poverty and are accused of neglect as their lawyer. I learn their stories in the context of a relationship I have with them, a relationship I hold out to them as confidential. Retelling their stories, even in the anonymous or composite ways narrative legal scholars traditionally tell stories, may yet be a misappropriation of those stories and a violation of the confidential relationship I hold out to them. I have not gotten their consent, and it would not be fair of me to ask for it. I may try to use a story anonymously without the client's consent. I may not use her name and I may change some identifying details, but I am not sure whether that solves the problem or makes it worse. Can I ever be sure whether she or someone she knows will not recognize her from what I write or say, or think they do?

Furthermore, while the stories I tell might be more accurate than those told by a journalist or politician, they are not necessarily the stories my clients would tell about their own lives. Any glimpse I have into a poor woman's life is at best incomplete. To me, she is a hero struggling against impossible odds; I am not sure she sees herself that way, or would appreciate my saying so. To me, someone who admits difficulty managing stress, her demeanor may appear incomprehensibly calm. To me, someone who values space and has the good fortune to live in a house, her apartment may appear dark, tiny, and cramped. I suspect she would resent that description.

In speaking out about welfare cuts, I have sometimes, in spite of my concerns, offered counterexamples of the prevailing negative images of poor women I saw portrayed, without names or much detail, that presented the world of welfare as punishing my clients for their responsibility, or standing in the way of their efforts to better themselves.[36] However, the stakes for a mother who confronts a charge of child neglect are greatly increased, and the safe spaces are few. If I share information about her with you, even in ways that purport to protect her identity, have I not appropriated her story and compromised my trustworthiness? Implicit in this criticism is a concern that the traditional ways that I (and others who employ narrative) shield identity is inadequate.

I am indebted to a group of young mothers for raising my consciousness about what it means to shield a client's identity and the problems associated with telling stories based on clients' experiences without seeking their consent. For the last several years, my law students have participated in a joint class with students from a teen parenting class in a local high school. In one class, I had the law and high school students participate in a case selection exercise. In the exercise, the students are put in the role of a lawyer with limited resources who must choose among a number of potential clients seeking her services. The client profiles were based on former clients of my office. As I always do, I changed the clients' names and certain details to preserve confidentiality.

Nevertheless one of the high school students believed she had recognized a client on whom the problem was based. The student asked me whether I had gotten permission to use the clients' stories. For the most part I had not.

The Lessons of Listening and Collaboration

There is a risk that not speaking is merely collaborating in the silencing of welfare recipients. When those of us with a more realistic view of mothers on welfare have ceded the ground to those who do not, politicians and journalists get away with calling the elimination of a safety net for poor families welfare "reform" and the elimination of food stamps for legal immigrants "immigration reform." The struggle remains to reveal the real issues facing welfare mothers respectfully. Respectful speaking out guards the confidentiality of women who entrusted their stories to the lawyer, acknowledges both that those stories belong to the client and the limits of the lawyer's standpoint, and minimizes the ability of less sympathetic and knowledgeable others to use the information the lawyer might provide in ways that harm her clients.

We can also take a less powerful, more collaborative role, however: one of listening and nurturing safe spaces where women can emerge to tell their own stories. We can do this both in the course of our individual advocacy and in our work with groups of mothers. The stories women cycling off welfare or accused of neglecting their children tell about their own lives are more authentic than any their lawyer might tell on their behalf. When those stories are heard, they will lead to a more constructive dialogue about the problems of work as a solution to poverty.

Some of these stories are already being told as current and former welfare recipients and welfare rights groups, sometimes with the assistance of lawyers, engage in narrative advocacy strategies orally, in writing, and in film. These individuals and groups have a sophisticated understanding of the risks of story appropriation by outsiders. They have taught us about how they are humiliated or ignored when they attempt to tell their stories, as, for example, when they have to testify in opposition to welfare benefit cuts and have persisted nonetheless.[37]

Conclusion

In the months to come, the connection between the elimination of cash assistance benefits and child protective activity will become more painfully apparent, as more TANF recipients are cut off from benefits because they reached their time limit. The lessons of the distant and recent past teach us that as benefits recede, the numbers of children separated from their parents will continue to grow.

What does it mean to access child care, even good quality child care, when added to the mother's list of worries about the safety of her child while she works is the fear that a child care worker may report her for neglect? How do the stakes for cycling off low-wage work change in the absence of a safety net, when loss of employment jeopardizes not only a source of income, but any income, as well as putting a mother's housing and her right to keep her children at risk? How do these harsh realities accompanying the end of welfare as we know it contribute to her stress? And how will that stress, when added to the everyday mundane stressors that include inadequate income, poor quality housing, and greater vulnerability as a crime victim, effect her ability to compete effectively in the job market, or parent her children, or stay away from an abusive relationship, or maintain fragile mental health or sobriety?

As the story of welfare disentitlement continues to unfold, painful, compelling stories of unfairness and harm to poor women and their children will abound. One of the many questions for lawyers will be how to assist their clients in making those stories heard. In the end, that question may more frequently be answered by listening than by speaking out.

Notes

1. Between 1995 and 1996, state AFDC caseloads decreased 9 percent. Robert Pear, "Most States Find Welfare Targets Within Reach," *New York Times,* September 23, 1996, p. A1; "Where Welfare Stands," *New York Times,* May 18, 1997, Section 4, p. 16.

2. Peter Kilborn, "Priority on Safety Is Keeping More Children in Foster Care," *New York Times,* April 29, 1997, pp. A1, A16, (citing American Public Welfare Association, "Status Report: Ballooning Ranks of Foster Care").

3. In New York City, more than 2,500 children entered the foster care system in 1997, an increase of 30 percent over the same period last year. Rachel L. Swarns, "Child Welfare Gets Extra Aid for this Year," *New York Times,* September 2, 1997, p. B1.

4. Even in the short term, the flexibility provided in the federal statute to use former AFDC dollars for a range of other purposes may result in disqualifying certain categories of recipients and reducing benefits to those who remain eligible.

5. In 1995, total annual AFDC expenditures dropped from $22,797,000,000 to $22,032,000,000 overall. U.S. House of Representatives, Committee on Ways and Means, *1996 Green Book: Background Material and Data on Programs within the Jurisdiction of the Committee on Ways and Means* (Washington, DC: U.S. Government Printing Office, 1996), p. 387 (hereinafter *1996 Green Book*).

6. Ibid.

7. U.S. Department of Health and Human Services, *Child Maltreatment: Reports from the States to the National Center on Child Abuse and Neglect* (Washington, DC, 1994), p. 3–1 (hereinafter Child Maltreatment).

8. Ibid., pp. 3–4, 3–6. These figures include cases substantiated and indicated.

9. The Temporary Assistance to Needy Families program is the successor to AFDC.

10. "A Year of the Child," *Connecticut Law Tribune,* May 27, 1996, p. 6. Interview with Linda D'Amario Rossi, commissioner of the Department of Children and Families.

11. In 1994, the last year for which statistics were available, 53 percent of the confirmed cases of maltreatment were for neglect, as compared to 25 percent for physical abuse. Child Maltreatment.

12. Department of Health and Human Services' National Incidence Survey estimates that children from families with annual incomes below $15,000 are 22 times more likely to experience maltreatment than children from families whose annual incomes exceeded $30,000. See also, Douglas J. Besharov, *Recognizing Child Abuse: A Guide for the Concerned* (New York: Free Press, 1990).

13. In Connecticut, for example, the foster care reimbursement rate is $567 or $637 per month depending on the age of the child. Connecticut Department of Children and Families, Policy Manual, 36–55–25.2. The average AFDC benefit level is only $222 per child.

14. For 1994, the percentage distribution of units receiving AFDC by race of the parent was as follows: 37.4% white, 36.4% black, 19.9% Hispanic, 2.9% Asian, 1.3% Native American. *1996 Green Book,* p. 485.

15. Based on preliminary data gathered by Jean Koh Peters, *Representing Children in Child Protective Proceedings: Ethical and Practical Dimensions* (Charlottesville, VA: Michie, 1997). Her preliminary findings based on data reported from the Connecticut Department of Children and Families suggest that a child in a white family had a 2.2% probability of being the subject of a confirmed report, a child in an African American family had an 8% probability, a Latino child has a 6.7% probability.

16. Sheila R. Zedlewski, *Potential Effects of Congressional Welfare Reform Legislation on Family Incomes* (Washington, DC: Urban Institute Press, 1996), p. 1.

17. Mark E. Courtney, Richard P. Barth, Linda Park, "Race and Child Welfare Services: Past Research and Future Directions," *Child Welfare* LXXV (March–April 1996): 99,100; Hampton and Newberger, "Child Abuse Incidence and Reporting by Hospitals: Significance of Severity, Class and Race," *American Journal of Public Health* 75 (1985): 56. In research connected to her book, *Representing Children in Child Protective Proceedings,* Jean Koh Peters gathered data on state reports of child maltreatment, and the outcome of state investigations of reports of child maltreatment, by race. Her preliminary findings suggest that at least with respect to the 44 states that provided data on the race of children subject to substantiated reports of child maltreatment, children of color are disproportionately represented in comparison to their numbers in the population generally.

18. In the states for which statistics were available, children of color were roughly twice as likely as white children to be the subject of a confirmed report of child maltreatment. Peters, "Who Are the Children in the Child Protection System?: Demographics," p. 15 (unpublished manuscript on file with the author).

19. The Adoption and Safe Families Act of 1997, PL 105-89, (H.R. 867), for example, requires states to define "aggravated circumstances" that would permit the state to bypass the federal reasonable efforts criteria and move expeditiously to terminate parental rights and make a child available for adoption. In addition, states would not be required to reunite families in cases where a parent has, among other things, lost their parental rights to a sibling. In addition, the act requires states, in most cases, to terminate the parental rights of the parent of any child in foster care for 15 of the last 22 months.

The act also provides financial incentives to increase the number of adoptions per year. It gives states $4,000 for each adoption above the number of adoptions in the previous year. Lastly, it provides for permanency hearings after 12 months rather than after the current 18 months. H.R. Rep. No.77, 105th Cong., 1st Sess. 1997, House Report No. 105-77, April 28, 1997 (p. 22).

20. Joel F. Handler, *The Poverty of Welfare Reform* (New Haven: Yale University Press, 1996), p. 19.

21. Winifred Bell, *Aid to Dependent Children,* (New York: Columbia University Press, 1965), pp. 124–36. Bell notes that local officials administering Mother's Pension programs in Florida (date) found 80% of the homes of families that applied for AFDC to be unsuitable. See also, Linda Gordon, *Pitied but not Entitled: Single Mothers and the History of Welfare* (New York: Free Press, 1994), pp. 47–48.

22. The United States Supreme Court invalidated the suitable home requirement in *King v. Smith,* 392 U.S. 309, 88 S. Ct. 2128 (1968).

23. HHS' National Incidence Survey projects that children of single parents are at an 87% greater risk of being neglected, also children in homes with incomes under $15,000 are at a greater risk of being neglected. *Survey*, p. 3.

24. *NIS Survey,* p. 3. (Finding from families with annual incomes below $15,000 22 times more likely to experience maltreatment.)

25. The Connecticut legislature subsequently authorized more limited disclosure of names, addresses, and phone numbers of welfare recipients to the Child Welfare Agency. See Connecticut General Statutes Section 17b-90(b)(2) authorizing disclosure "if the Commissioner of Children and Families has determined that imminent danger to such child's health, safety or welfare exists."

26. Jim Abrams, "Mrs. Clinton Should See Boys Town, Gingrich Says," *Associated Press,* December 4, 1994.

27. For examples of misappropriation by the media and legislators see, Lisa Crooms, "Stepping Into the Projects: Lawmaking, Storytelling and Practicing the Politics of Identification," *Michigan Journal of Race & Law 1* (1996): 1, and Lucy Williams, "Race, Rat Bites and Unfit Mothers: How Media Discourse Informs Welfare Legislation Debate," *Fordham Urban Law Journal* 22 (Summer 1995): 1159 (relating the misappropriation of stories of Latina and African American women in debates in Congress and the Massachusetts legislature in support of dismantling of AFDC program).

28. Barbara Leyser, *Welfare Myths: Fact or Fiction? Exploring the Truth about Welfare* (New York: Center on Social Welfare Policy and Law, 1996), pp. 11–12.

29. Kathryn Edin and Laura Lein, *Making Ends Meet: How Single Mothers Survive Welfare and Low-Wage Work* (New York: Russell Sage Foundation, 1997), pp. 38–39. Edin and Lein interviewed single mothers, some of whom were receiving cash assistance, and some who were not receiving cash assistance, but had low wage jobs. They identified the two groups using the terms "welfare-reliant" and "wage-reliant" "over the more commonly used term dependent, because neither welfare nor work provided enough income for families to live on," p. 6.

30. Lani Guinier, "The Miner's Canary: Race and the Democratic Process," *Dissent* (Fall 1995): 523, 525. The author acknowledges Lucie White for making this connection.

31. U.S. Department of Health and Human Services, *Child Maltreatment.*

32. See, e.g., 42 U.S.C.A. Section 10806(a)(Access to Records: Confidentiality), Gen. Stat. of Conn., Sec. 1-19, 120, Sec. 10-20 (Records not to be made public); Sec. 52-146 d-f (Privileged communications between Psychiatrist and Patient).

33. Besharov, *Recognizing Child Abuse,* pp. 99–100.

34. The vast majority of child abuse and neglect reports are closed as unsubstantiated. See U.S. Department of Health and Human Services, *Child Maltreatment,* pp. 3–5.

35. The intrusiveness of the investigation process is compellingly and realistically portrayed in the film, *Ladybird, Ladybird.* Based, according to the filmmakers, on an actual case in Great Britain, the film dramatizes a women's multiple encounters with the British Child Welfare system.

36. Such examples are included in "Listening to Welfare," *Yale Law Report* (Spring 1995).

37. Examples of this work include the following films, videos, and magazine and journal articles: Mothers for Justice and Warriors for Real Welfare Reform, "Welfare As We Know It" (1996), Kensington Welfare Rights Union, "Poverty Outlaw," Suffolk, N.V., "Welfare Warriors," Giovanna Shay, "The Phenomenal Women of Mothers for Justice," *Yale Journal of Law and Feminism* 8 (Winter 1996): 193 (Particularly pp. 221–228 (about media stereotyping) and 231–236 (about legislative advocacy), Rosemary Bray, "If Welfare Doesn't Work, Then How Did I Get Here?" *New York Times Magazine,* April 14, 1996, section 6, p. 111. (None of this work, for the most part, includes stories of women accused of neglecting their children.)

11

Fran Ansley

AFTERWORD

WHAT'S THE GLOBE GOT TO DO WITH IT?

Me: *Actually, I'm interested in finding out about Tennessee jobs moving down to Mexico, but I'm also interested in Mexican people moving up here to Tennessee.*
Him: *It's true—more and more Hispanics are moving here these days. You know over in Oakdale there is a big horticultural business with a work force that's practically solid Mexicans now. I talked to their manager not long ago, and he says you just can't get Americans to do that work.*
Me: *Meaning he can't get Americans to do that work for the wage he wants to offer.*
Him: *Exactly. You just can't get them to do it. And that's why we need this welfare reform.*[1]

As the chapters of this book were being conceived and constructed, the welfare repeal spectacle was in full swing, and government policy toward the poor was the subject of abnormally heightened interest and public scrutiny. For months it seemed that hardly a day could go by without some mention in the print or broadcast media of "moving people from welfare to work," or "getting mothers out of the system and into the work force," or some proud announcement that AFDC rolls in State X had plummeted after the imposition of time limits and work requirements. Much of this discussion centered around the welfare side of the equation: debates about the effects on recipients of public assistance, for instance, have loomed large, as have exoticized and sometimes horrific descriptions of life on the dole.

In the context of such a spectacle, contributors to this volume have performed an invaluable service by initiating a close and well-grounded examination of the work side of the (seriously overstated) dichotomy between welfare and work. This collection is crucially informed and influenced not only by recent scholarship but also by concrete conversations and collaborations with real live welfare recipients and low-wage workers. The authors have taken an important step in a badly needed process: bringing to the welfare reform conversation accurate descriptions and critical analyses of the low-wage labor market, a market that is at present the only opening to waged and legal work available to the vast majority of U.S. welfare recipients. In doing so, they also bring important themes around parenting, gender, and the structure of the social wage to public conversations and scholarly debates about labor markets and work. These latter conversations and debates have too seldom recognized the ways that welfare systems, household economies, and the low-wage labor market intersect and overlap, affecting each other both at a structural level and in the concrete lives of situated individuals and their social and family networks.

The term "labor market" as I use it here is intended to indicate, broadly and nontechnically, an array of people, social practices, and conditions of life. I mean to include, for instance, the terms upon which labor power is typically bought and sold within a given society or legal system, together with the social identity and relative social power of those who typically buy and sell it. An important part of labor markets defined in this way is the set of background rules—both formal and informal—that distribute default entitlements and punish their violation; that define legally protected property holdings; that work to generate initial expectations and limit or expand alternatives; that permit, prohibit, enforce, or ignore certain bargains, and in light of which various labor transactions are conducted and various individual decisions are made. A particularly important aspect of a given labor market is how responsibility for social reproduction of the work force is allocated (who is expected to carry out the work of social reproduction, who is expected to pay for that work and how), together with the ways work and household life are expected (or not expected) to accommodate and support each other. The characteristics of labor markets can vary from sector to sector. Within a national economy, different segments of its labor market can be quite similar and well-integrated or highly differentiated, even polarized. The labor market in the United States is highly segmented and becoming more so.

An interesting fact about labor markets thus conceived is that, for native members of a given society, many aspects of their "home" labor markets get taken for granted, either slipping altogether from conscious view, or presumed to be natural and universal features of all social landscapes.[2] The chapters in this book have the virtue of helping U.S. readers to see the low-wage sector of our own national labor market as strange: to view it with new eyes. The contributors reveal, in well-grounded detail, some of the ways that federal and state law—in areas as diverse as health care funding, unemployment compensation, professional ethics, tax policy, child care licensing, banking regulation, and labor law—have worked to help determine and reinforce the character of U.S. labor markets. In the process, they make it quite clear that different human decisions can and do produce different sorts of markets, with different sorts of impacts on particular groups. Their descriptions allow us to see legal rules emerging in various ways, sometimes from conscious political agendas and legislative campaigns and sometimes not, but almost always they are based upon social assumptions that the rules themselves then act to further reinforce and naturalize.

In describing and analyzing the U.S. low-wage labor market in the manner I have just suggested, this collection ends up delivering some bleak news about the lives and prospects of low-wage heads of household. And yet it is not a defeatist book. Several of the chapters presented here make the tonic move of pointing out recent astute interventions and innovative strategies that have emerged in particular sectors or regions in response to problems and injustices in the low-wage sector. These narratives suggest promising lines of further action that may be possible for low-wage workers and for their allies, collaborators, and advocates, even within the current set of fairly severe constraints on antipoverty policy. More fundamentally, all the authors speak with an edge of urgency rather than capitulation, with a clear belief in the efficacy of human agency, and with a mature appreciation of the deep resources that poor people themselves bring to the problems they confront.

Nevertheless, the book's message as a whole is clearly a disturbing one. Despite all the rosy talk in welfare reform circles about the goal of economic independence for families previously on welfare, the realities of today's low-wage labor market for workers who support and care for dependents are harsh indeed. Further, these realities are not just a one-time price of admission, some hard but finite rite of initiation that, like boot camp or a medical internship, can be endured and then surmounted by those properly armed with the right will and a reasonable modicum of preparation. Instead, these unblinking descriptions of real life for parents in the low-wage sector reveal a pattern of mutually reinforcing hardships and impediments that will make it exceedingly difficult, if not impossible, for the majority of ex-welfare recipients and other low-wage earners in the United States (especially those who are the sole support of dependent family members) to lift themselves and their households even above the official poverty level, much less provide a foundation that reasonably supports human flourishing.

The chapters in this volume, like parts of a larger mosaic, begin to compose a detailed picture of life in the low-wage labor market in the United States. The resulting pattern demonstrates only too clearly that a rhetoric calling upon welfare mothers to leave "dependency" behind by stepping into the world of waged work is a hoax. Large numbers of welfare recipients have already stepped into that world. In fact, many of them have done so repeatedly. But their experience shows (as it would seem even moderately well-informed and rational projections would foresee) that low-wage work in America cannot offer to families an independence worthy of the name, prevalent invocations of bootstraps notwithstanding. Jobs in the low-wage sector, even during times of relatively low official unemployment, are simply too inhospitable to achieve that: too rag-tag, too uninvested in individual job holders or specific communities, too ill-suited to the task of supporting long-term job attachment or providing reliable vocational advancement—especially for those workers who are asset-poor, who are likely targets of race and/or sex discrimination and of violence in various other interlocking aspects of their lives, and who have serious family obligations but little in the way of a family-linked material safety net.

My assignment in this Afterword is not to add more pieces to the mosaic that the chapters have begun to create, nor to analyze its various parts in closer detail, but rather to step back and suggest a larger frame that might help to put what has already been said in a somewhat different perspective. The editors of this volume are convinced—as am I—that it is impossible to understand recent changes in the nation's low-wage labor market or in U.S. welfare policy without placing those developments in the context of current global economic and political change.

In attempting to take that step back, I have found myself echoing the paradoxical joining of pessimism and hope that I believe characterizes this collection as a whole. In fact, if anything, the use of a global frame heightens the sense of paradox. Some of the worst features of the global economy look hauntingly familiar to critics of U.S. welfare policy, and the parallels indicate that what we see going on in our own country is part of something much bigger than either Newt Gingrich or Bill Clinton. In country after country around the globe, whether rich or poor, highly industrialized or underdeveloped, authoritarian or liberal democratic, governments are adopting similar measures, large corporations are pushing similar agendas, and similar social effects are being felt. A global frame thus offers a sobering view.

At the same time, the very rapidity and depth of the changes that are taking place, the reach of the global networks now linking more and more people and activities across old boundaries, the common cultural assaults on older ways of living are trends that result in new opportunities as well. They create conditions in which all kinds of people find themselves asking unusually large questions about economic histories and futures, about the sorts of societies they want and need to live in, about the lives and experiences of others far away, about their hopes and fears for coming generations. It is true that globalization allows "movers and shakers" to build transnational alliances, to create transnational organizations that advance their interests, to search the globe for the lowest wages and most business-friendly regulatory environments, to organize and carry out capital strikes against nations, localities, and work forces that resist compliance with their preferred policies. But globalization also creates pathways for new sorts of international communications between and among the "moved and shaken,"[3] groups of poor and working people who may be located at very different, but importantly related, nodes in the global economy and who have been ignorant too often in the past even of each other's existence.[4]

Although the use of a global lens cannot tell us whether our optimism or our pessimism will finally win the day, I want to suggest here some reasons why I believe the use of that lens is indispensable for those who want to understand or combat poverty in this country, who want decent jobs for all people who seek them, who want the dungeons of our economy opened up and cleaned out, who want *all* the children of the society loved and educated and well cared for. Labor markets in the United States—slave, free, and indentured—have long been global in important ways that are doubtless inadequately understood. But today our domestic labor markets, like the economy as a whole, are linked to and penetrated by the global economy to an unprecedented degree and in ways not seen before. The effects are as great for the low-wage sector, whose character will so strongly define the life chances of ex-welfare recipients and other poor parents in our society, as they are for jet-set executives who command the heights of multinational enterprises.[5]

Foreign and domestic labor markets affect each other in a range of different ways. Of course many U.S. manufacturing concerns have broken camp altogether, moving production entirely offshore. This has thrown large numbers of seasoned industrial workers onto the job market, with predictable results. Many such workers never recoup their former levels of wages or job security. They sink into lower-wage industrial jobs or finally switch to the service sector, where unions have traditionally been fewer, wages lower, career ladders scarcer, and job security thinner, but where at least these days there are jobs to be had. As these workers sink, they enlarge the pool of those competing for lower-wage jobs, a process that adds to the downward pressure on their wages. This pressure provides part of an explanation for the phenomenon so puzzling to the likes of Alan Greenspan: an economy where (at least at this writing) economic activity, productivity, profits and the number of jobs are up, while wages remain sluggish and many workers continue to voice an ominous sense of insecurity. A few laid-off manufacturing workers manage to join the small stream of upwardly mobile job seekers or to become thriving entrepreneurs. However, the proportion of such success stories after industrial dislocation is small and (not surprisingly) those success stories that do occur tend to be concentrated among the most socially privileged workers of the affected group.[6]

Impacts on U.S. labor markets are not restricted to job losses. For complex reasons—including advances in communication and other technology, changes in the law, and increased availability of support services tailored to transnational business—manufacturing employers are more able than ever before to issue credible threats that they will withdraw their capital and go elsewhere if they cannot inspire sufficient concessions or other inducements to stay. These threats, and the realities of global wage competition that lie behind them, significantly alter the atmosphere in the remaining industrial sector, exerting downward pressure on wages[7] and restricting the ability of industrial workers and their unions to organize either economic or political counterpressure in response.[8]

Of course, not all jobs are amenable to being relocated. In fact, some jobs that are emblematic of today's low-wage sector, such as those in home health care, food services, household domestic work, child care, or janitorial services are jobs that must be performed where the people who need the services live and work.[9] It may be possible for the postal service to send video images of hard-to-read envelopes to computer screens across the border for interpretation by low-wage eyes, but the wounds of the injured, the soiled diapers of the very young and very old, the discarded paper towels or dirty lunch dishes of the employed must be taken care of near the actual bodies of the people served.

Despite the relative immobility of such jobs, however, globalization is affecting them as well. In more and more communities across the country, newly arrived immigrants are filling these positions. Crisis conditions linked to economic restructuring and the impacts of globalization in many nations of the world's poor nations push many workers to migrate northward. At the same time, employers in developed countries, feeling their own kind of pressure from global and domestic competition, are more eager than ever to lower costs. Hiring immigrants is one way to do so. Their demonstrated willingness to hire undocumented or questionably documented workers then operates as a pull factor inducing more immigrants to come. Both push and pull impulses of immigration thus have much to do with globalization.

The immigration phenomenon is not restricted to any single pair of sending and receiving countries, or to any one region of the world. The International Labor Organization estimates that up to 20 million people around the globe are on the move in search of work. The introduction to a recent ILO study notes:

> As recently as the late 1980s, the migration of workers across international boundaries was a relatively minor phenomenon. Today, it is one of the most striking aspects of an intensive globalization of the world economy—with a major impact on the economies and labor forces of well over 100 countries.[10]

In the United States, much of this human movement is illegal under existing immigration laws, and that illegality has powerful effects. Some people view the significant presence of undocumented workers as a failed effort at law enforcement. To others, the lack of consistent and effective enforcement looks more like part of a rational, if somewhat messy and inconsistent, economic strategy. Important players in the U.S. economy want cheap labor. They are also enthusiastic about their experiences with a hard-working and seldom-complaining low-wage immigrant work force. The present system of immigration law and of border and workplace practice allows large numbers of immigrant laborers into the country for work in the low-wage sector, but it does so under circumstances in which it is clear to the laborers that their ability to stay here can be cut off at any time. Without genuine papers, even workers who know the law are afraid to demand compliance with it. And, of course, most undocumented workers know little about the formal rules that purportedly govern employment relations in the United States.[11]

The result is an increasingly degraded and hypocritical system. Laws setting minimum wages and maximum hours, laws prohibiting discrimination, laws regulating workplace health and safety, laws guaranteeing the right to collective bargaining, laws providing for police protection and outlawing police misconduct—all these rules remain on the books. But whole sectors of the work force can be treated for far too many purposes as though the laws did not exist. In addition, the *in terrorem* effect of being "illegal" makes undocumented workers vulnerable to abuse and extortion in spheres beyond the workplace, as well—as common stories of immigrant mistreatment at the hands of unscrupulous landlords, gouging creditors and money handlers, fake immigration lawyers, and similar unsavory characters can attest.

Of course, many employment laws are ignored in many low-wage workplaces, regardless of the immigration status of the employees there. Different legal standards and differential law enforcement create various kinds of differences among workers within our boundaries. For instance, right-to-work laws in the South have contributed to marked regional differences in the U.S. work force, and domestic and agricultural workers have long worked under "subnormal" rules.[12] More recently, the reemergence of prison labor as a significant factor in the larger economy raises other sorts of questions as well.[13] But certainly the burgeoning immigrant population toward the bottom of the U.S. work force now constitutes a special class of worker, confined in a special sort of highly exploitative market. Meanwhile, citizens—and noncitizens with legal work authorization—are freer to resort to law, but they must do so under conditions of job competition with those who are less so.[14] Ironically, the legal rules themselves end up deployed so as to create a class of people who are effectively "below the law."

Both these trends—the movement of manufacturing jobs to low-wage locations in the Third World, and the movement of low-wage immigrant workers into the United States—are signs that "U.S. labor market" is nowadays a concept that must be seriously qualified. At least for many workers, and in many important ways, the relevant labor market is now global, not national, and must be analyzed in that light in order to be adequately understood.

Capital flight and large-scale immigration are not the only global trends affecting low-wage workers in the United States. Both the post-NAFTA Mexican peso crash and the still reverberating Asian crises indicate the global nature of today's financial markets. In an international economy where stock markets never close, where governments must cope with the effects of "huge capital pools that race around the world in search of higher returns,"[15] countries are finding that their domestic economies are vulnerable to unexpected jolts as global investors react to developments many miles away.[16] Under the strictures of free trade agreements, and often under pressure from world financial institutions (both public and private), governments are severely constrained in what they can do to shield their domestic economies from such jolts or otherwise to adopt policies that are in conflict with a neoliberal agenda.

For instance, many underdeveloped countries in Latin America, Africa, and elsewhere for years have had their national economic policies dictated by the World Bank and the International Monetary Fund (IMF) in return for crisis loans or debt restructuring. Today, newspaper readers in the United States and other highly industrialized and wealthy nations also are feeling the chill as they watch places like South Korea, previously touted as a muscular development miracle, bowing humbly to the yoke of IMF disciplines in return for the country's "rescue." Meanwhile the terms of Korea's bail-out package suggest that only the boats of a few will in fact be bailed and patched (perhaps in some cases lavishly refurbished), while others will likely be scuttled, with their occupants told to start austerely, but flexibly, swimming as best they can toward a brighter, fitter, and more entrepreneurial future for all.

More economically dominant countries, like our own, have up to this point not been forced to become direct clients of the IMF, but they too are now affected by deficits and debt service pressures, and are increasingly vulnerable to dictates of globally active financial power centers. Even before the 1997 tremors in Asia, William Greider had observed:

> The wealthiest industrial societies, the very ones that first promoted the globalization of commerce, find themselves governed now by unforgiving imperatives from the capital market—a commandment to undertake a forced march to reduce living standards for their own citizens, discard old political commitments to social equity, and reduce benefit systems for pensions, health care, income support and various forms of ameliorative aid.[17]

These "unforgiving imperatives" are not motivated by some capricious lender's sadistic desire to do harm. They are rooted in a set of ideas about economic development—ideas that have gained tremendous currency in today's global economy. In fact, the spread of these ideas and the strength of the consensus that has emerged around them among many world leaders highlights one of the most striking things about what we call globalization: that it is importantly an ideological process, as well as a material one. Promoters concede that implementation of these ideas enriches some groups in society and greatly enhances their social power, but the theory is that in the long run the policies will redound to the benefit of all.

The new post–Cold War orthodoxy in development theory and in global economic policy circles goes by different names in different places. Some community activists and development professionals refer to the theory and its accompanying bundle of policy prescriptions as "structural adjustment," taking the name from the "structural adjustment loans" available from the IMF for countries that agree to undertake IMF-style reform.[18] In some international circles this development model is dubbed "the Washington consensus," in reference to the dominant role of the United States in framing World Bank and IMF policy, and generally in setting terms for global economic activity. In Latin America, the new orthodox approach is more often called neoliberalism.[19] In the United States, we are short on vocabulary. I once attended a gathering of U.S. grassroots community organizers where an African visitor listened for a while to the conversation and then exclaimed, "You Americans have structural adjustment too, it's just that you don't have a name for it!" For Americans, developing a vocabulary that feels comfortably our own, and yet is cosmopolitan enough to equip us for active learning and participation in global dialogue, is itself an important project yet to be achieved. At present, the outdated term "Reaganomics," or the more durable "trickle-down economics," might be the closest we have come to putting a popular label on the generally conservative, procorporate and pro–free trade, antilabor ideology of which welfare reform is but one manifestation.[20]

By whatever name, this new orthodoxy has been imposed on some countries against the express desires or better judgment of their elected officials. In other cases, political leaders have embraced it as morally right, practically effective, or both. In either event, its world dominance as the preferred model of economic development is at this point unquestionable, and for countries in need of aid from abroad, it is pretty much the only game in town.

Certainly there are disputes at the margins among proponents of this model, such as the differences between the Clinton administration and many in the Republican Party over the inclusion of labor and environmental standards within multilateral and regional trade agreements. Each year a freshet of research and analysis is produced, which debates and reflects salient disagreements within the development establishment.[21] Nevertheless, the general pattern of consensus is strong and clear.

In many important ways, U.S. domestic policy has begun to follow the neoliberal script as closely as other countries, though many Americans are un-aware of the global dimension to these changes. Policy prescriptions favored by the new orthodoxy include the following measures familiar to U.S. ears: cuts in social spending; holding down of wages for most workers; privatization of pre-viously state-run functions, agencies, and enterprises; high interest rates and other controls on inflation (even at the expense of substantial unemployment); promotion of production for export (even at the expense of curtailing basic labor rights); a hostility toward laws that directly or indirectly restrict capital mobility; and a deep reliance on traditionally measured economic growth as the only acceptable program for closing the yawning gap between rich and poor.

Effects of the widespread adoption of these policy perspectives are, natu-rally enough, hotly debated. Defenders point with pride to the fact that some countries and regions that have embraced the program have experienced strong economic growth, something that they believe is a foundation and key to any viable strategy for addressing world poverty. Critics counter that the growth has failed to take place in many regions of the world, and that even where it has occurred, it has been troublingly uneven both across and within countries—not so much lifting all boats as increasing the polarization of wealth, income, and life experience between the rich and the poor. The critics also maintain that the unleashing of world investment activity has led to speculative excesses, that environmental depletion and destruction continue and even escalate despite growing awareness of their dangers, and that the globalization of communication under conditions of near monopoly by a small group of media conglomerates is threatening to homogenize many of the world's cultures, penetrating and conquering not only local markets but local homes, personal worldviews, and intimate practices as well.

Since the new orthodoxy began to gain a dominant position, it has been subjected to a determined international chorus of protest from the left by a range of non-government organizations; church groups; labor unions; guerrilla soldier-poets; organizations devoted to the promotion of indigenous and women's and human rights; academics; dissident development professionals; environmentalists; and others in countries around the world.[22] These voices have raised awareness about problems associated with this development model, have provoked some important though relatively marginal reforms, and have certainly helped to show that consensus around the new orthodoxy is far from universal. Interestingly, the key terms with which these critics attempt to articulate their critique (words like participation, democracy, and sustainability, for instance) are repeatedly absorbed into the dominant discourse, but with remarkably little effect on core policy or practice.[23] And critics have not yet succeeded in articulating or demonstrating an alternative development strategy with wide appeal and credibility. Meanwhile, around the world there are also critics to the right of conventional neoliberalism. Some of these rightward critics are tied to fundamentalist religions. Many call upon strong patriarchal traditions—both secular and religious. Many play intensely to local xenophobias and narrow protectionism.

In my own view, sharp critique of the reigning model and the development of viable alternative programs are defining challenges for progressives at this juncture. In the years immediately ahead, those tasks must and will engage the hearts and minds of people all over the world who are working for a more equitable, democratic, and sustainable order. In fact (and despite how silly it sounds to say so), the future of the planet depends in important part upon the development and communication of those critiques and alternatives.

Such aspirational talk brings me back to the paradox with which I began these reflections. For people concerned about conditions of life in the low-wage labor market in the United States, the view through a global lens can be disheartening. Such a lens makes clear that many changes afoot in our own country—everything from a radically altered antipoverty policy to the reconception of the employment relation and the virtual collapse of enforceable accountability to employees or communities on the part of footloose corporations—are part of a much bigger set of developments that the U.S. electorate could not dream of controlling, even if we were to wrest back our electoral system tomorrow from the campaign finance networks in which it is currently entangled. This global lens makes clear that fields of social contest are shifting to transnational places and spaces where democratic institutions have barely been imagined, much less won, that the ideological assumptions and rhetorical strategies deployed in the debates over welfare reform in the United States are not the products of a short-term political wind within our national borders, but are part of a global ideological project whose present dominance, although unstable and under challenge, is nevertheless profound and far-reaching.

In the context of these global developments, it is apparent that many of the policy directions suggested by contributors to this book are running counter to a powerful current. For instance, several of the essays call for much fuller social integration of the costs of production and reproduction, rather than letting those costs fall so heavily, and often catastrophically, on the households of individuals who are unemployed or working in low-wage positions.

Such integration might be achieved in a fairly direct way by requiring more internalization of costs by the specific enterprises that help to generate them. We could require, for example, that present systems of employment-linked health insurance, retirement benefits, and unemployment insurance be stretched to include many of those workers currently left out, such as part-time, or short-term, or otherwise contingent employees. Or we could raise the minimum wage to a "livable" level, or impose tougher standards restricting industrial pollution of dumpsites near and far.

But such suggestions cut directly against the grain of current global trends. In today's globalizing economy, businesses—often with great success—are fighting against internalization of impacts and for the precisely opposite strategy. They are shedding costs, externalizing responsibilities, and shifting all kinds of risks down and away, rather than shouldering them. Today's business enterprises are becoming lean and mean: downsizing, outsourcing, disinvesting, hiring temps, and hollowing out their corporate shells—with the result that workers and local communities are generally finding themselves more marginalized than integrated, more thrown back on their own resources than folded into a corporate plan, less able to rely on their jobs to provide day-to-day or year-to-year security.

Of course, requiring direct cost internalization by firms is only one possible approach. Alternatively, some of the chapters in this book suggest that social integration of costs might be achieved in a more indirect way through social provisioning funded through taxes or similar redistributive mechanisms. We could greatly enhance the public services provided as a matter of course to all residents, including, for example, more accessible and serviceable systems of public transportation, universal health care regardless of employment status, or public education upgraded, enlarged, and transformed to include infant and toddler care, sick-child care, second- and third-shift care, adult retraining, and the like. This universal approach would also alleviate some of the present pressure on small business and would avoid marginalizing and excluding the significant numbers of people who, for many different kinds of reasons, lack an active individual or family link to waged work.

However, calls for increased social provisioning as a response to the long-standing inadequacies and recent disintegrations of the legal employment relation are no more acceptable to the new orthodoxy than direct internalizing of costs. Social provisioning has always been sparser in the United States than in other industrialized countries, but what little there was is now quite dramatically in decline, with the drive for welfare reform being only one example of the trend.

Despite the fact that taking a global view reveals powerful forces arrayed against the convictions and strategies voiced in this collection, I believe that taking a global perspective will ultimately bring energy and hope to the antipoverty fight in the United States. Certainly my own work has been immeasurably enriched in recent years by my attempts to find and understand "the global economy," both at home and abroad. Doing this work has opened a new circle of teachers, students, and collaborators and introduced me to a new set of potential tools. It has allowed me to gain new perspective on our own legal and social culture and, thereby, to realize that there are more alternatives and possibilities than I would have otherwise imagined. It has surprised me with the amazing strength of people working to survive and flourish under all but unimaginable conditions. Accordingly, I will close this chapter by recounting some abbreviated examples of these experiences, as a way of conveying the paradoxical sense of hope that my own exposures to the global economy have given me.

In a workshop at the Highlander Research and Education Center in southern Appalachia, I have watched as two $30-an-hour white and African American tire builders from Birmingham, Alabama, talked turkey with Mexican, Haitian, and Guatemalan immigrant farm workers, who were being cheated out of the minimum wage in labor camps in Florida. They were talking across tremendous and glaring differences, and yet could clearly see in each other crucial commonalties and shared interests, as well.

The Birmingham rubber workers, for instance, could report about the union-busting strategy they were experiencing at the hands of a Japanese-headquartered transnational venture, and about what they and their union were doing to try to combat that strategy—including an eye-opening trip to Japan for union representatives where they were greeted warmly by blue-collar Japanese trade unionists. The farm workers, in turn, could talk about what it was like to try to organize migrant laborers across cultural, racial, and language barriers, under the threat of potential deportation, and what the U.S. economy, with its range of low- and high-wage sectors, looks like from the Caribbean or from Central America, or from the orange groves and tomato fields of an increasingly transnational Florida.

In another instance, I attended part of "Lessons without Borders," a gathering sponsored by the U.S. Agency for International Development (AID) at the University of Tennessee. I listened as development practitioners of various stripes from the U.S. Southeast and from Third World countries on three continents compared notes on microenterprise development. Participants discovered both differences and common themes in their efforts to develop independent survival strategies for the very poor in the face of sometimes extreme marginalization and rapid economic transformation. They exchanged concrete experiences (for instance, the apparently international difficulties married women entrepreneurs encounter with possessive husbands, anxious about their wives' involvement outside the home). They exchanged sardonic remarks (for instance, noting how convenient it would be if only microentrepreneurs could eat microfood, live in microhouses and pay for all their needs with micromoney). They worked to identify best practices (for instance, stressing the development of strong peer networks among microborrowers).

These practitioners also discovered important similarities in their approach to development. Specifically, many people talked about the importance of working at a local level, respecting and building on networks of human capital already in place. They voiced a preference for working on a scale and in a manner that allowed individuals and communities to give voice to their own aspirations and to build economic institutions from the bottom up, not according to the dictates of distant funders or experts. These people were convinced that democratic, grassroots institutions would be better-suited to the actual and concrete needs of individuals, their households, and their communities, and could avoid some of the problems they had experienced in other kinds of projects—both in the south-eastern United States and in the Third World—where new policies were imposed from above, often with disastrous results.

Meanwhile, however, critics at the meeting raised sharp questions about how the grassroots, bottom-up, participatory side of AID efforts abroad could be reconciled with the rest of the agency's agenda—its better-funded and larger-scale program of required neoliberal-style economic "reform." They argued that the main thrust of AID's program has often worked to exacerbate the very problems reported by the people that the agency was purportedly trying to support through microenterprise and other small-scale programs.[24]

Of course, the issues raised by the critics were not resolved in the space of one conference. But the dialogues and debates that took place around the gathering—both the friendly "horizontal" exchanges between practitioners about concrete practices, and the more conflictive points raised by critics of broader AID and U.S. State Department policy and practice—are an indication of the learning opportunities that globalization can make available to people interested in U.S. antipoverty policy and community economic development.

I have had another chance to see the potential represented by global grassroots networks through a longer-term collaboration with a group called the Tennessee Industrial Renewal Network (TIRN). As part of this project, I have watched displaced and vulnerable factory workers from Tennessee gain strength and knowledge from participating in a series of two-way, worker-to-worker exchanges with their counterparts from the maquiladora zones of Mexico. These trips have taught Tennessee workers much about Mexico, but even more about themselves and about the multinational corporations for which they labor. Participants have gone on tours of factories and industrial parks, have met with grassroots groups, have visited workers in their homes, have been filmed and taped and interviewed, and have watched themselves portrayed to make someone else's point on television.

Overall, the TIRN exchanges and interchanges have been brand new experiences for the people involved. They have been galvanizing and energizing ones for the Tennessee participants, despite the fact that at their best these trips have also brought moments of disorientation and fear. TIRN members who traveled to Mexico have often spoken of our admiration for the workers we met at the border, for their families, and for the organizations they are working to build. The astounding, stubborn resilience of Mexican workers in the face of tremendous hardship has worked to shame, inspire, and amaze us, functioning as a much-needed antidote to the fear and despair that realities of life on the industrial border can also produce in visitors from the north. For myself, after several trips with TIRN delegations to the maquiladoras, after witnessing the savage development pattern that has taken hold there, and after hearing the theories offered by government officials and corporate managers to justify that pattern, it has become harder and harder to ignore the global dimension of economic trends taking place in our own country, as well as the domestic impact of economic trends taking place far away.

The trips to Mexico led not only to new insights but to new action by TIRN members. They spurred the organization to become involved in local advocacy around issues of the North American Free Trade Agreement (NAFTA) and free trade. Eventually they have led to TIRN's participation in an international network of people from around the hemisphere and the world, people who are talking about things like international human rights, the incorporation of labor standards into regional and global trade agreements, strategies for securing capital for local community development projects in both the United States and elsewhere, and the possibilities for cross-border labor organizing and solidarity.

A document that may give some sense of the excitement of these new cross-border and cross-sectoral collaborations is the Belo Horizonte Declaration. It is one in a series of international papers produced in response to NAFTA and hemispheric economic integration by a steadily, if unevenly, expanding network of labor, church, and community-based groups and nongovernmental organizations (NGOs) in the Americas.[25] I believe it is worth quoting at this juncture, not because it represents a completed process but because the consensus-under-construction reflected by it and by other documents in the series offer an important international counterpoint to the domestic themes and concerns identified by contributors to this book.

Declaration

At the Third Trade Union Summit, held parallel to the Trade Ministers' Meeting on the Free Trade Area of the Americas (FTAA) in Belo Horizonte, Brazil May 12–13, 1997, representatives of the trade-union organizations of the Americas, affiliated and fraternal organizations of the ORIT/ICFTU, and a number of important social organizations have had the opportunity to share our respective work on the social dimension of economic integration.

As part of this meeting, the trade-union movement has reviewed the joint statement prepared by citizens' networks from Mexico, the United States, Canada, Chile and El Salvador and presented to U.S. President Clinton during his recent tour of Mexico, Central America, and the Caribbean.

As an example of the intention to achieve effective complementarity between the perspectives and action strategies of the trade-union movement and those of other social movements, we have approved this declaration, based on the aforementioned document and on the trade-union experience gained in various subregional integration processes. Therefore, this declaration should be seen as complementary to that issued by the Third Trade Union Summit.

1. There should be no Free Trade Area of the Americas (FTAA) if it is to be created along the lines of other existing agreements such as NAFTA. We need an agreement that promotes genuine development for all of the peoples of the hemisphere, one that recognizes and attempts to reduce the differences in levels of development, ·one that allows for integration of our economies based on democratically determined national development models, and one that is based on consensus. Strong national economies must be the basis for a strong hemisphere. We are proposing an agreement designed for sustainable development rather than for trade liberalization.

Any trade agreement should not be an end in itself, but rather a means toward combating poverty and social exclusion and for achieving just and sustainable development. We do not support isolationism or traditional protectionism. We are not nostalgic for the past. We are looking forward, and we have viable proposals. We know that our economies cannot be isolated from the dynamics of the world economy, but we do not think that free trade is the solution. The problem is that free trade involves more than the opening of borders; it involves the abandonment of national development models and poses a serious threat to democracy.

Any national development model, to be viable, must take trade and world economic conditions into account. It must also build on each nation's potential and develop a strategy to establish its unique position in the world. It has never been demonstrated that the market achieves an optimal distribution of resources or the benefits of development. So-called free trade is actually trade regulation that increases the advantages of international capital, speculative or not, over productive investment and over the rights and well-being of workers.

2. There should be no FTAA if it does not include a social agenda that contains at least the following fundamental elements:

i) broad-based citizen participation in the negotiation of any agreement, and its ratification must occur in each country through genuinely democratic means.

ii) respect for an improvement of the social and economic rights of workers, women (who have suffered the greatest impacts of the restructuring of production), campesinos, indigenous peoples, and migrant workers. ·

3. Our countries' competitiveness must not be based on the exploitation of workers or social dumping. The current tendency toward downward harmonization of working conditions and wages must be stopped, promoting instead an upward harmonization of working conditions over the medium term, as well as recovery of wage levels. The starting point should be ILO conventions that guarantee freedom of association and collective bargaining, that prohibit child labor and forced labor, as well as discrimination based on sex, race or religion. Moreover, we demand a Charter of Social and Economic Rights for the Citizens of the Americas, accompanied by democratic and transparent enforcement mechanisms.

4. There should be no FTAA if it does not include protection and improvement of the environment, ensure respect for the rights of migrant workers and devote special attention to food security. Therefore, it must also include protection and support for campesinos, small-scale farmers, and the social sector, without subsidizing large agribusiness corporations. It should also protect and promote micro- and small urban enterprises because of their capacity for generating employment.

5. There should be no FTAA if it does not protect people from the vulnerability and instability caused by speculative capital and fly-by-night investments. Chile, despite the fact that it is the Latin American pioneer in free trade, has protections on portfolio investment: authorization is required; a percentage must be deposited in the Central Bank; and it must be held in the country for a minimum period. Performance requirements on foreign investment must be negotiated, along with regulations to protect labor rights. Intellectual property, which is primarily held by large corporations, should be protected, but not at the expense of global progress toward a social dimension in trade or of national sovereignty. The subject of foreign debt must also be taken up again, as it continues to reduce the ability of governments to act in such key areas of development as housing, health care, education, and the environment.

6. On trade issues, the problem of non-tariff barriers must be resolved. The elimination of non-tariff barriers to legitimate trade should not be confused with lowering sanitary and phytosanitary barriers that protect the environment. Interactions among our economies must support national integration of linkages among productive sectors, for which we demand rules of origin with national content requirements.

We will work in our respective countries to defeat any agreement that is not consistent with these demands.

Belo Horizonte, Brazil, 15 May 1997[26]

As the declaration suggests, domestic attempts to articulate and fight for a more equitable and sustainable development strategy in the United States will take place in the context of worldwide economic changes that currently exert tremendous pressure on popular movements but also offer real opportunity. Those of us who live in the United States now have an unprecedented chance to enlarge our perspective and to situate our experience in a larger global context that we have too long chosen or been led to ignore. It is heartening that such exciting possibilities are emerging from within and despite the destructive dynamics of globalization as we currently know it.

The frame I have proposed for situating this volume in the present global moment suggests that many of the proposals put forward by the authors, like those of the proposals put forward in the Belo Horizonte Declaration, will meet powerful opposition. We contributors should not deceive ourselves or our readers about the strength of the neoliberal, structural adjustment, trickle-down ideology now loose in the world. It is an ideology that works to the enormous short-run benefit of some powerful players in the global economy, and consequently it will not be abandoned lightly, certainly not on the strength of good ideas proposed by a few rarefied academics or isolated welfare mothers, or embattled trade unionists, no matter how well-articulated, deeply-felt, or otherwise terrific those ideas may be.

Nevertheless, the state of the world today should also remind us that the neoliberal project is not as strong as it may seem. Its problems are severe. For instance, environmental constraints are blatant and pressing, but current growth-hungry development strategies do not appear to recognize their urgency or the power shifts that would be necessary to meaningfully address them. Similarly, the unprecedented and increasing polarization of the world's economy into ever-more-distant camps of rich and poor, together with the resulting scandalous disparities in consumption levels and in human well-being, are unstable in the extreme. In response to these disparities, governments and wealthy individuals and households alike feel compelled to spend ever greater sums in the finally hopeless task of repressing and containing the have-nots, and in futile attempts to distance themselves and their present entitlements from danger. Meanwhile, the growing homogenization of cultures threatens to liquidate irreplaceable parts of the world's human inheritance, and to trigger regressive backlash in the face of their disintegration. The breakdown in previous systems of caregiving at the societal, community, and household levels, together with the failure to develop or support adequate and more equitable new ones, impoverishes all of us in ways that are becoming increasingly evident. In sum, although the new orthodoxy is unquestionably dominant, it has also proved incapable of satisfactorily addressing many of the world's most basic development problems. In fact, in only too many instances, it appears to be exacerbating them.

Accordingly, critics of present economic arrangements and of the prevailing development model should not despair. Now, more than ever, it is important to take up the sorts of appropriately modest and ridiculously ambitious tasks undertaken by the contributors to this volume: to discover facts, to raise criticisms, to tell stories, to denounce greed, to admit frailty, to stand with those hurt by orthodox economic "reforms," and to promote widespread discussion and action around questions of justice, sustainability, and human flourishing. What I hope to have suggested in this closing essay is that if critics work with a conscious awareness of the larger international frame that so surrounds and affects the American scene, they will be better enabled to carry out these tasks in a powerful way. Likely they will encounter daunting news, but they will also discover new and real inspiration. The global economy promises both new friends and vital lessons for critics who venture out to find them.

Notes

1. I have reconstructed this exchange (with altered identifiers) from an actual conversation with a government researcher in the Southeast whose job includes gathering and analyzing state employment data.

2. The tendency to naturalize power and resource allocation in familiar labor markets is, I think, enormously reinforced by the fact that race and gender—two categories that thus far have great salience in ordering labor markets—are widely perceived as physiological, rather than social, categories. Labor market inequalities that might be recognized as unjust, anomalous, and remediable if they were visited upon "equals," are perceived as natural and independent of human agency if they seem to be based on innate differences among different kinds of workers. In U.S. labor markets, for instance, significant gains have been won in formal equality for white women and for people of color. (In fact, a brand of formal equality has been taken up by racial conservatives under the banner of "color blindness" to fight against racially redistributive schemes, such as affirmative action.) Nevertheless, assumptions about innate genetic or cultural gender and race differences are endemic in American society, and, for the most part, they are assumptions that work to justify and explain the glaringly skewed distribution of power and resources within the economy and across the segmented labor market.

3. I can't take credit for this wordplay on movers and shakers. Nor, unfortunately, do I know who can. I saw it recently in print. Somewhere.

4. Some of my own work has involved finding and developing cross-border pathways between industrial workers in Tennessee and their counterparts in the maquiladora region of northern Mexico. See, "Women and Borders on the Move: Tennessee Workers Explore the New International Division of Labor," in *Chains of Iron, Chains of Gold: Women, Race and Class in the U.S. South,* ed. Barbara Smith (Philadelphia: Temple University Press, forthcoming 1998); Frances Ansley, "The Gulf of Mexico, the Academy, and Me: Hazards of Boundary Crossings," *Soundings* 78 (Spring 1995): 68; Frances Ansley, "North American Free Trade Agreement: The Public Debate," *Georgia Journal of International and Comparative Law* 22 (1992*): 329; Frances Ansley, "U.S.-Mexico Free Trade from the Bottom: A Postcard from the Border," *Texas Journal of Women and the Law* 1 (1992): 193; and *From the Mountains to the Maquiladoras: A TIRN Educational Video* (Tennessee Industrial Renewal Network, 1993) (available from TIRN, Knoxville, Tennessee). Political scientist and participatory researcher John Gaventa describes three examples of "bottom-up" North-South linkages that developed in the course of his work at the Highlander Research and Education Center. John Gaventa, *Crossing the Great Divide: Building Links between NGOs and Community-Based Organizations in North and South,* Issue Paper (Brighton, England: Institute for Development Studies, University of Sussex, 1997). See also, Maria Riley, *Women Connecting: Report on the NGO Forum '95 and 4th World Conference on Women* (Washington, DC: Center of Concern, 1995).

5. The streams of low- and no-wage labor that have driven both agricultural and industrial development in the United States since before its founding are well-known features of our economic history, but they bear new examination in light of present developments. For one thought-provoking contribution to such a process, see Charles Bergquist, *Labor and the Course of American Democracy: U.S. History in Latin American Perspective* (Verso: New York, 1996). See also Carl Nightingale, "The Global Inner City: Towards an Historical Analysis" (unpublished paper, 1995) (on file with author).

6. See generally John Gaventa, "From the Mountains to the Maquiladoras: A Case Study of Capital Flight and Its Impact on Workers," in *Communities in Economic Crisis: Appalachia and the South,* ed. John Gaventa, Barbara Ellen Smith, and Alex Willingham (Philadelphia: Temple University Press, 1989), also reprinted in *Appalachia in Interna-*

tional Context: Cross-National Comparisons of Developing Regions, ed. Phillip Obermiller and William Philliber (Westport, CT: Prager, 1994). See also Louis Jacobson, Robert Lalonde, Daniel Sullivan, *The Costs of Worker Dislocation* (Kalamazoo, MI: W.E. Upjohn Institute of Employment Research, 1993).

7. Lawrence Mishel, Jared Bernstein, and John Schmitt identify what they say is an incomplete list of six ways that international trade has a depressing effect on wages under current conditions: first, competition from imports of finished manufacturing goods eliminates manufacturing jobs; second, imports of labor-intensive intermediate manufactured goods do the same; third, price competition by domestic firms forced to respond to lower-priced imports depresses wages of workers who remain employed in domestic manufacturing; fourth, threats of plant relocation induce worker concessions; fifth, large increases in international manufacturing investment have upgraded foreign facilities and allowed domestic ones to decline, with resulting stagnation or decline in productivity for those who work there; sixth, the inflow of displaced workers into the service sector helps to keep wages in that sector low as well. Lawrence Mishel, Jared Bernstein, and John Schmitt, *The State of Working America, 1996–97* (Armonk, NY: M.E. Sharpe, 1997), pp. 190–1. Not all economists would agree. The World Bank, for instance, in its *World Development Report 1995: Workers in an Integrating World,* acknowledged widespread wage decline in countries all over the world that were undergoing "adjustment" according to the bank's prescriptions (which include a requirement that adjusting economies open themselves to the global market). However, the report argued that these wage declines were often caused by failed past policies rather than current ones, that they could sometimes be helpfully ameliorated by careful expert planning from the top, and that they were, in any event, a temporary phenomenon as long as adjusting governments would stay the course. The World Bank, *World Development Report 1995: Workers in an Integrating World* (1995), pp. 103–5. Major points of view are summarized in Richard B. DuBoff, "Globalization and Wages, the Down Escalator," *Dollars and Sense,* September/October 1997, pp. 36–40.

8. One important recent study documenting the frequency of threatened plant closures and their impact on unionization efforts is Kate Bronfenbrenner, "The Effect of Plant Closing and Threat of Plant Closing on the Right of Workers to Organize." This study helped to inform a later report, "Plant Closings and Labor Rights: The Effects of Sudden Plant Closings on Freedom of Association and the Right to Organize in Canada, Mexico, and the United States" (1997), submitted by the Secretariat of the Commission for Labor Cooperation (a trinational body created under the North American Agreement for Labor Cooperation, or NAALC). Bronfenbrenner discusses her study in "Organizing in the NAFTA Environment: How Companies Use 'Free Trade' to Stop Unions," *New Labor Forum,* Fall 1997, pp. 51–60.

9. On the other hand, some land-based nonmanufacturing jobs that one might have thought were firmly tied to place are becoming less so. For instance, large-scale coal operators use an increasingly global strategy in choosing which of their reserves to mine at which times and for which markets. Similarly, transnational agribusiness concerns can now pick up and move many of their operations with relative ease.

10. Peter Stalker, *The Work of Strangers: A Survey of International Labour* (Geneva: Migration International Labor Organization, 1994).

11. The U.S.-Mexico border region is surely the globe's most intense greenhouse for propagating a full range of sometimes hilarious, often horrendous, practices and happenings rooted in the contradictions of the immigration system. One particularly sharp observer of this real and imagined space is El Paso independent journalist Debbie Nathan. See, e.g., Debbie Nathan, "Love in the Time of Cholera: Waiting for Free Trade on the U.S. Mexico Border," in *The Late Great Mexican Border: Reports from a Disappearing Line,* ed. Bobby

Byrd and Susannah Mississippi Byrd (El Paso, TX: Cinco Puntos Press, 1996); and Debbie Nathan, *Women and Other Aliens: Essays from the U.S.- Mexico Border* (El Paso: Cinco Puntos Press, 1991). See also, Robert Kahn, "Operation Gatekeeper: Keeping Illegal Workers Male, Young and Fit," *Los Angeles Times,* July 6, 1997 (arguing that the heightened arduousness of border crossings in the wake of greater militarization of the U.S.-Mexico boundary serves to enhance the "quality" of the immigrant pool).

12. See, e.g., Guadalupe Luna, "Agricultural Underdogs and International Agreements: The Legal Context of Agricultural Workers within the Rural Economy," *New Mexico Law Review* 26 (1996): 9; and Marc Linder, "Farmworkers and the Fair Labor Standards Act: Racial Discrimination in the New Deal," *Texas Law Review* 65 (1987): 1335. See also David Griffith, *Jones's Minimal: Law-Wage Labor in the United States* (Albany: State University of New York Press, 1993); and Troy Duster, "Individual Fairness, Group Preferences, and the California Strategy," *Representations* 55 (1996): 41.

13. The specter of reborn prison labor is especially disturbing given the racial characteristics of the U.S. criminal justice system and the history of coerced African American labor that burdens our national past. For a glimpse at part of the history of the convict leasing system that emerged in Tennessee, as in many areas of the South after Emancipation, see Fran Ansley and Brenda Bell, "Miners Insurrections/Convict Labor," *Southern Exposure* 1, nos. 3, 4 (1974): 144–59 (based primarily on oral testimonies of miners gathered in the 1930s by Jim Dombrowski).

14. In conversations with East Tennesseans from depressed mountain communities, I have been told anecdotally that white Appalachians, who used to comprise a distinct and regular subgroup in the Florida winter citrus harvest, are now experiencing great difficulty in getting jobs in that industry. Over the last several seasons, according to these narratives, white people who have worked for two and three decades in the harvest have arrived in Florida with the season, only to be told that work crews will now be exclusively Latino and Latina. Landlords at the places they used to stay refuse to rent to them on the grounds that the apartments are for migrants only. Reportedly, African Americans—who also made up a segment of the citrus work force in Florida for decades—have been similarly affected.

These phenomena, a fascinating part of the long story of racial formation in America, deserve greater study. Currently in the Southeast a number of job categories are undergoing pronounced racial change, as employers make conscious decisions to incorporate Latinas and Latinos as a significant addition to or wholesale replacement for prior employee complements. The occupations involved are often the heaviest, dirtiest, most dangerous in the local economy. (For an instance that ended up backfiring on the employer involved, see Barry Yeomans, "Spiritual Union: A Case Study," *The Nation,* December 1, 1997, pp. 15–9.) The practice in many instances proves locally "catching." Often the first employers to make the move are large enterprises with branches elsewhere and a global outlook, perhaps a large agribusiness. Then as the word spreads through local networks, a range of smaller and more local enterprises begin to follow suit.

In one area near my home, the chain of "Latinizing employers" went from a large absentee-owned vegetable grower, to a locally owned poultry-processing plant employing several hundred workers, and on to smaller local service and industrial enterprises. Now the latest move is even to the level of the part-time family farm. In Tennessee, many squeezed rural families have been able to hold onto farmlands by raising a small tobacco allotment as a supplement to the waged work of one or more family members. (The federal system of tobacco price supports is structured in an unusual way that actually sustains small units at this level, though of course concentration in the tobacco industry at the upper end is pronounced.) In the past few years, some families that used to hire white youth in the short, but intense, tobacco harvest have begun tapping into the new rivers of migrant labor flowing into East Tennessee. They too find that they can hire Mexican and Guatemalan workers at bargain basement prices.

15. Richard W. Stevenson and Jeff Gerth, "IMF's New Look: A Far Deeper Role in Lands in Crisis," *New York Times,* December 7, 1997. p. A1 at A10, col. 2.

16. See, "Focus on Finance," special section in *IFG News* 2 (Summer 1997) (available from the International Forum on Globalization, San Francisco).

17. William Greider, *One World, Ready or Not: The Manic Logic of Global Capitalism* (New York: Simon and Schuster, 1997).

18. For critical discussion of the IMF role in the global economy, see Kevin Danaher, ed., *Fifty Years Is Enough: The Case against the World Bank and the International Monetary Fund* (Boston: South End Press, 1994). For a more favorable view of the IMF's sort of approach, see John Williamson, *The World Economy: A Textbook in International Economics* (New York: Basic Books, 1991).

19. This Latinate term seems to roll from Spanish-speaking tongues more easily than it does from English-speaking ones. In Mexico City, you can hear it embedded in popular songs blaring over the radio in taxicabs, but, to many Americans, the term sounds fancy and academic. In the United States, it has the added disadvantage that it can easily be misread as a reference to "liberalism," as that term is used within the domestic electoral context, rather than being understood as a broader ideological reference to classical liberalism and its descendants.

20. A shorthand reference to the dominance of the new orthodoxy is the ominous acronym "TINA." Coined, I understand, by Margaret Thatcher, the term stands for "There Is No Alternative." In the near term it is no doubt accurate to say that mendicant states have little choice but to accept IMF conditionality. Further, it is true that critics of neoliberalism do not currently have a coherent alternative to offer to the neoliberal project. But in the long run, present trends are far too precarious, environmentally and politically, to be sustainable. Most important, the seeds of resistance to the present order, and the passionate belief that more just arrangements are indeed within human grasp, are regularly reflected and refreshed in the work and practice of grassroots and rank-and-file groups around the world. South African scholar/activists Patrick Bond and Mzwanele Mayekiso recently reported on the intense (and often successful) pressures exerted on the new South African government to conform to the neoliberal agenda, and conceded the strength of the TINA slogan in that context. But they also went on to observe that:

> . . . there are the occasional moments when "TINA," uttered by facile bureaucrats (from both Old and New South Africa) is answered by a resounding cry from [the] social movements: "THEMBA!" (Zulu, for hope)—"There Must Be an Alternative!"

Patrick Bond and Mzwanele Mayekiso, "Developing Resistance, Resisting 'Development': Reflections from the South African Struggle," *The Socialist Register,* (1996): 42–43.

21. A look at the annual reports from the World Bank will give some flavor of both the reigning orthodoxy and the tactical disagreements within it. See, e.g., "World Development Report 1997: The State in a Changing World," and "World Development Report 1996: From Plan to Market."

22. Selected primary and secondary sources for these critiques include: Chadravarthi Raghavan, *Recolonization: GATT, the Uruguay Round and the Third World* (Penang, Malaysia: Third World Network) (non-governmental); Pamela Sparr, *Global Economics: Seeking a Christian Ethic* (Cincinnati: General Board of Global Ministries, United Methodist Church) (church); International Labor Rights Education and Research Fund, *Trade's Hidden Costs: Worker Rights in a Changing Economy* (Washington, DC: ILRERF, 1988)

and "The Morning NAFTA: Labour's Voice on Economic Integration" (Ottawa, Ontario: Canadian Labour Congress) (labor); *Shadows of Tender Fury: The Letters and Communiques of Subcomandante Marcos and the Zapatista Army of National Liberation* (1995) (soldier-poet); Neil Harvey, *Rebellion in Chiapas: Rural Reforms, Campesino Radicalism and the Limits to Salinismo* (La Jolla, CA: Ejido Reform Research Project, Center for U.S.-Mexican Studies, University of California, San Diego, 1994) (indigenous); Julia Cleves Mosse, *Half the World, Half a Chance: An Introduction to Gender and Development* (Oxford: Oxfam, 1992) (women); *No Guarantees: Sex Discrimination in Mexico's Maquiladora Sector,* Report of Human Rights Watch, (New York: Human Rights Watch, August 1996) (human rights); Leslie Sklair, *Sociology of the Global System* (London: Harvester Wheatsheaf, 1991) (academic); and David Korten, *When Corporations Rule the World* (West Hartford, CT: Kumarian Press, 1995) (development professional); Sierra Club, *Bankrolling Disasters: International Development Banks and the Global Environment* (San Francisco: Sierra Club, 1986) (environmentalist).

23. Of course, observers differ on the nature of the reforms that have been adopted by international finance bodies. For a view regarding the World Bank that there is a significant "metamorphosis taking place at the premier multilateral institution for assisting the world's poor," see George Gedda, " 'Poverty Week' Enlightens Professionals," *Knoxville News-Sentinel,* December 30, 1997, p. C3.

24. For a recent discussion of AID policy that accedes to these sorts of criticisms of past AID practice, but voices cautious optimism about more recent developments in Central America, see Lisa Haugaard, "Development Aid: Some Small Steps Forward," NACLA Report on the Americas, Vol. XXXI, September/October 1997. For a highly critical account of AID activities in Haiti, see Lisa McGowan, "Democracy Undermined, Economic Justice Denied: Structural Adjustment and the AID Juggernaut in Haiti," *The Development GAP,* January 1997. For a more approving perspective, see Paul Mosley, Jane Harrigan, and John Toye, *Aid and Power: The World Bank and Policy-Based Lending in the 1980s* (New York: Routledge, 1991).

25. Earlier documents in this lineage include a 1991 statement on "Public Opinion and the Free Trade Negotiations: 'Citizens' Alternatives," developed by a trinational group that convened in Zacatecas, Mexico, at the same time that U.S., Mexican, and Canadian trade ministers were there to negotiate NAFTA; a 1993 "Just and Sustainable Trade and Development Initiative for North America," and a related 1994 "Just and Sustainable Trade and Development Initiative for the Western Hemisphere," both developed jointly by the Alliance for Responsible Trade, the Citizens Trade Campaign and the Mexican Action Network on Free Trade, and both endorsed by the Action Canada Network.

26. The following organizations signed the Belo Horizonte Declaration at the time of its original drafting: Inter-American Regional Organization of Workers/International Confederation of Free Trade Unions (ORIT/ICFTU), Mexican Action Network on Free Trade (RMALC), Alliance for Responsible Trade (ART-U.S.), Common Frontiers (Canada), Action Canada Network, Chilean Network for a Peoples' Initiative (RECHIP), Brazilian Association of NGOs (ABONG), Coalition for Justice in the Maquiladoras (U.S.), National Indigenous Council of Mexico, National Union El Barzon (Mexico), Reseau Quebecois sur l'integration continental Confederation de syndicats nationaux (CSN-Quebec), Canadian Association of Labour Lawyers. Belo Horizonte was one in a series of meetings that began as unofficial parallel assemblies at the occasional trinational gatherings of trade ministers that accompanied original negotiation of NAFTA. Since Belo Horizonte, other gatherings of FTAA oppositionists have taken place in various meeting locations around the hemisphere. At this writing in June 1998, the most significant meeting since Belo Horizonte has been the "Peoples' Summit of the Americas," convened parallel to the Presidential Summit in Santiago, Chile in April, 1998. That gathering,

endorsed and supported by the AFL-CIO, the regional Organization of Workers (ORIT), and the main Brazilian and Chilean labor federations (the CUT-Brazil and CUT-Chile), as well as a broad spectrum of non-governmental organizations and community-based organizations, brought together for the first time trade unionists and representatives of hemispheric social movements for an integrated conference. Participants hammered out another generation of documents, including a set of concrete alternatives to the neoliberal approach already embedded in NAFTA and urged upon the rest of the world by proponents of the FTAA and the Multilateral Agreement on Investment (MAI). Some of these documents are available, in English and Spanish, from the Peoples' Summit Web page at: http://ourworld.compuserve.com/homepages/oca-chile-rm/.

See also Alejandro Bendaña, "Santiago People's Summit: A Report," *The Progressive Response* 2, no. 16 (May 16, 1998), (published jointly by the Interhemispheric Resource Center and the Institute for Policy Studies), and Victor Menotti, "Santiago's Other Summit," *San Francisco Bay Guardian,* April 29, 1998.

For more information on the MAI, see: "A Guide to the Multilateral Agreement on Investment," (New York and Washington, DC: United States Council for International Business, January 1996 (laudatory) and Tony Clarke and Maude Barlow, *MAI: The Multilateral Agreement on Investment and the Threat to Canadian Sovereignty* (Toronto: Stoddart, 1997) (critical).

ABOUT THE EDITORS AND CONTRIBUTORS

Fran Ansley teaches law at the University of Tennessee in Knoxville. She is working to gain a view of the global economy that is grounded in the experiences of blue collar and low-wage workers in East Tennessee and northern Mexico, and then to develop accessible ways of sharing what she has learned .

Mark H. Greenberg is a senior staff attorney at the Center for Law and Social Policy (CLASP) in Washington, D.C. Since coming to CLASP in 1988, he has focused on issues relating to federal and state welfare reform efforts. He has written extensively about the requirements of federal law and the nature and direction of welfare reform. Prior to joining CLASP, he worked for ten years in legal services programs, first at Jacksonville Area Legal Aid in Florida, and then at the Western Center for Law and Poverty in Los Angeles.

Joel F. Handler is the Richard C. Maxwell Professor of Law at UCLA Law School and a professor of policy studies at the UCLA School of Public Policy and Social Research. He has served as a member and chair of several committees and panels of the National Research Council. A Guggenheim fellow, he is a prize-winning author of more than a dozen books on poverty and social welfare policy.

Yeheskel Hasenfeld is Professor of Social Welfare in the Department of Social Welfare, School of Public Policy and Social Research, University of California, Los Angeles. He has written extensively on human service organizations, and he current research focuses on the implementation of welfare reform initiatives. His recent publications in this area include *The Moral Construction of Poverty: Welfare Reform in America* and *We the Poor People: Work, Poverty and Welfare,* both written with Joel Handler.

Julia R. Henly is an assistant professor at the University of Chicago in the School of Social Service Administration and a faculty affiliate of the Northwestern–University of Chicago Joint Center for Poverty Research. Dr. Henly's work examines the coping strategies and social networks of low-income populations, especially low-income mothers. Her work explores the intersection of public assistance policies with informal means of support, and the ways in which parents manage the multiple demands imposed by poverty, caregiving, and paid labor.

Susan R. Jones is Professor of Clinical Law at the George Washington University law school. As the director and supervising attorney of the Small Business Clinic/Community Economic Development Project, she represents small businesses and nonprofit groups including microbusinesses and nonprofit microenterprise development organizations and teaches business law and the law of nonprofit organizations. She is the author of *A Legal Guide to Microenterprise Development: Battling Poverty Through Self-Employment* (American Bar Association Commission on Homelessness and Poverty, 1998).

Peter Pitegoff is Vice Dean and Professor of Law at the State University of New York at Buffalo School of Law, where he teaches corporation law and finance, community development law, ethics, and business transactions. He has worked and written extensively in the areas of economic development, labor and industrial organization, worker ownership of enterprises, welfare and employment policy, and urban revitalization.

Kathleen A. Sullivan is Clinical Professor of Law at Yale Law School, where she teaches courses on poverty law and child welfare law advocacy. As supervising attorney with the Jerome N. Frank Legal Services Organization, Yale's clinical law office, she represents current and former welfare recipients and families involved in child welfare cases.

Louise G. Trubek is Clinical Professor of Law at the University of Wisconsin Law School. She also serves as Senior Attorney at the Center for Public Representation, a nonprofit public interest law firm where she directs a health law clinic. She is co-author of the casebook *Poverty Law: Theory and Practice* (West Publishers) and has written articles on health law and public interest lawyering.

Lucie White, previously a professor of law at the University of California at Los Angeles, is the Louis A. Horvitz professor of law at Harvard Law School. She teaches courses on civil procedure, social welfare policy, and community-based advocacy around poverty issues. She is writing an ethnography of women in two local Head Start programs as an example of the law's potential to support grassroots community building among poor women. Professor White has also written about lawyer—client roles, social power, and institutional arrangements in contexts of extreme poverty, as well as change-oriented lawyering practices in apartheid South Africa.

Lucy A. Williams is a professor of law at Northeastern University School of Law and was the School's 1994–1995 Public Interest Distinguished Professor. She has written and lectured widely in the area of welfare law and poverty. In August 1994, she was appointed by President Bill Clinton to the three-year Advisory Council on Unemployment Compensation, which evaluated all aspects of the unemployment compensation program and made policy recommendations to the president and Congress. Prior to joining the faculty at Northeastern, she was an attorney at Massachusetts Law Reform Institute for thirteen years, where she specialized in employment and governmental benefits law.

INDEX